ALL-ROUND GUIDE TO THE
Isle of
MAN

BY FAR THE MOST COMPREHENSIVE GUIDE

Compiled and edited by
Trevor Barrett

Managing editor: Miles Cowsill

New 2010/2011 edition

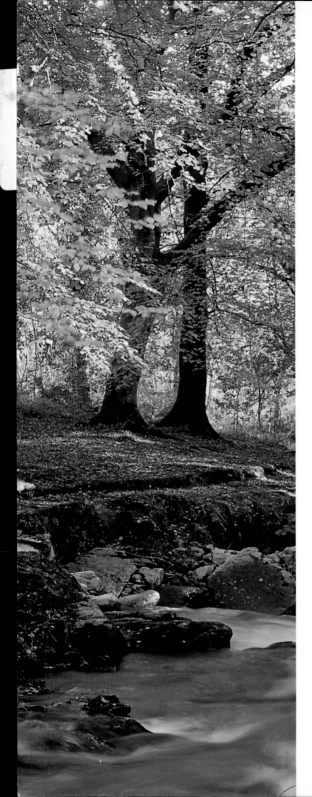

CONTRIBUTORS

Stan Basnett, Duncan Bridges, Frank Cowin, Yvonne Cresswell, Andrew Douglas, Mick Duckworth, Barry Edwards, John Hellowell, Nick Pinder, Andrew Scarffe & Chris Sharpe

PHOTOGRAPHS

Lily Publications, Vicky Harrop, Dave Collister, Manx National Heritage & Isle of Man Department of Tourism & Leisure

Published by Lily Publications Ltd., PO Box 33, Ramsey, Isle of Man, IM99 4LP
Tel: +44 (0)1624 898446, Fax: +44 (0)1624 898449.

www.lilypublications.co.uk   lilypubs@manx.net

ISBN 1 899602 47 X

CONTENTS

Contents

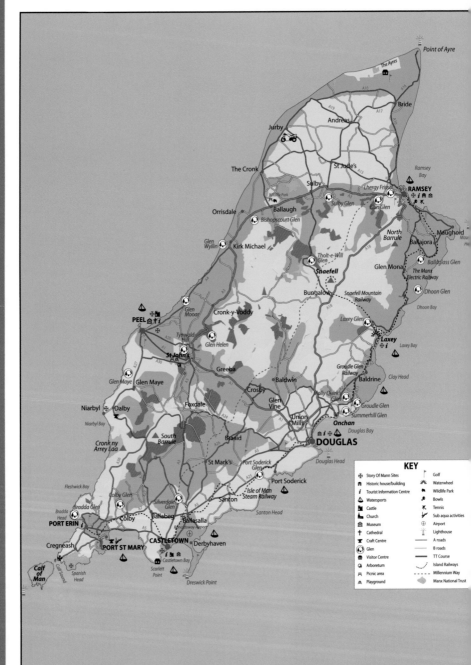

Point of Ayre

The Ayres

Bride

Jurby

Andreas

The Cronk

St Jude's

Sulby

Ramsey Bay

Lhergy Frissel

RAMSEY

Wildlife Park

Sulby Glen

Orrisdale

Ballaugh

Glen

Bishopscourt Glen

North Barrule

Maughold

Ballajora

Ballaglass Glen

Maugh Hei

Glen Wyllin

Kirk Michael

Tholt-e-Will Glen

Glen Mona

The Manx Electric Railway

Snaefell

Bungalow

Snaefell Mountain Railway

Dhoon Glen

Dhoon Bay

Glen Mooar

Cronk-y-Voddy

Laxey Glen

PEEL

Tynwald Hill

Glen Helen

Laxey

Laxey Bay

St John's

Greeba

Glen Maye

Glen Maye

Baldwin

Groudle Glen Railway

Baldrine

Clay Head

Niarbyl

Dalby

Foxdale

Crosby

Glen Vine

Molly Churn Glen

Groudle Glen

Niarbyl Bay

South Barrule

Braaid

Union Mills

Summerhill Glen

Onchan

Douglas Bay

Cronk ny Arrey Laa

St Mark's

Port Soderick Glen

DOUGLAS

Douglas Head

Fleshwick Bay

Colby Glen

Silverdale Glen

Port Soderick

Isle of Man Steam Railway

Santon

Santon Head

Bradda Head

Bradda Glen

Colby

Ballabeg

Ballasalla

PORT ERIN

Ronaldsway Airport

CASTLETOWN

Derbyhaven

Cregneash

PORT ST MARY

Castletown Bay

Calf of Man

Spanish Head

Scarlett Point

Dreswick Point

KEY

Story Of Mann Sites		Golf	
Historic house/building		Waterwheel	
Tourist Information Centre		Wildlife Park	
Watersports		Bowls	
Castle		Tennis	
Church		Sub aqua activities	
Museum		Airport	
Cathedral		Lighthouse	
Craft Centre		A roads	
Glen		B roads	
Visitor Centre		TT Course	
Arboretum		Island Railways	
Picnic area		Millennium Way	
Playground		Manx National Trust	

A **PEEP BENEATH** THE CLOAK

Although well patronised since Victorian times by generations of holidaymakers, particularly from the north-west of England – given its location in the Irish Sea, 60 miles off Lancashire's Fylde coast – it's surprising that in this age of global travel the Isle of Man remains relatively 'undiscovered'.

On the other hand, there are frequent visitors who jealousy guard the secret of this holiday gem.

Perhaps they fear that too many feet stepping ashore will stampede the Island's quiet, unhurried lifestyle and trample its great natural beauty. Or, more likely, maybe they just want it all to themselves.

In the pages of this guide the Isle of Man is available to everyone. From the comfort of your armchair you can begin to appreciate the Island's many attractions – and the differences which set it apart from anywhere else in the British Isles.

Chief among these is Tynwald - the system of self-government established by Norse rulers more than a thousand years ago and still effective today. Empowered to make their own laws, the Manx enjoy a sense of freedom and independence which is reflected in the warmth of their welcome and the easy and relaxed pace of life – one of the Island's most endearing and contagious qualities, encapsulated in the Manx saying *traa dy-liooar*, meaning time enough.

If you are one of the many who enthusiastically admit to being intrigued by the prospect of visiting the Isle of Man, but have never quite made it, this guide could be just the motivation you need.

As you turn the pages, you will gradually unravel all that lies beneath Manannan's Cloak. As old as time itself, and conjured up at will by the ancient sea god Manannan Mac Lir to protect the Island from the envious eyes of invaders, this shroud of mist is a local weather phenomenon romanticised in Manx mythology – one of many legends, superstitions and tall tales which help make the Isle of Man an even more enigmatic and appealing holiday destination.

FASTFACTS A-Z
THE ISLE OF MAN
IN A NUTSHELL

ACTIVITIES & SPORTING ATTRACTIONS

- The Isle of Man has 9 golf courses and is popular for angling (licences are required), outdoor pursuits, walking, watersports and many other leisure activities.
- The legendary TT (Tourist Trophy) motorcycle racing event takes place in early summer on the challenging and tortuous Mountain Course – 37.73 miles of public roads.

CURRENCY AND POSTAGE STAMPS

- Manx currency is the equivalent of sterling and all UK currencies and euros are accepted. Manx stamps, much prized by collectors worldwide, are produced by the Isle of Man Post Philatelic Bureau (www.gov.im/post/stamps).

EATING OUT & EATING IN

- Many generations of Manx crofters and farmers have managed the land to reap the benefits of the island's rich pastures and largely unpolluted environment. Consequently, quality and flavour are key words on any Isle of Man menu, from prized and unique Manx Loaghtan lamb to award-winning cheeses, Peel kippers (still smoked in the traditional way) and delicious seafood. For self-caterers, farmers' markets help guarantee a ready supply of fresh island produce.

ENTERTAINMENT

- Painstakingly restored over a 10-year period, and a listed building since 2002, the Gaiety Theatre on Douglas seafront is a magnificent example of the work of Frank Matcham (1854- 1920) – one of Britain's most revered Victorian theatre architects. Today the Gaiety is part of the Villa Marina and Gaiety Theatre Complex, which is also home to the Sayle Gallery (named in memory of Manx artist Norman Sayle).
- Erin Arts Centre in Port Erin is another important and long-established Manx venue for the performing arts, regularly hosting major international festivals of music and song.

EVENTS

- Every year across the island there are many celebrations of Manx culture and tradition in all its forms, along with a busy calendar of sporting and other colourful events which guarantee great spectacle and entertainment from early spring through to late autumn.

FINDING YOUR WAY AROUND

- OS Landranger map 95 is an invaluable source of reference and information for exploring and discovering the Isle of Man.

HISTORY & HERITAGE

- 10,000 years of Manx history is brought vividly to life in the innovative and captivating *Story of Mann*, presented island-wide at Manx National Heritage attractions such as the Manx Museum in Douglas, medieval Castle Rushen in Castletown, Peel's House of Manannan and the Great Laxey Wheel.

LANDSCAPE

- With much of it given over to farming, and more than 40% of it uninhabited, the landscape is largely unspoilt – a haven for wildlife, supporting a great variety of habitats. Tranquil countryside, wooded glens, high hills, uncrowded beaches and dramatic coastline are the main features. The highest point is Snaefell (2,036 feet – 635 metres), accessible on foot or by mountain railway. Much of the 100-mile coastline can be walked on Raad ny Foillan (Road of the Gull) – the signposted coastal footpath (95 miles/153km).

LANGUAGE

- English. Manx Gaelic, derived from Irish and Scottish Gaelic, is being encouraged and revived in education. In Manx the Isle of Man is called Ellan Vannin.

LOCATION & TRAVEL

- Location: North Irish Sea, off the coastlines of Lancashire, Galloway, Northern Ireland and North Wales. Well served from airports across the British Isles (flights take as little as 20 minutes) and by sea from England and Ireland (approximately 4 hours by conventional ferry, 2 hours 30 minutes by fastcraft).

MOTORING

- There are more than 500 miles of roads. Driving is on the left and road signs are in English. Car hire is widely available. Parking discs (free of charge and easily obtained) are required in towns. Touring caravans are prohibited because of the island's narrow roads and winding country lanes.

PUBLIC TRANSPORT

- The Isle of Man is famous for its remarkable vintage railways and trams: the Isle of Man Steam Railway (Douglas-Port Erin), Manx Electric Railway (Douglas-Ramsey, via Laxey), Snaefell Mountain Railway (Laxey to the summit) and Douglas horsetrams

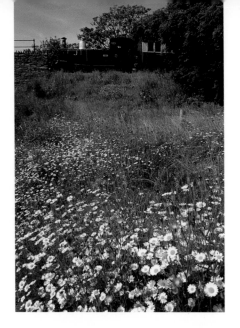

(promenade, summer only).
- Frequent bus services operate all over the island. Money-saving Explorer Tickets cover all bus and public transport train travel as listed above.

SIZE & POPULATION

- Approximately: 33 miles long, 13 miles wide at extremities; 200 square miles in area; population 80,000.

TOWNS AND RESORTS

- Douglas is the capital and Castletown is the former capital. The other main centres are Ramsey, Peel, Port Erin, Port St Mary and the villages of St John's and Laxey.

TYNWALD DAY

- Held early in July (usually 5th) at Tynwald Hill in the village of St John's, this is a national celebration of the Isle of Man's 1,000-year-old parliament and independence.

GATEWAYS TO
MANANNAN S KINGDOM

Steam Packet's fastcraft *Manannan.*

TRAVELLING BY SEA

Manannan's Cloak makes for an interesting legend, but the mist is no barrier to the ferries and aircraft which serve the Isle of Man on a regular basis from many parts of Britain.

Flying gives you an obvious time advantage, whereas a ferry can accommodate your car too. If you're travelling in the high season, or busy school holiday periods, it's sensible to book your flight or sailing well in advance.

The information given in these pages was correct at the time of going to press (March 2010) and is intended as a general guide, but contacting individual operators will give you a completely up-to-date picture.

Ferry services are operated by the Steam Packet Company, based at the Sea Terminal on Douglas harbour – your arrival point on the Isle of Man. The fleet comprises the conventional ferry *Ben-My-Chree* and two fastcraft. All vessels carry cars and foot passengers.

From England you have the choice of two departure ports. Heysham in Lancashire is 9 miles from the M6 and the average crossing time is 3 hours 30 minutes by conventional ferry and 2 hours by fastcraft. Sailing from Liverpool averages 4 hours and 2 hours 30 minutes respectively.

From Belfast (fastcraft only) it takes 2 hours 45 minutes, whereas Dublin gives you the choice of conventional ferry (4 hours) or fastcraft (2 hours 50 minutes).

You can pack so much more into an Isle of Man Steam Packet Company getaway

Belfast
(seasonal)

Isle of Man

Heysham
(year round)

Dublin
(seasonal)

Liverpool
(year round)

STEAM-PACKET.COM

Take your car. Take your gear. Take the ferry.

Whether you're planning a family holiday or a short break, you'll always find great ways to save if you take the ferry. The Isle of Man Steam Packet Company takes you there in comfort and you can bring your car for the ultimate freedom. Set your own itinerary or get a helping hand from our tour operator, Steam Packet Holidays.

Find the best ferry fares at **STEAM-PACKET.COM**
Or find the best holiday packages at **STEAMPACKETHOLIDAYS.COM**

ISLE OF MAN
STEAM PACKET COMPANY

TRAVELLING BY AIR

As at March 2010, airports and airlines serving the Isle of Man daily were as follows:

- Belfast (Manx2)
- Birmingham (Flybe)
- Blackpool (Manx2)
- Bristol (Flybe)
- Dublin (Aer Arann)
- East Midlands (Manx2)
- Edinburgh (Flybe)
- Glasgow (Flybe)
- Gloucester (Manx2)
- Guernsey & Jersey (Blue Islands)
- Liverpool John Lennon (Flybe & EasyJet)
- London City (Aer Arann)
- London Gatwick (Flybe)
- London Luton (Flybe)
- Manchester (Flybe)
- Newcastle (Manx2)
- Southampton (Flybe)

CONTACT DETAILS

- Steam Packet Company: tel 01624 661661 www.steam-packet.com
- Aer Arann: (UK) 0800 587 2324 (Ireland) 018447700 www.aerarann.com
- Blue Islands: 08456 202122 www.blueislans.com
- Flybe/Loganair: 0871 522 6100 www.flybe.com
- Manx2: 0871 24 22 226 www.manx2.com
- Easy Jet: www.easyjet.com

Ronaldsway Airport.

Niarbyl

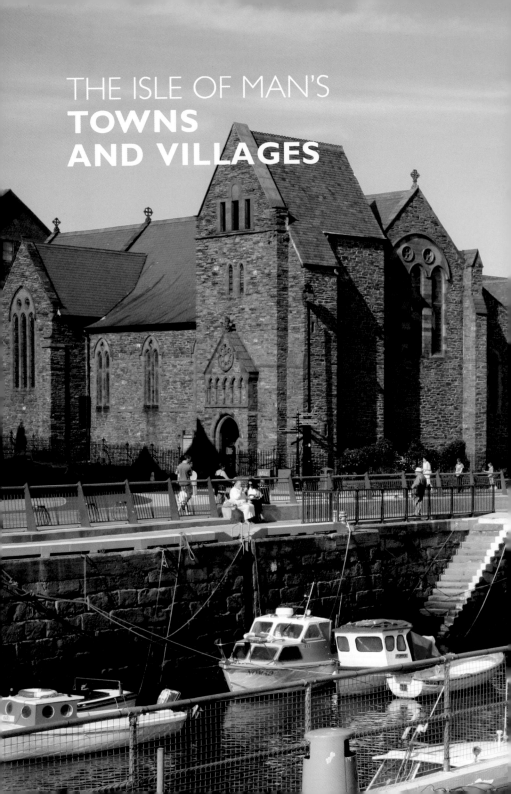

THE ISLE OF MAN'S
TOWNS
AND VILLAGES

Douglas marina: pleasure boats and leisurely strolls.

TOWNS AND VILLAGES IN THE EAST

DOUGLAS

In the last few decades the transformation of Douglas from tired Victorian resort to vibrant international offshore banking and finance centre has been dramatic.

Along the sweeping promenade – best viewed from the top of Douglas Head, where the two-mile crescent of Douglas Bay spreads out invitingly before you – grand old architecture rubs shoulders with luxury apartments and towering statements of 21st-century corporate clout.

Morning and evening rush hours may be a new and inevitable consequence of this progress, but for all this the Isle of Man capital still retains its relaxed and welcoming easy come easy go holiday charm and appeal: the great variety of accommodation, pubs, restaurants, entertainment and other attractions new and not so new make sure of it.

It was largely due to its sheltered position on the east coast that Douglas became the

The marina has completely transformed the old inner harbour.

island's major port and the focus of trade in salt, herring, hides, soap and beer. During the 18th century it was also a centre for the 'running trade', by which merchants avoided high British tariffs on imported goods such as tea, tobacco, wine and brandy by importing them legally into the Isle of Man, paying lower taxes to the Lord of Mann, and then 'running' the goods to colleagues waiting along the shore on the British mainland.

'Running' increased the wealth of the town, but in 1756 the British government brought an end to the business by purchasing the rights of the Lord of Mann so that all goods entering the island paid British taxes. The Royal Navy and British customs officials controlled this, and the effect was a drastic drop in the wealth and living standards in the town. Interestingly, a commander of one of the revenue cutters was Lieutenant William Bligh, later of mutiny on the Bounty fame, who married a local girl, Elizabeth Betham. Peter Heywood of Douglas was also on the Bounty crew as, of course, was Fletcher Christian, whose family had strong Manx connections.

In 1787, during a terrible storm, a gale off Laxey wrecked the island's herring fleet. Many boats and lives were lost as they headed for the shelter of Douglas's crumbled pier, and in 1801 a new Douglas pier was constructed.

Shipwrecks were a fact of life for the island's sailors. In 1822 a Royal Navy cutter ran aground in the harbour entrance at Douglas and 97 men were saved. The rescue was organised by Sir William Hillary, who had moved to the Isle of Man after triumphs in the Napoleonic wars, and in 1824 he launched the appeal which led to the formation of what was to become the Royal National Lifeboat Institution.

Hillary was involved in many other rescues, including that of the paddle steamer *St. George* in 1832 after it had become stranded on the treacherous Conister Rock reef near the entrance to Douglas harbour. Although a

Victorian ingenuity restored:the Great Union Camera Obscura, Douglas Head.

non-swimmer, he took out the lifeboat with his crew and saved all 22 aboard. In 1832 he was also responsible for building the rock's Tower of Refuge for shipwrecked sailors – a sight long familiar to all ferry passengers arriving at the Sea Terminal.

The town spread out from the harbour in the 19th century; first as Georgian residences were built for affluent arrivals from England attracted by the low cost of living, and later for the wealthy holiday visitors from the factory towns of northern England who came on the steamships from Liverpool and Whitehaven. In 1830, to cater for this increased sea traffic, a group of local businessmen decided to build the passenger ship *Mona's Isle* – an enterprise which led eventually to the formation of the Isle of Man Steam Packet Company.

In the decades since, the twin piers of Douglas have welcomed the arrival of millions of holidaymakers, and today cruise ships are regular visitors too. There are two interesting anecdotes relating to the piers: King Edward Pier is the only public work

named after the uncrowned sovereign, and at Victoria Pier the 'Dawsey' memorial commemorates David 'Dawsey' Kewley, a ropeman with the Isle of Man Steam Packet Company, who is reputed to have saved 24 men from drowning.

The holiday trade boomed for Douglas and the Isle of Man in the late 19th century and well on into the 20th. In 1866 Douglas took over from Castletown as the island's capital, and the latter half of the 19th century saw major developments of hotels and boarding houses, the construction of Victoria Pier in 1872, the erection of splendid theatres and ballrooms, and improvements to municipal facilities and housing for local residents.

The great benefactor Henry Bloom Noble funded the town's public baths, a park, a hospital (recently replaced by a new modern hospital) and, in the middle of the promenade, the original Villa Marina, which was a focus of entertainment in Douglas from 1913 up until its decline in the 1990s. The nearby Gaiety Theatre, designed by Frank Matcham and another celebration of

the Isle of MAN

18

Douglas's Victorian and Edwardian heritage, was saved from demolition at the eleventh hour in 1971 when Tynwald approved the purchase of it for the nation. From a sad and sorry state of neglect, the Gaiety was completely and authentically restored under the direction of manager Mervin Russell Stokes, who was rewarded with an MBE for his work. The painstaking 10-year restoration culminated in 2000, the theatre's centenary year, and it now stands proud as one of the finest surviving Matcham theatres in the British Isles. The new Villa Marina underwent a similar rebirth in 2004, following significant

and sympathetic redevelopment, and is a major modern venue for a wide variety of live shows and other entertainment, including cinema, dance and events.

Other investment in visitor facilities over recent years is apparent in Douglas's fine restaurants, fashionable shops, wine and tapas bars, yacht marina and attractions such as the excellent award-winning Manx Museum and restored Victorian Camera Obscura.

Traditional attractions are still going strong too. The Victorian horse trams ply the wide two-mile promenade in summer months, and Douglas is the hub of the island's vintage

towns **and** villages in the **EAST**

Michael Sandle's RNLI Memorial on Douglas promenade.

railways. From here you can enjoy all the delights of both the Isle of Man Steam Railway, which takes you to beautiful Port Erin in the south, and the Manx Electric Railway. This heads north to Laxey and Ramsey along the spectacular east coast. At Laxey you can temporarily interrupt one great Isle of Man railway journey to experience yet another – by disembarking for the 5-mile ascent to the island's highest point on the Snaefell Mountain Railway.

LAXEY

Laxey ('Salmon River' in old Norse) sprawls along the sides of a deep glen, running down from the mine workings in its upper reaches to the tiny harbour at the north end of a wide bay.

Old papers of village life record that in the 18th century large shipments of fish were sent from the port to Sicily. The main products today are flour (still produced on the site of the 1513 mill) woollen goods and Meerschaum and Briar pipes. The factory

shop of Laxey Pipes on the quay offers an astonishing choice of fifteen styles and six finishes in the Meerschaum range.

It was in about 1780 when the small community of Laxey discovered that a fortune lay at its feet. Substantial deposits of lead, copper, zinc and silver were soon being exploited by a thriving mining industry which reached its peak in the mid 1870s. A thousand men were employed here and the operation was highly profitable, producing as much zinc as all other zinc mines in Britain could muster between them. From 1876 to 1882 the Great Laxey Mines paid out the highest total in dividends of all the lead mines in the British Isles, ensuring a reasonable standard of living for the people of the village.

Transporting the ore from the mines to the washing floors further down the valley, where it was cleaned and made ready for sale, was the work of pit ponies, hauling tramway wagons. But in 1877 they were replaced by *Ant* and *Bee* – two 19-inch gauge steam

Lovely, leafy Laxey belies its rich mining heritage.

locomotives which remained in service until the mine closed in 1929. Today, thanks to the dedicated work of the Laxey and Lonan Heritage Trust, the quarter-mile surface section of the tramway has been restored and two replica locos take passengers through what is the island's longest railway tunnel to a picnic site not far from *Lady Isabella* – better known as the Great Laxey Wheel.

One of the world's biggest ever waterwheels, it pumped water from the mines from depths of up to 2,000 feet. At 72 feet in diameter, with 95 steps leading to the viewing platform 75 feet above the ground, the wheel presents a breathtaking sight. Nearby, in Laxey Valley Gardens – once the washing floors – is *Lady Evelyn*. At a mere 50 feet in diameter, this restored wheel first served the remote Snaefell Mine, which closed in 1908, and then a Cornish china clay

works. The Trevithick Society preserved it and returned it to the Isle of Man, where it has been on show at Laxey since 2006.

Another of the village's attractions is the Laxey Heritage Trail – a leisurely and fascinating 2-hour circular walk from *Lady Isabella*. It takes you to a variety of interesting places, such as the woollen and flour mills, Quarry Falls, Old Laxey, Laxey Glen and the former 18th-century water-driven corn mill.

The Laxey and Lonan Heritage Trust, a voluntary organisation, has an information centre and gift shop located in the old fire station on the road just before you arrive at *Lady Isabella*. Lower down the glen are gardens, the beach and a small folk museum near the station. From the station you can get high aboard the scenic electric mountain railway on a 5-mile climb to the summit of Snaefell.

ONCHAN

This ancient parish immediately north of Douglas has grown rapidly since the Second World War, becoming something of an overspill for the capital although under the separate administration of the Onchan District Commissioners.

The patron saint of the parish was St Christopher, better known by his Gaelic name of Conchenn, meaning dog-head or wolf-head. In the porch of the present parish church, built in 1833, there are Norse carvings which depict dog-like monsters set on Christian crosses.

The church register dates back to 1627 although the first vicar was appointed in 1408. Interestingly, the church features some modern stained glass and in the churchyard there are headstones designed by Archibald Knox and the grave of Lieutenant Edward Reeves RN, the last surviving officer to fight with Nelson at Trafalgar. An earlier church on the site witnessed the marriage of Captain Bligh of *Bounty* fame to Elizabeth Betham, daughter of the Collector of Customs, who lived in Onchan and also lies buried in the churchyard. Beneath the churchyard wall stand two electric lamp standards, originally erected in 1897 to commemorate Queen Victoria's Diamond Jubilee and now the island's oldest street lamps.

Close by is chapel-like Welch House, a former infant school and Sunday school now used as an office. Above that is Molly Carrooin's Cottage. It is 300 years old and up to 100 years ago had a thatched roof. The recently-created village green connects with the Onchan Wetlands, an urban nature reserve on the site of an old mill dam.

The old part of the village grew up around the church – a process repeated with Onchan's rapid expansion, the old village now fringed by a large number of estates and a modern shopping precinct, as befits the second most populated area of the island.

Onchan, very close to Douglas and easily

Onchan Parish Hall, designed by Baillie Scott (1864-1945).

reached, is of interest to visitors for its country walks, King Edward Bay Golf Club, horseriding establishments, and Onchan Park and Stadium – a big magnet for all ages in summer months for activities such as boating, tennis, bowls, miniature golf, squash, go-karts and stock car racing.

PORT SODERICK

Popular with Victorian holidaymakers for its beach, bathing huts, refreshments and walks, Port Soderick lies only three miles south of Douglas on the east coast. This small resort and the capital were connected by road with the construction of Marine Drive, on the headland above Douglas harbour, but separated again when a landslide cut the road in two, as is still the case today. They were also once connected by the Douglas Southern Electric Tramway – the only railway on the Isle of Man ever to use the standard British gauge of track. Despite its demise, Marine Drive still provides an appreciation of the spectacular coastal views the tramway's passengers were treated to.

Port Soderick and Port Soderick Glen are still accessible by road using the A37.

Port St Mary is the island's main sailing centre.

TOWNS
AND VILLAGES
IN THE SOUTH

BALLASALLA

J ust north of Castletown and
Ronaldsway Airport, on the main A5
road south out of Douglas, is the village
of Ballasalla. Within its boundaries are
the extensively restored ruins of Rushen
Abbey. The interpretive centre explains the
site's history and significance, and the summer
2010 opening of the new Abbey Restaurant
is a development which many visitors will
welcome.

It is believed that the abbey was founded in

1098 by Magnus, King of Norway,
construction commencing in 1134. As with
many ancient sites, over recent centuries it
has provided a ready-made source of building
materials, but fortunately much of the fabric
of the original buildings has survived.

The abbey's Cistercian monks engaged in
all sorts of work – draining the land,
straightening the course of local rivers and
streams, and generally influencing the way of
life here. Close to the abbey is an example of
their achievements – Monks Bridge, dating
from the 14th century. With three arches but

Historic and charming Castletown.

a width of just four feet, it crosses the Silverburn River and is one of only a few packhorse bridges still standing anywhere in the British Isles. It is also referred to as the Crossag, a Gaelic word meaning little cross or crossing.

Records prove that a number of kings and abbots lie buried within the abbey's precincts. Excavation in the early 20th century unearthed a skeleton of a man buried with a bronze figure representing the Egyptian god Osiris, pointing to him having been a Crusader. Chronicon Mannia (*Chronicles of Mann*), a valuable reference work of the island's early history, was written at Rushen Abbey. It contains an account of the murder of Reginald II, King of Mann, by a knight called Ivar.

A little further upstream from the bridge, the Silverburn is joined by the Awin Ruy, or Red River. It flows down from Rozefel – Granite Mountain, or Stoney Mountain as it is called today – and its bed is strewn with boulders. The mountain was the source of

much of the building material used in the construction of the new Douglas breakwater in 1979. Norse settlers who recognised the colouring of the granite, exposed as it was to the elements, named the mountain Rjoofjall – Ruddy Mountain.

In summer months nearby Silverdale is one of the island's most frequented glens. It was originally the site of the Creg Mill and its dam is now a boating lake, very popular with children. There is also an unusual water-powered carousel here, along with a craft centre, café and wildlife and nature trails.

Ronaldsway Airport is easily reached from the village by bus or taxi. Ronaldsway, meaning Reginald's Ford in Norse, is reputedly the site of King Orry's castle and has been the scene of many battles.

CASTLETOWN

Sited at the edge of a long extinct and almost untraceable volcano, Castletown was for centuries the capital of the Isle of Man, its medieval limestone castle a symbol of

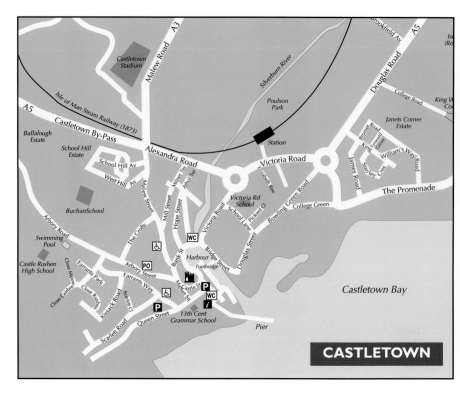

CASTLETOWN

strength, power and authority, guardian of the Manx in times of war and peace. It wasn't until the 1860s that the status of capital passed to Douglas, under the governorship of Scotsman Henry Loch.

Castletown today has a quiet but distinctive charm. Not only is the fortress which gave the stronghold its name still standing: it is in remarkably good nick – one of the most complete castles in the British Isles – and well worth seeing for its period recreations, fine views and deep sense of history. Castle Rushen dominates the southern lowlands and is visible for miles around. As well as being an impressive historical attraction it is also a working castle, its courthouse and precincts still in traditional use. A point of early military interest is that the staircases spiral to the right, obliging any uninvited swordsmen with hostile intent to grip their weapons left handed as they ascended so that right-handed

defenders had an obvious advantage.

The castle overlooks the harbour, which is built on a shelf of lava, clearly visible at low water. A walk along the shoreline from the harbour towards Scarlett Point shows you more evidence of this past volcanic activity in the area. Aeons of tide and weather have exposed the volcano's surviving plug, and the Scarlett Visitor Centre and nature trail make for an informative excursion.

The virtual end to commercial seaborne traffic into and out of Castletown came in the 1970s. Now banking and finance are the mainstays of the town's fortunes and have helped stimulate a revival in business. An innovative but sympathetic new purpose-built development in the heart of the old town is Callow's Yard, linking Arbory Street and Malew Street. Close to the harbour and castle, this upmarket shopping experience offers within one site a unique combination of select foods, places to eat and relax, facilities for functions and conferences, and apartments created specifically for holiday or business use.

Practically all of the town's ancient buildings are grouped around the harbour and to the seaward side of the castle. Among them is a cluster of small but fascinating museums. The Nautical Museum, Old House of Keys and Old Grammar School are all significant in the telling of the island's *Story of Mann* and attract many visitors, particularly in summer months.

The Nautical Museum's main exhibit is the remarkable 18th-century armed sailing schooner *Peggy*, built in 1789 but rediscovered by chance in 1935, walled up in her original harbourside boathouse (now the museum) a hundred years after the death of her owner Captain George Quayle. *Peggy* was involved in local smuggling and trade, and is officially recognised by Britain's National Historic Ships Committee as being 'of extraordinary maritime importance'– a distinction shared

with more than fifty other historic vessels, including Henry VIII's *Mary Rose*, all deemed worthy of preservation.

The Old Grammar School, built in approximately 1200, was originally the town's first church. Nearby is the old garrison church of St Mary's, built in 1826 to replace Bishop Wilson's church of 1698 and saved in recent times from dereliction. On his first visit to the Isle of Man in 1777, founder of Methodism John Wesley preached in front of the castle and noted in his journal of the 30th June of that year, "A more loving, simple-hearted people than this I never saw."

The Old House of Keys building was the seat of the Manx government from 1709 until 1869, when population and commercial pressures forced the move to the new capital of Douglas. Visitors are now welcome to sit in on live recreations of the debating process, sitting times (as advised at the time of this guide going to press) being 11.30am, 2.00pm and 3.00pm.

Castletown's market square is little changed

Medieval Castle Rushen keeps a watchful eye over the swans.

Have your say in a debate in the Old House of Keys.

since the 1800s. In the centre stands Smelt's Memorial, erected in 1838 to honour Governor Cornelius Smelt (1805 to 1832) – and to this day still incomplete. The people of Castletown refused to contribute for a statue to grace the column, the erection becoming known as the 'Castletown Candlestick'.

Across from the Smelt Memorial and close to the George Hotel is the former home of Captain John Quilliam RN, who fought at the Battle of Trafalgar and at the height of the fighting saved *HMS Victory* from destruction by rigging a jury (temporary) rudder.

Looking down on the square is a clock presented to the island by Queen Elizabeth I. Curiously, it has only ever had one finger – but is still going strong after 400 years!

Both anglicised and Norse names are much in evidence in the town and surrounding area – the legacy of Castletown's long association with the seat of government and early colonisation by Viking settlers. Look out for Bowling Green, Great Meadow, Paradise, Red Gap, Witches Mill and the Rope Walk, and homestead names such as Grenaby, Tosaby and

Orrisdale.

The outskirts of Castletown have almost as much history as the town itself. Lying to the east is King William's College, a long-time site of public school education, its great central tower dominating the landscape. Facing the school is Hango Hill, where the Manx patriot William Christian was shot (though posthumously pardoned of treason) for leading a revolt against the Countess of Derby when Charles II was England's king. The Norse name for the hill was Hangaholl, or Hill of Hanging, and Christian was the last person to be executed here. It is also an important archaeological site, with ruins of a blockhouse built by the seventh Earl of Derby at the time of the unrest in England.

To the west of the town is the Balladoole estate, centred on Balladoole House – for centuries the home of the Stevenson family. Evidence in Douglas's Manx Museum shows that at least six generations of the family lived on the estate prior to 1511.

John Stevenson, Speaker of the House of Keys (1704-1738), is remembered for the

These pepper pot lights welcome vessels into Castletown harbour.

The entrance to the Speaker's Garden, Castle Rushen.

manner in which he led the Keys in their patriotic struggle against the tenth Earl of Derby. Bishop Wilson called him 'the father of his country' and at one time he was imprisoned in Castle Rushen for championing the rights of his fellow countrymen.

To the west of Balladoole, where the coastal footpath Raad ny Foillan (Road of the Gull) joins the main A5 road, is the area known as Poyll Vaaish – easily reached by car or on foot from Castletown. There are superb views of the surrounding countryside, especially the panorama northwards as the low hills of the coastal areas roll ever upwards to the central mountain range, with Snaefell visible in the far distance.

Poyll Vaaish in English means Death Pool or Bay of Death. There are legends galore about this corner of the island – stories of shipwrecks, pirates and looters. In fact, the name probably derives from the black marble which comprises the sea bed in the vicinity, the ripples of lava evident at low water. Just after dropping down from the basaltic rock stack of Scarlett, you will come upon a small quarry where the black marble is worked. This was the source from which the steps of London's St Paul's Cathedral were made – a gift from Bishop Wilson – and in recent years replaced due to wear.

Close by the Stevensons' ancestral home is the site of a Viking ship burial mound – one of a number of ancient sites which make this area well worth exploring. Also of interest is Strandhall, where a spring flows down to the shore. Legend has it that although the source of the spring lies many feet above sea level, it is a salt water spring with petrifying powers. No doubt the story has taken credence from the fact that at exceptionally low tides – and particularly after a storm has moved the sands – the remains of a large petrified forest can sometimes be seen.

Visiting Castletown and its immediate area is easy, particularly if travelling from Douglas. There is a regular year-round bus service and

the steam railway operates in both directions several times a day from early to late summer. Driving is very easy too, although the narrow streets of Castletown itself make park and walk a better option for exploring the town which is also known for hosting major agricultural shows and the slightly more eccentric World Tin Bath Championships.

COLBY AND BALLABEG

To the east of Port Erin (and north-west of Castletown) in the flat lands of the parish of Arbory are the villages of Colby and Ballabeg. Colby (Kolli's Farm) stands at the entrance to the delightful Colby Glen.

A walk up the glen takes you alongside a brook which runs its lower course through wooded glades and higher up where the gorse is a blaze of yellow. Further up the glen again there are the remains of Keeill Catreeney (keeill meaning church or chapel) and a burial ground. The ancient St Catherine's or Colby Fair used to be held here. Nearby is Chibbyrt Catreeney (Catherine's Well), and it was said that anyone who drank from it would be forever afflicted with an unquenchable thirst.

Another fair, which still survives, is Laa Columb Killey (St Columba's Day Fair). Held in a field in either Colby or Ballabeg at the end of June each year, it attracts people from all over the island and gives a glimpse of Manx country life as it used to be.

Ballabeg is on the ancient quarterland and the village is named in the Manorial Roll of 1511 as Begson's Farm. The area is very rural and foxgloves and wild fuchsia line the quiet sheltered lanes. Weedkillers and pesticides are not used on Manx hedgerows and it is still possible to see wild flowers which have disappeared from other parts of the British Isles; the lanes of Arbory and the neighbouring parishes of Malew and Rushen display excellent examples. In fact, Manx Wildlife Trust in partnership with other bodies has introduced an initiative known as the Wild Flower Project to both conserve

Manx native wild flowers and encourage the planting of them wherever possible.

Churches have always played an important part in the life of the south of the island and none more so than Kirk Arbory. Built in 1757, the present church has an oak beam supporting the roof, the beam having belonged to two previous churches. An inscription on it mentions Thomas Radcliffe, Abbot of Rushen, and appears to refer to the influential Stanley family crest of an eagle and child. The grave of Captain Quilliam of *HMS Victory* and Trafalgar fame (see under Castletown) is in the churchyard.

Along the road from the church towards Castletown is Friary Farm, and clearly visible from the road are the remains of the Friary of Bemaken, founded by the Grey Friars in 1373. The friars were assisted in its completion by stonemasons who were on the island working on Castle Rushen. Employed by William de Montacute and later by his son, the masons were on the move around Britain strengthening castles and fortifications between 1368 and 1374. Two Ogham stones were found on the site and are now in the Manx Museum, Douglas. They are inscribed in the ancient Ogham script which was used in much of western Britain from the 4th to early 7th centuries.

CREGNEASH

Tucked away on a hillside of the Mull peninsula, in the Isle of Man's south-west corner, is the lovely village of Cregneash – referred to on some maps in its Gaelic spelling of Cregneish, meaning Rock of Ages. You can get to it very easily by road from Port St Mary, the A31 climbing Mull Hill and giving excellent views of the uplands rising to the north. The village is the oldest on the Isle of Man and its 19th-century thatched crofters' cottages are a folk museum representing yet another story in the Manx National Heritage *Story of Mann*.

The museum has a working farm and in summer there are authentic demonstrations of how life was for the island's crofters in the 1800s. The cottages nestle in and around a sleepy hollow. Views over the coastline and the nearby Calf of Man and Sound are stunning. Close by this 'modern' village are the remains of an older one. The Mull Circle (Meayll in Manx, meaning Bald or Bare Hill) dates back to the late Neolithic or early Bronze Age. Used primarily as a prehistoric burial place, it is unique in archaeological terms, combining the circle form with six pairs of cists (stone coffins), each pair having a passage between which radiates outwards. The prehistoric village was below the circle, and hut foundations and other relics were discovered on the site.

On the hilltop above the village is a radio beacon used by transatlantic airliners. The huddle of buildings nearby houses a similar system for Irish Sea shipping. Walking on past the beacons brings you to Spanish Head, so called because a galleon of the Spanish Armada was reputedly wrecked here. Also here is an area of land known as the Chasms – huge fissures, some a hundred feet deep,

A white thatched cottage? It has to be Cregneash.

Derbyhaven – forerunner to Epsom's famous horse race.

covered by gorse and heather and very dangerous for those foolish enough to ignore the warning signs and stray from the footpath.

From the village of Cregneash the road drops down to the Sound Visitor Centre, with its cafe and panoramic window overlooking the swirling tidal waters of the Sound and the Calf of Man beyond. This is one of the most scenic spots on the island and a haven for birds and wildlife. With binoculars you may be lucky enough to spot grey seals sunbathing on the rocks of Kitterland – another small island not far from the shoreline – or even basking sharks, feeding on microscopic plants and animals just below the surface.

Walking from the Sound – the Land's End of the Isle of Man – to Port St Mary or Port Erin is also a pleasure not to be missed.

DERBYHAVEN AND LANGNESS

A close neighbour of both Castletown and the extremities of Ronaldsway Airport is the picturesque hamlet of Derbyhaven, and stretching south behind its sheltered bay into the Irish Sea is the narrow finger of the Langness peninsula.

Ideal for windsurfers and small boats, Derbyhaven was a thriving port in the days of the Vikings and their medieval successors. It was here that blacksmith John Wilks, from whom two former Governors of the Bank of England are directly descended, made the island's first penny coins, an action which Tynwald authenticated by declaring them legal tender. The remains of the old smelthouse, probably dating from around 1711, are still visible. There is also evidence that Manx coinage was minted here by one John Murrey, a merchant of Douglas in 1668 and the probable owner of the Derbyhaven Mint.

The sandy turf of the Langness peninsula is home to the Castletown Golf Links. Close to the ruins of John Wilks' smelthouse is the 10th hole and it was here, 153 years before it was transferred to Epsom Downs in 1780,

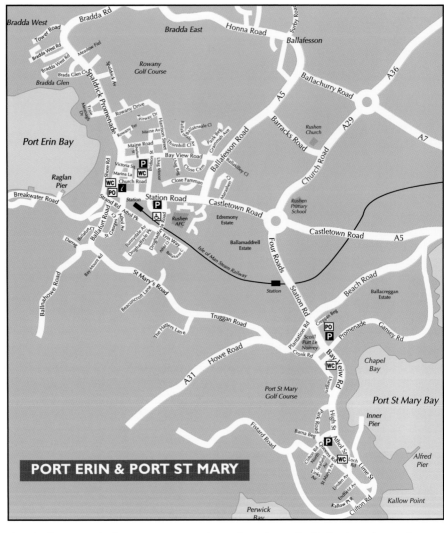

Bradda West
Bradda Rd
Tower Road
Bradda West Rd
Meadow Fiel
Bradda West Rd
Spaldrick Av
Brada Glen Clo
Bradda Glen
Spaldrick Promenade
Train Meadragh Dr

Bradda East
Honna Road
Surby Road
Ballafesson
Ballachurry Road
A36

Rowany Golf Course
Rowany Drive
Airway Dr
Rowany Ter
Maine Av
Ballaneale Cl
Thornhill Cl
Park Ter
Graemah Ave
Rushen Church
A5
A29
A7

Port Erin Bay
Maine Road
Bay View Road
Llag Doo
Ballafesson Road
Barracks Road
Church Road

Raglan Pier
Victoria Sq
Marina La
Church Road
Close Cam
Close Famman
Marathon Cl
Ballakilley Cl
Rushen Primary School

Breakwater Road
WC
PO
i
Strand Rd
Athol Pk
Station
Station Road
Rushen AFC
Edremony Estate
Castletown Road
Castletown Road
A5

Ballafurt Road
St Georges La
Sunnydale Av
Droghadfayle Rd
Erin Way
Ballahane Cl
Ballamaddrell Estate
Four Roads

Durrat
Bay Mount Rd
Isle of Man Steam Railway
Station
Station Rd
Beach Road
Ballacreggan Estate

Ballnashowe Road
St Mary's Road
Beaconcroft Lane
Truggan Road
Creggan Beg
Promenade
Gansey Rd

The Hatters Lan e
A31
Howe Road
Plantation Rd
Scoill Purt Le Noirrey
Cronk Rd
Bay Veiw Rd
WC
Chapel Bay

Port St Mary Golf Course
Fistard Road
Barna Beg
Park Rd
High St
Athol St
Port St Mary Bay
Inner Pier

Clifton Rd
Queens Rd
Seafield
St Mary's Av
Linden Av
Endfield Av
P
WC
Loch Rd
Lime St
Alfred Pier

Links Av
Perwick Bay
Kallow Pk
Clifton Rd
Kallow Point

PORT ERIN & PORT ST MARY

that the famous Derby horse race originated. It seems that the seventh Earl of Derby wished to encourage the breeding of Manx horses and as an incentive presented a cup to be won in open competition. One stipulation he put on the race was that only those horses that had been foaled within the island or on the Calf of Man could be entered. The Manx horses of that period were small and very hardy, renowned for their speed, surefootedness and stamina. It may well be that prior to the Derby the only time horses were in competition was after a wedding when the guests raced back to the bridegroom's home to claim the honour of breaking the bride cake over her head as she entered her new home!

Langness is very well known for its wildlife, especially birds – skylarks in particular - and it's often possible to see seals at Dreswick Point, the southernmost tip of the peninsula and indeed of the Isle of Man.

The waters here conceal a reef called the Skerranes which has claimed many lives. In 1853 the crew of the Plymouth schooner *Provider* perished and their bodies were buried in sight of the wreck, the grave marked by a nearby natural tombstone of rock carved with the vessel's name and the date of her loss.

The Langness lighthouse was built in 1880. It became fully automated in 1996, but prior to its construction another landmark was erected on the peninsula and is still here – the cylindrical structure known as the Herring Tower, built in 1811.

Pretty, popular, picturesque Port Erin bay.

PORT ERIN

Sitting close together but on opposite shoulders of the Mull peninsula – that is to say on its west side and its east side – are the popular summer seaside resorts of Port Erin and Port St Mary.

Whether you approach Port Erin by land or by sea the views are impressive. Port Erin translated means either Lord's Port or Iron Port and in Manx Gaelic is written as Purt Chiarn. Latter-day smugglers came to know

Port Erin very well, using the solitude of the bay to mask their activities and hidden from observation by the steep hills and perpendicular cliffs surrounding the village. In the 19th century the village became the playground of the Lancashire mill owners and their employees.

Situated at the head of an almost landlocked bay, which is guarded to the north by lofty Bradda Head and to the south by Castle Rocks and the peninsula, Port Erin

Port Erin station doubles as a museum of railway memorabilia.

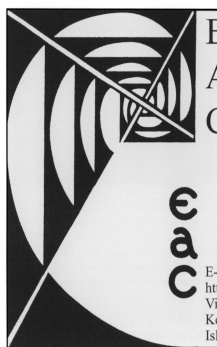

ERIN ARTS CENTRE

LAARE ELLYNYN PHURT CHIARN

Tel: 01624 832662
(Box Office)

Tel: 01624 835858
(Administration)

Fax: 01624 836658

E-mail: information@erinartscentre.com
http://www.erinartscentre.com
Victoria Square, Port Erin,
Kerrin Victoria, Phurt Chiarn,
Isle of Man IM9 6LD

offers shelter in most weathers. Pretty white-painted cottages trim the inner edge of the bay, bordered by grassy banks, rising up to a more formal promenade fronting a traditional line of seaside hotels.

The combination of sea, sand, cliffs, hills and heather makes Port Erin very photogenic. Add the appeal of cloud shadows, and brilliant sunsets often framed by Ireland's Mountains of Mourne, and you have some idea of the area's great visual attraction.

Port Erin is also popular for its fine 18-hole Rowany golf course and the Erin Arts Centre, a venue for regular events, exhibitions and the performing and visual arts.

More than a century ago the quality of the waters offshore from Port Erin motivated the establishment of the Marine Biological Station at the seaward end of the bay. In 2008 the staion closed but it is hoped that it wlll re-open again under local managment.

Directly opposite are the remains of a breakwater started in 1864 and which was meant to turn the bay into the national harbour of refuge. William Milner of Bradda Head was a staunch supporter of the breakwater and he along with everyone else on the island must have felt a great sense of loss when one night in January 1884 it was destroyed in a storm.

A notable son of Port Erin was William Kermode, born in 1775. Seeking fame and fortune, he crossed the world to take up a grant of land in Van Diemen's Land – now known as Tasmania – and did indeed amass a fortune and contributed valuable service to the Tasmanian Legislative Council. Ambushed in his coach by two bush rangers demanding his money or his life, he smacked their heads together, bound them up and drove to Hobart where they were arrested.

PORT ST MARY

Only a few miles from Port Erin across the neck of the Mull peninsula is the attractive fishing village of Port St Mary. The peninsula

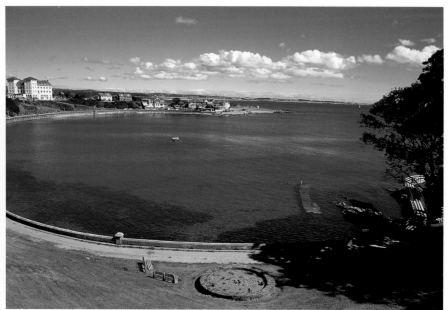

Port St Mary: a beautiful bay and great golf.

forms an impressive backdrop, its steep slopes and fields rolling right down into the village. The golf course here is the only 9-hole course on the island, but no less challenging for that, designed by the 1920 British Open Champion George Duncan. And the views from the sixth tee are spectacular.

Once a thriving fishing port and home to both Manx and Scottish vessels, Port St Mary has a factory which processes the delicious local shellfish delicacy known as queenies – a variety of small scallop. The harbour is full of pleasure boats of all types. The breakwater gives good shelter and its deepwater berths are popular with visiting sailors and the few remaining fishing vessels. The inner Alfred Pier, named after a previous Duke of Edinburgh who laid the foundation stone in 1882, shelters the smaller craft and is a very picturesque part of the port.

Clustered round the harbour are old Manx cottages, their original thatched roofs having long ago given way to Manx slate. The newer part of Port St Mary lies above the sandy beach of Chapel Bay. Linking the harbour and the bay is a fine walkway winding its way close to the water's edge.

Across the headland from Port St Mary Bay, on the southern side of Kallow Point, is Perwick Bay. This owes its name to the old Scandinavian word for Harbour Creek. In very recent times the hotel that once stood at the edge of the cliff has been developed for private housing but the beach is still worth a visit, particularly if you have more than a passing interest in geology: there is a noticeable fault on the bay's south-east side. The rocky pools and small caves at the foot of the cliffs make a good play area for children. Sitting high on the hillside above Perwick Bay is the village of Fistard.

From castle and cathedral to kippers and Celts, Peel's great appeal is multifaceted.

TOWNS AND VILLAGES IN THE WEST

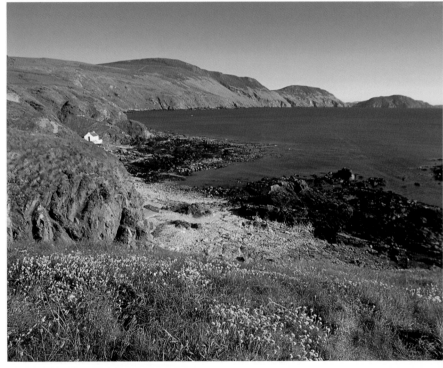

GLEN MAYE AND NIARBYL

Glion Muigh (Glen Maye) means Yellow Glen, and this is a village sitting on steep hillsides at the bottom end of the mining glens of Glen Mooar and Glen Rushen. It is easy to see that the village owes its existence to the farming and mining industries, and much of its original character has been retained.

Beyond the village the river plunges over a series of waterfalls, before finishing its dash to the sea between high cliffs which are clad in gorse and heather.

Niarbyl (or to give it its Manx name Yn Arbyl, meaning The Tail, on account of the long reef jutting out from the shoreline) is an ideal place for picnics, with superb views to the north and south and boasting an attractive new cafe and visitor centre on the approach road down to the sea. The grandeur of the west and south-west coast is probably best experienced from this isolated but marvellously relaxing spot – a favourite location for film and TV productions. Massive

Peel's castle and cathedral ruins, St Patrick's Isle.

PEEL

cliffs stretch away southward in a series of giant headlands and bays before Bradda Head, at Port Erin, briefly interrupts the flow. The Mull Hills continue the vista and from this angle it almost seems as if the Calf of Man is joined to the main island. You'd also be hard pushed to find better walking country than this.

FOXDALE

Foxdale is a cunningly misleading name, because it actually translates as Waterfall Dale – very apt in view of the area's abundance of streams. The village was once a centre for lead mining and from the 300 or so tons of ore mined each month, some 15 to 20 ounces of silver per ton were extracted. When the industry ceased in the early part of the 20th century, many of the miners emigrated to the colonies, and it has taken a long time for the village to begin to recover some of its lost prosperity.

Draw a straight line from west to east approximately half way down a map of the Isle of Man and you will see that Peel and Laxey are exactly opposite each other on their respective coastlines, separated by a distance of about 13 miles. But while Laxey is relatively close to both Douglas and Ramsey, Peel is the west coast's only sizeable town – and the only one on the Isle of Man to have a cathedral.

In fact, Peel has two cathedrals. One is the medieval ruin of St German's, located within the walls of Peel Castle on St Patrick's Isle, the isle being accessible via the causeway. The other, the present Pro-Cathedral in the centre of the town, is a fine building which technically speaking gives this ancient fishing port the status of a city.

Peel takes its name from an abbreviated form of St Patrick's Isle and has only been known as this since the name came into regular use in the 19th century. The town has played a significant role in the development of the island's nationhood, and excavations of the area's Viking settlement have uncovered important burial sites.

One site revealed the remains of a female subsequently known as 'The Pagan Lady'. The grave was unusual in that it was a curious mixture of Christian and Pagan rituals, and a very fine bead necklace was recovered and is one of many artefacts displayed in the Manx Museum in Douglas.

Celebrated prisoners have been incarcerated in Peel Castle over the ages. Shakespeare makes mention in *Henry VI* of one such famous detainee – Eleanor, Duchess of Gloucester, who for 14 years was imprisoned in the cathedral crypt, accused of treason and sorcery against Henry VI as she sought to advance her husband's claim to the English throne. Her fellow plotters were not so fortunate: Roger Bolingbroke was executed and Margery Joudemain, the Witch of Eye, was burnt to death. History records that the duchess was a difficult prisoner, capable of escape or even suicide and in need of careful guarding. Her ghost is said to haunt

the cathedral's crypt.

For a long time Peel was the centre of the Isle of Man's once-thriving fishing industry, boasting a great maritime tradition and a considerable fleet. Today the port is still known for its traditional oak-smoked Manx kippers, the quayside factory and museum open to summer visitors.

Close to the harbour and kipper factory is the Manx Transport Museum – the smallest of the island's museums, and not to be confused with the much larger Transport Museum under development in Jurby. Only about 60 square metres in size, the Peel museum's unusual and rare exhibits include a P50 from 1962 – the world's smallest road-legal car ever produced, this example being one of just 100 made by the town's long-defunct Peel Engineering Company.

Peel's place and story in Isle of Man history is brilliantly told in House of Manannan – a waterside attraction that's not to be missed. Named in honour of the ancient sea god but very much a museum experience for the 21st century, this highly engaging interactive heritage centre presents the town's role

Former warehouses along Peel's inner waterfront are now fashionable apartments.

within the context of the *Story of Mann*. The centre is one of the island's major visitor attractions, as well as a successful educational aid for Manx school children.

But if history is not your thing, Peel merits a visit for other reasons too – notably the sands, ice cream, 18-hole golf course, fabulous sunsets and quiet relaxing charm.

ST JOHN S

Inland, 5 miles to the east of Peel, you will find the attractive village of St John's. Every year in early July (normally on 5th) this pleasant and quiet community is completely transformed by the colour, splendour and ceremony of Tynwald Day – the island's national celebration of more than 1,000 years of unbroken self-government.

Thousands of people crowd around Tynwald Hill to witness an ancient tradition which includes the proclamation, in both Manx and English but in summarised form, of laws enacted during the last year. These are read out by the Deemsters – the Manx equivalent of British High Court Judges – and also in attendance are the Lieutenant Governor of the island and a whole assembly of dignitaries, civil servants and others. On occasions, Her Majesty the Queen or other member of the British royal family is guest of honour.

But it's not all pomp: many of the spectators are here to enjoy all the fun of the fair which is an important element of the day's celebrations.

The village of St John's has several important everyday attractions too, none more popular than Tynwald Mills Centre – relaxing country shopping in quality outlets housed under the roof of the spacious former woollen mills. Close by is Manx Wildlife Trust (a mine of information and excellent books) and, within easy walking distance, St John's stately Royal Chapel, the beautiful and not-to-be-missed national arboretum and park, and the showcase Manx Wild Flower Garden.

Stay on a Manx Farm

"Staying on a farm - b&b or self-catering - has lots of natural appeal, particularly when you're talking Isle of Man."

There can be few finer ways to get an authentic snapshot of Isle of Man life than to stay at one of the beautifully located properties that make up the Stay on a Manx Farm initiative. A group of working island farmers have opened their doors – and their unique rural lifestyle – to guests who are looking for a genuine Manx hospitality in a truly idyllic setting.

You can choose from purpose designed self-catering premises to cosy bed and breakfast rooms with en-suite facilities. A stay on a Manx farm can be as energetic or as relaxing as you choose to make it, but you can always rely on warm hospitality and high quality accommodation.

allachrink Bungalow, Bride	Tel: (01624) 880364
allachrink Farmhouse, Bride	Tel: (01624) 880364
allacricket Farmhouse, Ronague	Tel: (01624) 823696
allavair Farm House, Bride	Tel: (01624) 880830
allavell Farm, Grenaby	Tel: (01624) 824306
olooneys Farm Cottages, Cooil	Tel: (01624) 611898
raig Cottage, St Judes	Tel: (01624) 880242
raig View Cottage, St Judes	Tel: (01624) 880242
roit-ny-Bane Farm, Kirk Andreas	Tel: (01624) 880316
errowgarrow Barns, Greeba	Tel: (01624) 801871
ionslieu Farm Cottages, Higher Foxdale	Tel: (01624) 801349
nockaloe Beg Farmhouse, Patrick	Tel: (01624) 844279
meale Farm Cottage, Smeale	Tel: (01624) 880888
he Stable at Glendown Farm, Port St Mary	Tel: (01624) 834699
he Stables, Knockaloe Beg, Patrick	Tel: (01624) 844279
hie y Ribbeyder, Smeale	Tel: (01624) 880888

www.stayonamanxfarm.com

Seeing the light: Maughold Head is a distinctive landmark and the nearby village of Maughold was an important centre of Celtic Christianity.

TOWNS AND VILLAGES IN THE NORTH

ANDREAS, BRIDE AND JURBY

This is very much farming country. The relatively flat northern plain, easy for walking and cycling, is a maze of roads and lanes zigzagging between the villages. Andreas, Bride and Jurby are the island's three most northerly parishes (central, east and west respectively) and share virtually the same scenery, the Bride Hills providing the only high ground in the area.

Jurby though is now developing at a pace

calculated to transform it from the small community which grew up around the Royal Air Force base in the years of the Second World War into a west coast village in its own right. The famous old airfield, which has served many purposes since those war years – not least as the very popular motorsport and gliding venue which it is today – is the focal point of this activity and is attracting attention for a variety of reasons.

One is the creation of the new Manx Transport Museum, housed in Hangar 230

Ballaglass Glen, near Maughold – a favourite haunt of Manx poet T.E. Brown.

and (at the time of going to press) due to open at Easter 2010. The museum is dedicated to the island's road transport heritage, particularly buses, which unlike railway heritage has been largely neglected over the decades. Consequently, many of the older buses and other road vehicles which served the Manx community throughout the 20th century and before have been long forgotten or scrapped. Manx Transport Trust, responsible for the new museum, is redressing the balance by salvaging and preserving as many relevant vehicles as possible and displaying them as a prized collection. Seeing old buses and the like being restored to first-class condition and working order on site will be one of the many attractions for visitors.

Another enterprise which is highly likely to benefit from the new museum's presence is the nearby and long-established Jurby Junk. Proprietor Stella Pixton started the business in the 1970s with the aim of providing long-term security for her young son, but when he grew up and moved on she persevered and

now occupies two industrial units on the airfield-cum-industrial estate – one offering a choice of any sort of junk imaginable and the other a selection of as many books as you can cram into 3,000 square feet! Over the years, Stella's customers have included not only locals and holidaymakers but also many film and TV companies in search of props for their Isle of Man-based productions. Stella's other claim to fame is that she is the proud daughter of a very distinguished and celebrated father – pilot and aviation pioneer Charles Howard Pixton, who in 1914 won the Schneider Trophy for Britain and went on to become a key figure in British and Manx aviation history and development. He died in 1972 and is buried at the churchyard in Jurby.

In fact, Jurby's old garrison church merits a visit. The porch has a fine collection of stone crosses, and wandering through the churchyard and reading the inscriptions on the old headstones evokes many images of local history. In the new part of the churchyard, the well-kept graves of Polish,

Canadian, Anzac and British airmen are laid out in neat rows. On a clear day, from the back of the church, you can see Scotland's Mull of Galloway and its lighthouse.

Andreas has always been a pleasant village with a peaceful rural existence, largely uninterrupted since the end of the Viking era. In the 1940s, the land to the north and east of the village served as a base for the RAF. Roads and lanes accustomed to carrying nothing bigger than a horse and cart were widened, and it was not unusual to see large aircraft being manoeuvred on the roads skirting the edge of this ancient village. In 1995 the old airfields of Andreas and Jurby were used as locations for the film *The Brylcreem Boys*.

The parish church of Kirk Andreas with its Lombardic campanile is unexpected, but the Italian style sits well with the Manx countryside. It was built in 1802 to replace a parish church from the 13th century, the time when parishes were first formed on the island. In 1869 Anglo-Saxon coins were discovered during the building of the bell tower. Dedicated to St Andrew, probably during the period of Scottish rule (circa 1275 to 1334), there are indications that a much earlier church, whose name has been lost, occupied the site. During the Second World War the spire was removed from the church to give a clear flight path for the planes using RAF Jurby and RAF Andreas.

The Andreas carved stones are very fine examples of Dark Age craftsmanship and one, a pillar, is particularly interesting with an inscription in Roman capitals and letters from the Ogham alphabet. Such carvings are seldom found outside Wales.

Not only the hills on whose slopes it sits but also a new rose share their name with the village of Bride. But looking at the village's past, the romance ends there. Bride was frequently raided by pirates and marauders, on clear days the smoke from the village's chimneys visible on the Galloway coast and tempting the villainous chieftain Cutlar MacCulloch and his men to set sail for a free Manx feed. On one occasion, arriving at a wedding feast just after soup had been taken, they deprived the guests of the meat by eating it all themselves.

To the west of Bride is Thurot Cottage, a private house built using timbers from the ship of a defeated French fleet led by the vessel *Bellisle*, under the command of Captain Thurot. The battle, in February 1760, was witnessed by Bishop Hildesley and probably seen – and certainly heard – from Bride.

Bride church and its Celtic cross are interesting, and this is a very pleasant area for walking.

BALLAUGH

The comparatively modern north-west village of Ballaugh is within easy reach of the west coast and straddles the A3 between Kirk Michael and Ramsey. It marks the beginning of the scenery that is so typical of this corner

Ballaugh – the newer of the parishes
two churches, built in 1832.

of the island: remote glens running down to low sandy cliffs and shoreline against the hills of the northern uplands. The new church, built in 1832, is clearly visible from a distance. Approximately a mile and a half nearer to the sea is old Kirk Ballaugh Church, with its very distinctive 'leaning' gate posts. Ballaugh has the oldest parish register in the island, dating from 1598.

KIRK MICHAEL

On the west coast and a few miles south of Ballaugh, Kirk Michael (previously called Kirk Michael Towne or Michaeltown) sits at the junction of the spectacular A4 coast road to Peel and the picturesque A3 to St John's and the south.

It is also on the famous TT course, and the spotlight falls on the town in late May and early June every year when the races pass through; the inhabitants of Kirk Michael are said to have the flattest feet in the Isle of Man because their houses edge right up to the race course! A good place from which to watch the racing is the Mitre. Very close to the town is Glen Wyllin (meaning Mill Glen, and sometimes spelt without a break between the words). At one time a bridge carried a railway line high above the glen and helped make it a very popular spot with holidaymakers. Nothing remains of the railway now except for the two redundant sandstone bridge supports, but the beauty of the glen is undiminished and still attracts many visitors, the lower section leading to the shore.

Five bishops are buried within the grounds of the local church. There is a memorial stone to the popular cleric 'The Good' Bishop Wilson, who did much for the people of the island in his long and beneficial stewardship.

MAUGHOLD

In the north-east of the island close to Ramsey (Maughold Head overlooks Ramsey Bay) is the village of Maughold. It enjoys stunning views of coast and countryside and was the most important centre of Celtic

The cross house at St Maughold church contains fine examples of carved Celtic and Norse crosses.

RAMSEY

Ramsey Bay

The Mooragh

A9 Andreas Road
Bride Rd A10
Thorn Hill Park
Thorn Hill Cl
Ormley Avenue
Ormley Road
Rheast Mooar Lane
Rheast Mooar Cl
Rheast Mooar Av
Cooil Breryk
Grovemount West
Moorgh Park
Grovemount
Richmond Road
Richmond Gr
Crowe Mount West
Ash Gr
Hospital
Jurby Road
Whitebridge Av
Gardeners La
Mt Auldyn
Cumberland Rd
St Olaves Cl
Bay View
Coburg Road
Lakeside Centre
Moorgh Promenade
Park Road
Premier Rd
Moorgh Lake
Ballacloan Road
Windsor Road
Windsor Mount
Windsor Gr
Crowells Ter
Westfield Dr
Bowring Road
Riverside
Ramsey Football Stadium
North Shore Road
Old River Road
Hope St
Templar Ter
Teare's
Ship Yard Road
Gibson St
Marsden Ter
Sulby River
PO
WC
Gladstone Park
Gladstone Av
Station Rd
Parliament Sq
Derby Road
Close Claddagh
Close Kella
Lezayre Estate
Bircham Avenue
Bircham Av
Close
West St
Auckland La
West Quay
West Quay
Neptune St
East Quay
Dale St
Swimming Pool
Queens Promenade
Auldyn Infants School
Fairfield Av
Taubman St
Christian St
Parliament St
Water St
St Pauls Square
Marine Gr
Lezayre Road
Ramsey Grammer School
Ramsey Grammer School
Albert Square
Albert Rd
Albert Rd School
Station Albert St
The Strand
Fairway Drive
Brookfield Avenue
Brookfield Cres
Westbourne Rd
Queens Pier Road
Tower Rd
Parsonage Rd
Summerland
Waterloo Road
Approach Rd
Queen's Pier (The Iron Pier)
Ramsey Golf Club
Crook Elfin
Princes Road
Vernon Road
Seamount Rd
Manx Electric Railway
Brookhill Rd
Pier Road
Queens Drive
Stanley Mt West
Walpole Rd Dr
Walpole
Mountain Road
May Hill
Glen Elfin Rd
Beaumont Road
Lheaney Road
Lheaney Gr
Killeba Road
Crescent Road
Queens Gr
Ballure Rd
Ballure Road
Claughbane Av
Claughbane Drive
Ballastowell Gdns
Barrule Park
The Cres West
The Crescent
Claughbane Walk
Mountain Road A18

Christianity on the Isle of Man.

The church, Kirk Maughold, which dates from the 12th century, is dedicated to St Maughold, who is said to have been cast ashore near the headland.

The churchyard contains the remains of four ancient keeills (churches or chapels) and beautiful carved stone crosses found in the area are on display in the cross house. Of both Celtic and Norse origins, they are among the finest examples of the many carved crosses which have been discovered throughout the island's landscape.

A path from the village takes you to the lighthouse on Maughold Head and those breathtaking views.

PORT E VULLEN

This small and attractive sheltered bay snuggles between Maughold Head and Ramsey Bay.

RAMSEY

Ramsey, the second largest town on the Isle of Man, is blessed with a wonderful setting: cradled by the 10-mile sweep of the crescent bay, whose sandy shoreline extends to the northernmost Point of Ayre, against the backdrop of the high hills of North Barrule.

Chronicles of Mann of about 1250 records this north-eastern town as Ramsa – seemingly drawn from the old Scandinavian language and meaning Wild Garlic River – yet there are no buildings of great antiquity in Ramsey other than Ballure Church. The Burial Register dates from 1611 and in 1637 the building was reported to be in a near ruinous state. At various times over the years it has been restored.

The probable reason for Ramsey's lack of old buildings is that it suffered much turmoil throughout its early history. Olaf, King of

The long twin breakwaters at the harbour entrance identify this as Ramsey.

towns **and** villages in the **NORTH**

Historic Milntown promises a variety of novel attractions.

Mann, was murdered by his nephew Reginald near the harbour in 1154. Somerled, the 12th-century Thane of Argyll, made a historic landing here, and a century later Robert the Bruce passed through on his way to besiege Castle Rushen.

Centuries on, landing in Ramsey became a lot easier when the magnificent Queen's Pier was built in 1886. Thrusting out into deep water for a distance of 2,248 feet, it established Ramsey as a popular stopping-off point for steamers en route to other ports of call. Today Ramsey harbour, with its twin forcep-like breakwaters at the entrance, offers shelter to yachts, coasters and trawlers. It is the headquarters of the Manx Sailing and Cruising Club, which organises local races and is responsible for the prestigious Isle of Man Round the Island Yacht Race every summer.

Another very distinctive feature of Ramsey's harbour is the iron swingbridge, 225 feet long, which came into operation in 1892. On the landward side of the bridge is Ramsey shipyard, which constructed one of the world's first iron ships as well as *Star of*

India, now displayed as an attraction in the American port of San Diego. The yard also built the world's first two ships specifically designed as oil tankers.

Flowing into the bay via the harbour is the island's longest river, the Sulby. In fact, Ramsey was once an island. In 1630 the town was virtually destroyed by the sea, a continuous threat until the early years of the 19th century.

In 1881, Mooragh Park was created on reclaimed wasteland, protected by a new promenade and sea wall. It is a very popular spot and a great attraction for all ages, with 40 acres of gardens and a 12-acre boating lake. Canoeing, sailing and other water-based activities are part of the draw, as are the summer concerts and galas held in the park and the Lakeside Centre.

Ramsey hosts several major annual events, including Yn Chruinnaght – the week-long Celtic festival of music, dance, art and literature – and vintage motor rallies add to the fun and excitement of spectaculars such as the TT Festival and Manx Grand Prix, and also complement Ramsey's Fun Carnival Day

✚*Milntown*

Lezayre Road, Ramsey IM7 2AB

An historic House set in 15 acres of
outstanding Gardens and Grounds,
which include a Watermill and Millpond.

Fine Café and Restaurant
serving a wide selection of light
refreshments and meals.

Gardens and Café open
March to October 10.00am - 5.00pm.
Café open most weekends during the
Winter season 11.00am - 4.00pm.
Please phone for Restaurant
opening times.

Tours of the House by arrangement.
Occasional events and exhibitions.

For Café, Restaurant and Functions
telephone (01624) 818091
For all other information
telephone (01624) 812321

www.milntown.org

in July.

The town has other big sporting attractions. The summer angling festival pulls in many keen fishermen, and golfers now have a choice of two 18-hole courses in the area – Ramsey's long-established club and Glen Truan, a newer course at Bride.

For visitors with a preference for history, the Grove Museum of Victorian life in Ramsey – part of the *Story of Mann* – presents an interesting country house preserved as a period museum, with 19th-century furnishings and fittings.

A larger and much older historic Ramsey house is Milntown. For over 400 years, up to 1886, this was the residence of the Christian family, members of which famously included William Christian (1608-1663 – the last man to be executed at Hango Hill near Castletown but posthumously pardoned of treason), Fletcher Christian (notorious leader of the mutiny on *HMS Bounty*) and Ewan Christian (the only person ever to have been both an MP in the House of Commons and a member of the Isle of Man's House of Keys).

The Milntown estate, which adjoins the entrance to Glen Auldyn, originally covered about 500 acres and is now a more modest but very impressive 15 acres, comprising the historic house, extensive gardens and collections of vintage cars and motor cycles. Plans to open Milntown as a visitor attraction will come into effect from early 2010, beginning with the opening of the restaurant and gardens. House and ghost tours are scheduled for later in the year. Milntown is reputedly the Isle of Man's most haunted house, as featured on TV's *Ghost Hunting* with invited guests from the cast of *Coronation Street*.

The vintage vehicles of the Milntown collection are all roadworthy and are frequently displayed at major events such as the Isle of Man TT Festival. The house also contains fine collections of paintings, furniture, ceramics and silver.

Set yourself free!

Imagine a place which is far away from the hustle and bustle of everyday life, yet is so close to home. A place with breathtaking scenery and a relaxed and un-demanding pace of life, where you're guaranteed a warm welcome, friendly service and the very best of hospitality. Imagine the Isle of Man.

For more information on travelling to the Isle of Man, the events and attractions on offer or to request a 2010 holiday guide please visit our website:

www.visitisleofman.com

In Victorian times the beach at Port Soderick (just right of centre) was very popular, at that time connected to Douglas by tramway.

THE
NATURE
OF THE LANDSCAPE

There's no better place to appreciate the topography of the Isle of Man than from the top of the island's highest peak. At 2,036 feet Snaefell is certainly no giant, but on a clear day you can see much of the island itself and, across the Irish Sea, the Cumbrian Mountains to the east, the purple hills of Galloway to the north, Snowdonia to the south and, to the west, Ireland's Mountains of Mourne in the north and Wicklow Mountains in the south. The view from the top of Snaefell also throws light on the fact that more than forty per cent of the island's land area is uninhabited.

Snaefell stands in the middle of the ridge of hills which runs through the Isle of Man on a north-east to south-west axis, from Ramsey to Cronk ny Arrey Laa (thought to mean 'hill of the day watch') south of Niarbyl, where the cliffs drop steeply into the sea.

Cutting across the ridge and dividing the uplands into north and south is a central valley extending from Peel to Douglas.

The large slate massif responsible for Snaefell also produced 25 peaks exceeding 1,000 feet in height. In the process it created a very pleasurable walk; you can spend a day striding across the uplands, through gorse and heather, taking in the wonderful panoramas of the Isle of Man's east and west coasts without any great rollercoaster variations in descent and ascent.

In fact, walking in the hills will take you to some of the wildest places on the island. The scenery is spectacular, particularly with the purple heather of late summer, and the heathland is a diverse wildlife habitat of international importance. Ling, western gorse, bell heather and bilberry are the dominant plants. Blanket bog is another globally-rare habitat found in the uplands.

Birdwatchers too will have a field day. Curlew, skylark, meadow pipit and wheatear are among the species which do well up here. The island as a whole supports a great variety of birdlife and is recognised for its healthy populations of chough, peregrine falcon, raven and hen harrier, the latter representing somewhere in the order of ten per cent of the total hen harrier population in the British Isles. Since the 1960s the Calf of Man bird and nature reserve has been home to an officially-designated British Bird Observatory.

The hills have broad ridges with relatively smooth slopes merging into wide drainage basins. Streams cutting into the hillsides have produced the glens which collectively are one of the Isle of Man's great natural attractions.

Large areas of the uplands were once covered in forest. Tree loss in Neolithic times probably resulted in waterlogging and the formation of the peat on which the Manx people relied for fuel until relatively recently. In Viking times, many people lived on the uplands in summer, grazing livestock on the common pasture. The remains of their settlements, called 'sheilings', can still be seen.

GLENS

Though there are few valleys of significance, the Isle of Man is known for its glens, many of which have been purchased by the Manx Government as national treasures. There are 17 of these national glens – and others besides – and broadly speaking each is categorised as either mountain or coastal in nature. They vary in physical length, breadth and isolation but each is beautiful in its own way.

The national glens are also the largest areas

Peel's enticing beach, bay and medieval castle and cathedral ruins.

of established broad-leafed woodland. Many are characterised by tumbling waterfalls, and the rushing waters of the steep glens were once put to good use for milling, mineral extraction and to drive turbines in the manufacture of paper. Relics of such enterprise can be found in the shape of disused mine shafts and buildings.

When Victorian holidaymakers started coming to the island in large numbers, pleasure gardens, railways, follies and other attractions were created to further romanticise and popularise the glens.

A fine example of a mountain glen is Sulby (also known as Tholt-e-Will Glen). It starts from a spring in peat moss on the west slopes of Snaefell and runs down to Sulby. It is river-worn (the Sulby River is the island's longest), deep and bold and represents an image of the grandest of Manx scenery in miniature. One of the glen's most charming attractions is the Tholton craft studio and shop. This produces only genuine Manx crafts, including the Isle of Man's only handmade teddy bears.

Glen Auldyn is perhaps the gentlest of Manx mountain glens and starts on the north of Snaefell as a trickling rill, then runs down through forest and a couple of hamlets to Milntown on the B17. The views at the top end are splendid.

One of the loveliest of the short coastal glens is Ballaglass, near Maughold Head in the north. It is easily accessible by Manx Electric Railway. You can walk its total length or just a section of it nearer the sea. The lower wooded part is wonderful in spring when coloured by bluebells, and the area is rich in folklore. Here you might just encounter the spectre of the giant Irish deer, the 'Londhoo'.

Dhoon Glen, a little further south and also on the route of the Manx Electric Railway, is typical of the quaint coastal glens. From the car park the walk down to the beach takes about half an hour.

Country walks in the glens.

PARKS AND GARDENS

The Victorian tourist boom spawned a good number of parks. Many have lost their grandeur but are still very pleasant and relaxing, most with free access.

The Arboretum at St John's is a fine spot for a picnic. The park's abundant trees and shrubs were gifted to the Manx nation by world governments in celebration of the Tynwald Millennium, the 1,000th year of the Manx Parliament, in 1979. Nearby are the Manx Wild Flower Garden and the nursery gardens of the Forestry Department.

Douglas has many parks and gardens, tended with great pride. Best known are undoubtedly the sunken gardens on the promenade. Noble's Park, with its sporting and leisure facilities, and the Villa Marina's attractive colonnaded gardens were donated to the town by Henry Bloom Noble.

From July to October, Summerhill Glen is a joy for children, the evenings brightened by fairy lights and illuminated animal displays.

Douglas even has its own special rose – the Douglas Centenary – which celebrated the capital's 100th year as a borough in 1996. To the north end of Douglas Bay, and within walking distance of most of the Douglas hotels, is Onchan Park, which offers a great variety of family entertainment through to late summer.

Laxey has fine natural gardens. The sheltered site of the old mine washing floors has been turned into a garden to blend in with the surrounding landscape.

The biggest park in Ramsey is Mooragh. There are rowing boats, canoes, pedaloes and sailing dinghies for hire and you can learn to sail, canoe or windsurf. There are also a bowling green, crazy golf and putting green, and along the banks of the Sulby River you can enjoy the nature trails of the Poyll Dooey (Pool of the Black Ford) wetlands.

ONSHORE AND OFFSHORE

The best way to appreciate the breathtaking beauty of the Isle of Man's 100-mile coastline is by following the Road of the Gull coastal footpath, as described in detail further on in this guide. However, for the moment, you can think of the island's coast in terms of two distinct sections.

Going clockwise from Maughold in the north-east to Peel in the west is maritime hardcliff. These rocky cliffs include some of the remotest places on the island, least affected by human activity and idyllic breeding grounds for numerous bird species. The vegetation along the footpaths is also of interest. The tall cliffs at Douglas Head diminish incrementally all the way down to Derbyhaven. Between the two, on a low promontory above Port Grenaugh west of Santon Head, is a Celtic fort called Cronk ny Merriu (which means 'House of the Dead'). The Vikings subsequently used the fort and there are remains of a rectangular Viking house within the original fortifications. On Langness and around Derbyhaven, there are large populations of wading birds and

Langness is a picture of wild flowers.

Further round the 'clock' are the dramatic sights of Spanish Head, the Chasms and the Sugar Loaf – a solitary conical rock 100 feet tall favoured by breeding guillemots, razorbills and kittiwakes. Along the edge of Bay Fine look out for basking sharks feeding just below the surface – sunglasses are a useful aid for spotting them. Other points of note along this first of the two sections of coastline include Milner's Tower on top of Bradda Head at Port Erin, the Bradda Hills, the tall cliffs 1,400 feet high shot for the opening sequence of the feature film *Waking Ned*, Corrin's Folly on Corrin's Hill above Peel, and St Patrick's Well, where legend has it that the horse St Patrick was riding shed a silver shoe and spring water immediately gushed forth, forming the well.

The other section of coast, continuing clockwise from Glen Mooar to Ramsey, is not as dramatic as the rocky extremities in the south but is of vital importance for its ecology. Predominantly sand and shingle, or maritime soft cliff and dune, it embraces the Ayres, which has several special habitats unique on the island and is both a National Nature Reserve and a designated Area of Special Scientific Interest (ASSI).

The Ayres derives its name from the old Norse word eyrr meaning 'gravelbank'. The soft cliff and dune here is still changing as the hills to the south are being eroded and some of this material is being deposited. Marram grass (used locally as thatching and known as bent) stabilises the dunes. Just inland, heath has developed on the thin soil, and heathers, western gorse and other grasses grow here. The Ayres is notable for small breeding colonies of Arctic and little terns, and other bird species you are likely to see here include mallard, shelduck, lapwing, curlew, oystercatcher, gannet, shag and cormorant. The Ayres also has a visitor centre and nature trails.

Offshore, the Calf of Man in the south is the only true island, but there are a number of small islets and rocks which are of interest historically or ecologically.

The Calf of Man is a bird sanctuary and nature reserve managed by Manx National Heritage. There is a resident warden and a bird observatory, and the cliffs and springy turf are nesting grounds for an impressive variety of species including chough and Manx shearwater. At one time the latter was harvested for food and for oil used in the treatment of wool and for cleaning firearms. The ground-nesting shearwater population was decimated in the 18th century, most probably by rats escaping to the Calf from a ship.

It is possible to visit the Calf during summer months, weather and visitor numbers permitting. Regular sailings operate from Port Erin and Port St Mary. With a circumference of 5 miles and an area of 616 acres, the Calf can be explored easily in half a day – although such is the peace and tranquillity of the place that you may well find it difficult to leave!

Just off the Calf is Chicken Rock, unmissable for the lighthouse built in 1875 to steer shipping well clear of the treacherous reef on the edge of a steep descent deep into the Irish Sea.

Of much greater significance in Manx history is St Patrick's Isle, Peel – the site of the remains of Peel Castle and its medieval St German's Cathedral. "No part of the Isle of Man has played so great and interesting a part in the history as the islet known as Peel Island, or St Patrick's Isle." So spoke Canon Stenning. And in any historical account or modern photographic portrait of the Isle of Man, the isle is present, the first mention of it occurring in *Annals of Ulster* for the years 797-798. In addition to the castle, numerous periods of architecture are represented, from prehistoric earthworks to Napoleonic fortifications, and the islet has served as a garrison, an armoury and an ecclesiastical prison. Eight bishops are believed to have been buried here. The castle ruins are a big

Autumn in St John's.

visitor attraction and the grounds a venue for open-air summer concerts and theatre.

Offshore in Douglas Bay, and easily visible to all arriving at the Isle of Man by sea, is Conister Rock and Sir William Hillary's Tower of Refuge.

In the south of the island, linked to the Langness peninsula by a short causeway, is St Michael's Isle. Here are the remains of a stone 17th-century round fort, built for the 7th Earl of Derby (Yn Stanlagh Mooar) and of much earlier earth embankments, thought to have been raised at the time of Magnus's landing here in 1250. There is also a ruined chapel, which stands on the probable site of an ancient keeill, and a close inspection of the building reveals alterations to its dimensions at different times. It is associated with the local legend of a priest who had a vision in which St Michael pointed to this location as the place for the building of a new church with a particularly fine altar. The church was duly built but to finance the altar the priest retrieved a hoard of gold buried in the churchyard by pirates – only to be later tricked and murdered by other pirates who knew of its existence. To this day it is believed that whoever strikes the walls of this ancient building will hear the moans of the priest and the jingle of coins.

THE
ISLE OF MAN
IN HISTORY

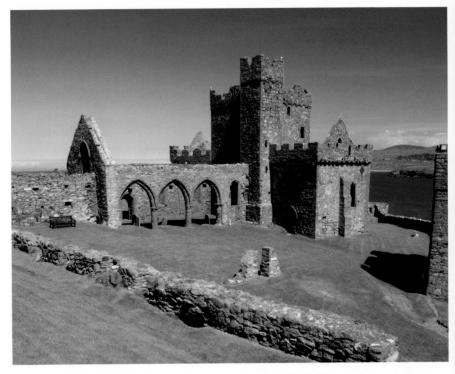

The earliest inhabitants of the island are believed to have been part of the original Celtic people of the British Isles. The Celts inhabited central and western Europe in pre-Roman times and in all likelihood derived, by assimilation, from the Neolithic people of Britain.

Not much survives from this period save for a few old names. In Manx Gaelic, the word for 'homestead' was 'balla' and there are still nearly 200 'balla' place names today. Of the original Manx place names, seventy per cent are Celtic. Many Manx surnames also date from the Celtic period, though they have been altered. Many begin with a hard C, K or Q – Corlett, Kelly and Quayle – which are all shortened versions of the Mac prefix. So Corlett is MacCorleod, son of the fierce one.

Excavations have revealed that the Celts were a prosperous and peaceful people, closely interwoven with the Irish. They lived in communities, with an idiosyncratic land tenure system which was largely unchanged by the feudal system, and they made the transition from pagan to Christian. They left behind 'monuments' in the form of Ogham stones, and there are four fine examples on the Isle of Man dating from the 4th century.

The Romans certainly knew of the Isle of Man, but they never came as settlers and their influence, though profound on mainland Britain, was negligible here.

The Norsemen were a different proposition altogether. Essentially a maritime people, they found fame and plunder on the high seas. They harried Scotland and established colonies in the Orkneys, the Inner and Outer Hebrides and Northern Ireland. It was inevitable that they would eventually land on the Isle of Man and disrupt its peace.

What is thought to be the earliest recorded attack on the island occurred in 798 when the Vikings landed on what is now St Patrick's Isle, off Peel. By the end of the 9th century there were Viking settlers and the island became a pawn in the fight between Ireland and the Kings of Scandinavia.

Understandably, historical evidence is obscure, but a character from this period has formed a great part of early Manx history. Though his identity is disputed, 'King Orry' is attributed with establishing three important bulwarks of Manx society – the State, a legislative body and a standing army. The chronicles of the monks of Rushen Abbey favour the Viking King Godred Crovan, son of Harald the Black of Iceland, as the real 'King Orry'. He reached Mann in 1075 but was heavily defeated by the inhabitants. He returned with a strengthened army and landed in Ramsey Bay. Legend has it that on landing he looked up at the clear night sky and the Milky Way and declared, "There is my path, running from my country to this place", or words to that effect.

Ever since, the Manx have called the Milky Way 'Yn Rad Mooar Ree Goree' (the great track of King Orry). King Orry was sufficiently fortified to defeat the Manx on this occasion, in battle on Skyhill. He spared his vanquished opponents and ruled for 16 years. The name of King Orry is still much loved and used on the island.

Godred Crovan established the Kingdom of Mann and the Isles and with him begins the real recorded history of the island. There are two important 'ship burial' excavations on the island, at Knock-y-Dooney, near Kirk Andreas, and at Balladoole, in Kirk Arbory, which date from this time. Chiefs were buried in this way. Their ship was drawn ashore and equipped with everything they might need for the 'journey to Odin', including a sword, spear, fishing gear, a bowl and a sacrificial knife.

The second Scandinavian period, started by Godred Crovan, lasted from 1079 to 1266. It is a period of great importance for the development of the Manx system of government. Godred ruled the British islands, from Dublin and Leinster to the Isle of Lewis. His descendants were to rule Mann for nearly two hundred years. At various times, the kings lived in Dublin, Northumbria and Mann. During the transition period from warriors of the seas to landowners and farmers, the Vikings left the Celts to run the farms and harvest the crops while they traded with the adjacent islands, Iceland and southern Europe.

The Cistercian Abbey of St Mary was built and constituted at Rushen Abbey during this period. It quickly became a source of great power on the island and was a huge influence on the lives of the islanders. Another important development near the end of this period was the tying of the island's fortunes to the English crown. Reginald, a tough Viking who reputedly spent three long years at sea, was desperate to hold on to Mann as part of his kingdom. In his anxiety, he swore to be a liegeman to Henry III of England, in return for two hogs' heads of wine and 120 crannocks of corn.

The Scandinavian influences have stood the test of time and still appear in a multitude of ways in everyday life on the island. The most marked features are the land tenure system, the legislature and the Diocese of

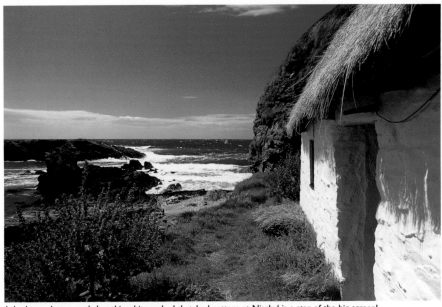

It looks modest enough, but this whitewashed thatched cottage at Niarbyl is a star of the big screen!

Sodor and Mann, all of which differ greatly from their counterparts in Great Britain. There are many words of Scandinavian extraction including Snaefell, the island's highest peak, which means 'Snow Mountain'. The Norse settlers used 'by' as the ending to many of their words and this remains a feature in many place names. Kirby meaning church farm, Colby meaning Kolli's farm, Jurby (Ivar's Farm) and Sulby are a few examples.

Although the Vikings eventually became Christians, it was not before they had extinguished the light of Christianity, which had burned brightly on Mann from the 4th century onwards. Around the beginning of the 11th century the Manx began, once again, to embrace Christianity. From the time of the founding of Rushen Abbey by the Cistercians of Furness Abbey in Barrow, it is possible to get a clearer picture of developments from the writings of the monks.

The Manx bishops are known as the Bishops of Sodor and Man, and the earliest reference to the Diocese of Sodor and Man seems to be in 1154. Consisting of the southern islands of Scotland, it extended from the Hebrides to Arran and the Isle of Man itself. Sodor owes its derivation from two Norse words meaning Southern isles, so in fact Sodor and Man means 'the southern Isles and Man'.

Bishops have always played an important role in the history of the island, sometimes leading the people by good example, at other times abusing their power and privileged position. In 1266 the connection between the Isles and Sodor came to an end, although the diocese continued to be under the rule of a distant Norwegian Archbishop until the 15th century. It was during this period that the island was divided into parishes.

After Norse rule had come to an end, the Isle of Man was the subject of many struggles, which saw its ownership passing between the Scots and the English. It was not until 1346 that the island came firmly and finally under English rule. During this period, immediately before the long reign of the Stanleys, the island's people suffered grievously. Contemporary writings of the time report that the island was 'desolate and full of wretchedness'. In another report the writer told of a great battle on the slopes of South Barrule, in which Irish freebooters who plundered everything of value heavily defeated the Manx. Only the purchase of corn from Ireland saved the people from starvation. So poor were the islanders that they could no longer afford to make the magnificent crosses for which they were renowned.

The Stanley dynasty ruled the Isle of Man from 1405 to 1736. The first King of Man, Sir John Stanley I, never came to the island and was succeeded by his son Sir John Stanley II, a wise but somewhat despotic ruler, who at least conferred some benefits on the people. It is recorded that there were two revolts against his authority. To prevent a repetition, he increased the power of the governors and substituted trial by battle with trial by jury as a means of settling disputes. Many of his successors did not visit their kingdom, and those who did come often paid only a fleeting visit.

The next major turning point in the story of Man came with the arrival of James Stanley, the 7th Earl of Derby, referred to by the Manx as 'Yn Stanlagh Mooar' ('The Great Stanley'). In 1643 he was ordered to the Isle of Man by Charles I of England to put down a threatened revolt by the Manx. Hiding an iron hand in a velvet glove, he soon made himself popular. Although the people of this period enjoyed the peace, they had less liberty.

With Charles II on the English throne, Yn Stanlagh Mooar proved his loyalty once more to the Crown. Leading his troops, 300 of them Manxmen, he set off in support of the King but was defeated and executed.

At this time, the great Manx patriot William Christian ('Illiam Dhone' to the Manx) anticipated punitive action against the islanders and ordered the militia to take all military installations. Everything was

Harry Kelly's Cottage at Cregneash preserves an earlier way of life.

The replica longship Odin's Raven in Peel's House of Manannan heritage centre.

captured, including Peel and Rushen castles – soon given up by Stanley's widow – and the island eventually surrendered to the Parliamentarians.

William Christian paid a terrible price for his actions. After the Restoration, some ten years after leading the revolt against the Countess of Derby, he was executed by shooting on Hango Hill at Castletown.

The 18th century was a turbulent period for the Manx. The end of rule by the Stanleys, serious disputes with the English Parliament, and the destruction of the smuggling trade (the only way the island had been kept afloat financially) all caused unrest. The period also saw the passing of the Act of Settlement in 1704, effectively the island's *Magna Carta*, and in 1736 under the rule of the 2nd Duke of Atholl, the Manx Bill of Rights was introduced. This Act in effect did away with despotic government and replaced it with an oligarchic government – the Keys (or the Lower House) of Tynwald. Constitutional government was just around the corner.

Working hard for the people for more than half a century during this era was the much-loved Bishop Thomas Wilson, Bishop of Sodor and Man for 58 years. He fed the populace in times of crop failure, promoted education, established schools and libraries, and laboured long on behalf of the Manx State.

On 11th July 1765 the island passed into the ownership of the British Crown. As the Manx standard was lowered at Castle Rushen and the Union Jack raised, George III was proclaimed King of Man. John the 3rd Duke of Atholl had sold the island to the Imperial Parliament for £70,000. The prosperity of the island, such as it was, disappeared overnight with the demise of the smuggling trade and London appeared well satisfied. This was not to be the end of the Atholl connections with the Isle of Man.

As the island fell into decay and its people into despair, the government in London felt obliged to try and rectify this state of affairs and in 1793 appointed the 4th Duke of Atholl as Governor. This was not a success and in 1829 he severed his relationship with the island for the sum of £417,000 and left.

George IV, King of Great Britain and Ireland, became Lord of Man. The period immediately after the Duke's departure saw little change. London continued to control the island's revenue, and the House of Keys still largely ignored the peoples' wishes by electing one of their 'own' whenever a vacancy in the House occurred. Help was at hand though, in the name of Mr Henry Loch, later to be Lord Loch and after whom part of Douglas promenade is named.

Appointed as Governor in 1863, Henry Loch brought energy and a real sense of purpose to the position. Working closely with Tynwald Court, lengthy negotiations with Her Britannic Majesty's Government were eventually concluded in 1866 to ensure that after the running expenses of the Manx Government were met, any surpluses could be retained on the Isle of Man for improvements to a fledgling infrastructure. Part of the agreement called for the House of Keys to be popularly elected and for the English Government to receive a sum of £10,000 annually from insular revenue as a contribution towards the defence of the realm, a payment that, although much increased, continues today.

Even before the arrival of Governor Loch, the island had achieved popularity as a holiday destination. Certainly with more and more of the revenue being retained locally and spent on improving the infrastructure, it was not too long before the population increased and communications to and from the island vastly improved. Towards the end of the 1800s, as the railways and their associated shipping companies opened up the adjacent islands to travel for all, a whole new industry mushroomed on the Isle of Man – tourism.

Much of the infrastructure that exists today owes its initial development to this period. Hotels, railways, piers, theatres, reservoirs, steamships and roads all played their part in thrusting the island to the forefront of the domestic British leisure market, such as it was.

As the new post-Victorian era arrived, the island rose to the challenge of mass tourism and for decades happily served the Lancashire cotton workers, Yorkshire miners, Scottish engineers, Geordie shipbuilders and many other working class families seeking annual escape from a life of hard work. During the 20th century the Isle of Man was not alone in experiencing huge changes to its economy with the decline of traditional industries and the lightning march of technology. It has been a period to challenge even the very cornerstone of Manx character and philosophy. As the inscription with the ancient Three Legs of Man symbol defiantly declares, 'Quocunque Jeceris Stabit' – Whichever Way You Throw Me I Stand.

Rolling countryside? The Great Laxey Wheel.

THE
WILD
ISLE

From the scent and semi-alpine conditions of mountainous heather moorland to the music of the Irish Sea as it laps and pounds bays and beaches, the Isle of Man is a creation of breathtaking natural beauty. It's an environment which supports a rich diversity of wildlife – on the land, in the air and in the sea. And enhancing the appeal of this feast of flora and fauna is the fact that the island's isolation from its mainland neighbours has had two positive effects: firstly producing a distinct Manx ecology, and secondly saving the resident

populations of Atlantic and grey seals from the ravages of the two outbreaks of phocine distemper which killed so many of these endearing animals along the eastern shores of the UK.

WILDLIFE ON THE LAND

At the end of the last ice age, around 10,000 years ago, rising sea levels submerged the last land bridge between the Isle of Man and the rest of the British Isles. This separation is the reason why there are no native large mammals to be found on the island. But although deer, badger, fox and otter are all absent, and there are no snakes, the upside is that many other species do very well here as a direct result.

For example, brown and mountain hares – both increasingly scarce in the rest of the British Isles – are relatively common. Polecats inhabit conifer plantations, and feral populations of goats, ferrets and even wallabies have established themselves, particularly in the north of the island.

Along the 100-mile shoreline, several places lend themselves perfectly to spotting seals and animals of the deep, and birdwatchers flock to the Isle of Man to appreciate such ornithological delights as choughs, wild red grouse, peregrines, Manx shearwaters and a good number of other species.

A summer walk in an upland valley or glen is almost certain to show you at least one hen harrier, hunting along the lines of the old walls. In spring, a courting pair engaged in their aerial dance over the heather moor is a sight and sound to remember. But for a really unique view of these truly magnificent

raptors, go to Manx Wildlife Trust's Close Sartfield nature reserve (described a few paragraphs further on) in late autumn and winter.

Stand on the rooftop platform of the reserve's hide in early evening and you'll witness large groups of hen harriers flying in to congregate at one of the biggest winter roosts in Europe. During 2000, one hundred and ten of these rare birds were seen here in just one short evening!

Another rarity which visiting birdwatchers may have the good fortune to encounter is the corncrake. Now absent from almost all of mainland Britain, this species is pretty much restricted to the Scottish isles and Northern Ireland. But small numbers continue to breed on the Isle of Man and it always pays to keep an ear out for the strange 'crek-crek' call of the males in spring, especially when near hay meadows. To actually see a corncrake now is a truly unusual event.

Particularly good places for bird lovers and wildlife enthusiasts are Langness in the south, where many migrant visitors make their

Walking along the south coast..

Looking north over Ramsey and the bay to the Ayres.

landfall, and the Ayres in the north.

The Ayres is of special note as it is one of those strange contrasts found on an island of this size. The northern plain is a post-glacial till and as a result has a low-lying rolling landscape not found anywhere else on the island. The strong coastal currents and substrata of soft rocks and glacial sands have formed the huge shingle dune formation that is the Ayres. Along with slacks and lowland, the dunes back a wide, open beach, 4 miles long, which looks like a piece of the north Norfolk coastline tacked on to the rocky shores of the Isle of Man. And the lichen heath ecology is almost unique.

As well as the sight of hundreds of orchids and nesting little terns in spring, you can enjoy watching seals, basking sharks, porpoises and whales passing through the fast tidal channel that lies just a stone's throw from the beach.

Another rewarding location at which to see the rich coastal wildlife is the Sound, at the south-west tip of the island. Here you can sit

and look across another fast-flowing – and deep – tidal channel towards the Calf of Man and listen to the call of adult male seals as they bask on the rocks. Harbour porpoise, dolphins, minke whales and basking sharks are all regular visitors, and views of the Sugar Loaf rock and its seabird colony are just a short stroll away.

Inland too there is an abundance of other wildlife to see. The island is ringed with numerous rain-fed rivers tumbling down from the uplands, many of them cutting steep winding gorges as they pass. Apart from the Sulby they are modest in size compared with rivers of mainland Britain, but most support trout, salmon and a range of aquatic life that is mostly free of pollution due to the lack of intensive industry. Many of these valleys were planted by the Victorians and are now classed as National Glens, freely accessible and open at all times. Awash with bluebells, violets and primroses in spring, these wooded valleys hold a special place in Manx natural history.

For botanists too there are rare treasures to

be discovered. Atop Snaefell you may be lucky in finding the small colony of alpine least willow, a last survivor of the ice ages, while lower down the mountainsides are cotton grass, bilberry, sundew and a variety of other upland species, sometimes in abundance. The dominant purple of the heathers in summer is characteristic of these habitats, but look closer below the heather's protecting arms and you'll find a miniature garden alive with mosses.

Also characteristic of the island's lowlands are the areas known as Curraghs (pronounced khur-ucks). These low-lying wetlands are a combination of small scrub woodlands dominated by willows and alder, with wet grassland, sedges and rushes often mixed in. Important for a variety of wildlife, they are particularly critical for plants, including the royal fern, and for many species of orchid such as the heath-spotted, northern marsh, butterfly, twayblade and others.

The gem of these sites is the Close Sartfield reserve in the northern Ballaugh Curraghs area. Here in late May and June you can walk amongst a colony of over 100,000 orchids growing together. Curragh habitat also occurs at the bottom end of valleys throughout the island, and little gems can be seen just a stone's throw from the centre of Douglas and Ramsey, as well as tucked away at the head of many river valleys and glens.

Out on the coastal cliffs and shores you can discover another range of wild flowers. The often steep rocky coastline is sometimes alive with the colours of a rock garden, decorated by a mosaic patchwork of thrift, spring squill, sea campion, harebells, maidenhair ferns and stonecrops formed around the exposed rocks and soil. Areas such as Scarlett outside Castletown, Marine Drive (Douglas Head) and the slopes around Niarbyl, to name just a few, can hold great swathes of these natural rock gardens in spring and summer.

Out on the open sand or shingle beaches, away from the steep rocky shores, look for the yellow-horned poppy as well as the scarce Isle of Man cabbage – a plant restricted to the island and other shores fringing the Irish Sea.

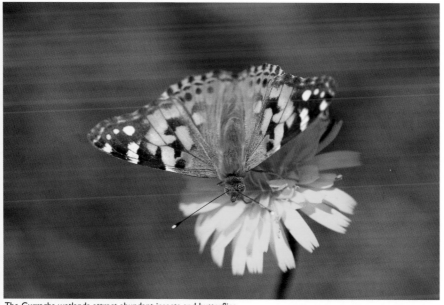

The Curraghs wetlands attract abundant insects and butterflies.

Braaid – not only lovely countryside but also the site of an important Norse settlement.

And as you drive or walk or ride around the island's roads, take a moment to look at the verges you pass. Traditional Manx sod hedges are solid, built of earth and stone, and home to a wide variety of plants and animals, typically orchids, foxgloves, lizards and butterflies.

Some hedges show handsome displays of bluebells, primroses and valerian, while others such as those around Archallagan plantation east of Foxdale present an orchid show to shame many a nature reserve. You can also see good populations of elm – a tree that has all but disappeared from much of England due to the ravages of Dutch elm disease – and in spring the powerful scent of abundant wild garlic can seal the picture of these green roadsides in your memory for life.

WILDLIFE IN THE SEA

As dedicated and patient observers have discovered in very recent years, the variety and nature of marine wildlife which can be seen close to the Manx shoreline is greater and even more astonishing than anyone had previously suspected.

Seals have long been a familiar sight, particularly on the rocks and in the fastflowing waters of the Sound, and basking sharks – the world's second biggest fish, up to 11 metres/36 feet long and weighing 10 tonnes or more – are regular visitors to the island's west coast waters from about the third week in May, saying their farewells in August, and best seen on an organised boat trip if you want to appreciate the sheer scale of these awesome creatures at close quarters as they feed on tiny plankton just below the surface of the water.

Much less familiar, except to the keenest observers, are rare dolphins and huge whales. They are drawn here by the abundance of their favourite foods – herring sprats, sandeels, mackerel, squid, cuttlefish and sardines – and they include fin whales, which are second in size only to blue whales as the largest animal ever to inhabit the planet.

In September, the perpetual quest to satisfy

a healthy appetite also brings minke whales to the Isle of Man. Their prize is the herring which spawn on the sea bed from Langness to the Point of Ayre. Minkes are not shy of coming close to the shoreline, and an autumn afternoon spent at the bay at Laxey can prove a very rewarding experience for spectators.

Then there are other impressive whale species which are familiar to these waters, including the orca (killer whale) and the rare sei. Killer whales make no bones about feasting on grey seals and other cetaceans. Humpback and sei whales are seen only occasionally, as are white-beaked dolphins.

Of all marine wildlife, dolphins seem to share a very special affinity for mankind which goes way beyond their natural intelligence and playfulness. Bottlenose (most prevalent from October to April) and common (summer) are two species which frequent the island's waters, but you could also catch sight of the wonderful and rare risso's dolphin.

The distinctive-looking risso's has a blunt snout, no beak and a torpedo-shaped body, and is very acrobatic. The Isle of Man is one of the world's few places where it can be seen close to shore. And it is here throughout spring, summer and autumn, sampling a Manx diet of squid, cuttlefish and mackerel.

Not far behind dolphins in the must-see popularity stakes, certainly for children, are seals – and on the Isle of Man you're guaranteed to spot them at fairly close quarters by looking no further than the Sound. In fact, you can watch them in their natural habitat while you enjoy all the comforts of the Sound visitor centre and cafe, where the wide panoramic window gives you a fabulous view over the tidal channel to the Calf of Man nature reserve and bird observatory.

Within the tidal channel, close to shore, is the tiny island of Kitterland, where seals bask openly on the rocks. This is an ideal and sheltered location for them, the water deep, fast-flowing and rich in fish.

Two seal species inhabit Isle of Man waters: Atlantic grey and common, the latter being slightly smaller and much scarcer. And it's not always easy to tell them apart, the main difference being that the common seal has a

Basking sharks are regular visitors to the Isle of Man waters.

Peel: Manannan's cloak of mist and a certain light create a moody beach and St Patrick's Isle.

more distinctive dog-like rounded head compared with the Atlantic seal's longer, more Roman snout!

Both species breed here. Common seal pups are born in early autumn and able to swim within hours of birth. The pups of Atlantic grey seals are distinctive for their white furry coats, and during the three-week weaning period they gain up to 2kg a day in weight. After this the white coat is shed. Although it keeps the youngsters warm and protected in strong autumn gales, the fur is easily waterlogged and grey seal pups are poor swimmers to start with.

During weaning, pups are often temporarily abandoed, left ashore on small beaches and coves, while their mothers fish for food. Occasionally, a mother fails to return because of accident or falling victim to a predator such as a killer whale, and her pup is orphaned. But if you see a young seal pup alone on a beach or cove, do not disturb it or assume it has been abandoned – it is much more likely to be awaiting the return of its mother.

WILDLIFE IN THE AIR

Boasting a unique avifauna, the Isle of Man is something of a paradise for birdwatchers. Here is an expert guide to some of the best locations.

I. THE AYRES.

Beaches are pebbly and support good breeding populations of oystercatcher, ringed plover and little tern. In late summer, sands exposed at low tide attract flocks of sandwich tern and kittiwake, as well as sanderling, dunlin and the occasional knot. The terns are frequently harried by skuas, mainly Arctic. Sea-watching along the coast reveals good numbers of Manx shearwaters, common scoters and eiders, and gannets from Scottish breeding colonies nearby fish the shallow waters. Dunes separate the shore from the heath, with stonechats plentiful in both habitats. Flocks of golden plover frequent the heath and shoreline during winter months, when all three divers appear offshore.

2. GLASCOE DUB.

Less than 4 miles south of the Point of Ayre, this little farm pond is the island's best site for shoveler. Winter months attract pinkfooted geese and several hundred wigeon.

3. RAMSEY.

In winter the harbour can have up to 40 mute swans and over 50 Canada geese. Little grebes occur regularly, and kingfishers are often seen just above the stone bridge. You may even spot a black redstart around the harbour entrance. The attractions at Mooragh Lake include goldeneye, which can number more than 50.

4. BALLAUGH CURRAGHS.

Not only the site of western Europe's largest communal hen harrier roost, but also the place to see (and hear!) water rails, greylag and long-eared owl. Summer attractions include wild orchid fields, grasshopper, sedge warbler, blackcap, redpoll – and maybe even a wild red-necked wallaby!

5. MAUGHOLD BROOGHS.

From the car park, coastal paths lead east and west. Take care along the path towards Maughold Head to see colonies of kittiwake and guillemots, scattered razorbills and fulmars, and peregrine, raven and chough. The path west gives views of black guillemots and maybe the odd puffin on the sea, but the main attraction is the island's largest cormorant colony – now accommodating more than 150 pairs.

6. PEEL.

An excellent year-round site. Summer views at Contrary Head include black guillemot, puffin, guillemot, kittiwake, fulmar, stonechat, chough and perhaps wheatear. Black guillemots nest in holes in the breakwater wall and there are usually eiders in the bay. Watching the sea from below the castle in late summer should yield plenty of gannets and Manx shearwaters, and possiby sooty shearwater, storm petrel, Leach's petrel and skuas, with kittiwakes plentiful around the breakwater. For most of the year purple sandpipers and turnstones frequent the castle rocks, and during winter it's often possible to see all three divers in the bay.

7. THE FOXDALE DAMS.

The two small dams – Eairy and Kionslieu – can attract an interesting variety of wildfowl: fair numbers of teal and tufted duck in winter, along with the odd goldeneye and pochard and a resident ruddy duck. Whooper swans appear from time to time, and other recent visitors have included gadwall and goosander. Common sandpiper are regular transient spring visitors. Green sandpiper has also been seen. Two or three pairs of tufted duck now breed here, and the songs of willow warbler, sedge warbler and whitethroat are constant in early summer.

8. MARINE DRIVE.

Take the easy walk from Douglas Head to Port Soderick and you can't fail to see stonechat, chough and raven – with every chance of a peregrine.

9. LANGNESS AND DERBYHAVEN.

Arguably the best site throughout the year. In winter a flock of perhaps 60 chough feed along the shore, and there are flocks of several hundred oystercatcher, golden plover and curlew. Brent geese frequent Derbyhaven Bay in increasing numbers and it's also good for great northern diver and grebes, especially Slavonian and great crested. The principal wildfowl are wigeon, teal, mallard and shelduck, but any of the less common ducks may also turn up. At any time there's a fair chance of grey plover, little egret and black-tailed and bar-tailed godwit. Other waders appear on passage, especially little stint,

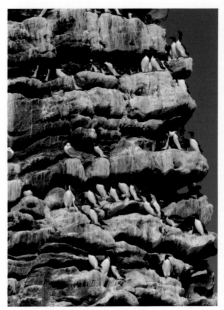

Seaside rock:: gull and guillemot colony.

curlew, sandpiper, whimbrel, ruff, and perhaps spotted redshank, greenshank and wood sandpiper, while rarities have included avocet, little ringed plover, Temminck's stint, both white-rumped and buff-breasted sandpiper, and long-billed dowitcher. Passerine migrants include flocks of skylark and white wagtail, plenty of wheatear and, especially around the ruined farmhouse, a variety of warblers. Stonechats, linnets, reed buntings, ravens and both carrion and hooded crows (and their hybrids) are ever-present.

10. POYLLVAAISH AND STRANDHALL.

These two sites and the intervening coast are very similar to Langness and Derbyhaven and seem particularly attractive to shelduck, wigeon and eider.

11. CHASMS AND SUGAR LOAF.

Spectacular for nesting colonies of kittiwake and guillemot, and excellent for chough and raven. On the Port St Mary side, black guillemots can always be seen and

the **wild ISLE**

Strange but endearing: seals are a common sight.

wheatears nest in the rocky field margins.

12. CALF OF MAN.

For most of the year the Manx National Heritage bird observatory is manned by wardens, and basic accommodation is available. Summer boats from Port Erin and Port St Mary serve this islet nature reserve, where regular breeders are eider, fulmar, Manx shearwater, shag, peregrine, kttiwake, auks, stonechat, chough and raven. Occasional breeders have included hen harrier, water rail and short-eared owl. Thousands of passerine migrants are ringed and overnight visitors have a fair chance of seeing a trapped rarity.

13. THE HILLS.

The variety of species is small, but driving through the hills is very likely to show you hen harrier, merlin, red grouse, wheatear and raven. In winter there's also the possibility of snow bunting. Particularly rewarding roads in the south are the A27 and A36, which meet at Round Table. In the north, you shouldn't ignore the narrow and mostly unfenced road which meanders from the head of the West Baldwin valley, through Druidale and down to Ballaugh. Recommended walking routes are the Millennium Way between Sky Hill and Crosby and – using the mountain railway – Snaefell summit to Glen Mona or Laxey.

WILDLIFE IN THE PARK

The Isle of Man has yet more wildlife to show you. And although Curraghs Wildlife Park puts the emphasis on wetland birds and mammals from around the world, rather than on native Manx species, there is a strong natural connection – because the park edges and partly embraces the Ballaugh Curraghs, an important wetland habitat and wildlife environment which has international recogntion. This Ballaugh Curraghs (pronounced khur-ucks) is an area of marshy woodland and grassland in the north – a surviving remnant of a habitat formed at the end of the last ice age as glacial meltwater was trapped against the hills. Over time the

European Lynx, Curraghs Wildlife Park.

majority of the island's other marshes have been drained for farming, but these five hundred acres or so have defied all similar attempts. Ballaugh Curraghs is designated as both an area of special scientific interest and a site of international importance for birds and other wildlife. Most of the habitat types present in the Curraghs can be seen along the park's nature trail, along with an explanation and history of the area's origin, ecology and land use. Curraghs Wildlife Park opened in 1965, purely as a tourist attraction. Today it is also a valued part of the international conervation scene, playing a role in explaining the need for wildlife consesrvation. The birds and animals are presented in suitably themed areas in a way designed to both entertain and educate. Kids particularly love the Humboldt penguins, the fervour at feeding time never failing to amuse an appreciative audience. The penguins' home is a landscaped enclosure, the rock work resembling the limestone slabs found around Castletown and Port St Mary. Their near neighbours are rheas, Patagonian hares, guanacos, geese, swans and flamingos, all happy to permit visitors to wander amongst them. The park has had great success in breeding flamingos from its modest population, defying the expert belief that this is only possible by keeping these long-legged birds in large numbers – a luxury the park doesn't run to. Similar success has been enjoyed with breeding demoiselle cranes, bar-headed geese and swan geese. They breed nearly every year and in summer months the downy young can be seen in the park's crèche. All the adults are exhibited in the Asian Swamp area, along with crab-eating macaques, short-clawed otters and fishing cats. In the wild, the macaques really do eat crabs and the cats really do go fishing, both species living in river valleys and swampy habitats, and surviving by foraging along the water's edge. The Flooded Forest of the Amazon presents several species of island-dwelling monkeys, including the breeding

troop of rare black-capped squirrel monkeys. Other species here are capybara, king vulture, spectacled owl, red-handed tamarin, black spider monkey, agouti and the spectacular scarlet ibis.

Follow the North American Trail to see raccoons and otters, and step into the Australian Outback to encounter wallabies, emus, galahs and various Australian waterfowl. There are two species of wallaby here: the smaller Parma wallaby, believed to be extinct for a hundred years before an introduced colony was identified on a small island in New Zealand, and the rare brushtail rock wallaby. In the wild, these animals have been repatriated to Australia in an attempt to restore the local vegetation on Kawau Island. One of the park's most informative and eye-opening themed areas is Life on Islands – a unique living exhibit which highlights the very real threat of extinction now facing many island species under pressure from increasing human populations. Here you can see lemurs, fruitbats, waterfowl and other species which, rare in the wild, are part of international breeding programmes and in the front line of wildlife conservation. It's a sobering fact that more than two-thirds of known animal extinctions in the last 400 years have been of island species.

Education is a key part of the park's work, and habitat loss, rarity and conservation are explained in The Ark. There's also a schoolroom where children can learn about the incredible diversity of wildlife and why we should look after it for the benefit of future generations. All of which very much reflects Curraghs Wildlife Park's role as a member of both the British and European Zoo Associations – as does the fact that more than a third of the park's mammal species are in European breeding programmes. But while the future for much of the world's most precious wildlife is uncertain, Curraghs Wildlife Park remains a relaxing, enlightening and enjoyable place to visit.

the **wild ISLE**

MANX
HERITAGE
AND THE STORY OF MANN

You won't see:
Badgers
Squirrels
Moles
Snakes

M anx National Heritage is one organisation but responsible for six distinctly different and wide-ranging functions. It is at once the Isle of Man's Museum Service, Art Gallery, National Library & Archives, Ancient Monuments Service, National Trust and National History Recording Service. The purpose of these varied roles is to care for and to tell the history of the island and to provide research facilities for students.

The island's history is presented by Manx National Heritage through the innovative and award-winning *Story of Mann*. From the hub – the Manx Museum ('Thie Tashtee Vannin', the Treasure House) in Douglas – the story radiates out to other Manx National Heritage sites across the island, encouraging you to interact with the story in the most interesting way possible and to see these attractions first hand.

Ideally, your starting point is to take a seat in the Manx Museum lecture theatre to view *The Story of Mann* – a 20-minute film normally shown every half an hour during the day. It gives you an overview of the island's history and landscape. The idea then is to proceed through the different areas of the museum, starting with the art gallery, where all the pictures are either of the Isle of Man or are by Manx artists – a policy common to all of the Museum's collections.

Art is followed by maps and geology and a never-ending argument about whether lead or slate is the most important. Prehistory, Celts and Vikings lead through to later history, tourism and war-time internment, with side paths of literature and home design.

Model boats and typical buildings take you to the exhibition gallery, which regularly hosts temporary displays of art or history. A small exhibition links the entrance to the reading room for the library and archives, and nearby are the Bay Room Restaurant and museum shop.

Throughout the museum trail there is generous use of videos and other electronic displays, with links to the other relevant sites,

monuments and landscape which are under the protection of Manx National Heritage.

Peel's interactive and ingenious House of Manannan may well be your next turn of the page in following the *Story of Mann*. It is very entertaining in bringing the island's Celtic and Viking past to life, using a combination of video, audio and authentic recreations such as a Celtic roundhouse centred around an imaginary family of the time. The magic and wizardry are led by Manannan himself, shape shifter that he is, as the video presenter of the documentary-style tale.

Moving on in time, a replica longship, two-thirds actual size, forms the link between the Vikings and maritime history. The ship, *Odin's Raven*, was built in Norway in 1979 and in that year sailed to the island to mark the Manx Millennium.

The House of Manannan also uses a dozen or so other characters from differing periods of the past to tell their stories. Other devices and subjects include a busy quayside scene, the natural history of the coasts, kippers and

Peel's attractive new inner harbour waterfront redevelopment.

There are stories to be seen and heard in Peel's House of Manannan.

in 1134 as a daughter house of Furness in Cumbria, it gives the opportunity to explore the remains of a small but important Cistercian abbey. Introductory displays give the history of the site and explain the background of 'the Church' then and now. At certain times of the year an archaeological dig is likely to be in progress with the possibility of being able to talk to those involved, either direct or via a video link. There are child-friendly areas where to a limited extent you can enjoy experiences such as an archaeological dig, identification of finds, building a Gothic arch and trying to produce your own version of the *Chronicles of Mann* as written by the monks.

the Steam Packet, all bringing you to a final section which introduces Peel Castle and urges you to make the short journey along the waterfront to visit it. When you do, Manannan's voice takes you wherever you want to go and explains the fortifications and buildings including the old cathedral.

More aspects of the *Story of Mann* are revealed at Rushen Abbey, Ballasalla. Founded

Not far away from the abbey is Castle Rushen – in centuries gone the main island home of the kings and lords and today one of the best-preserved medieval castles in Britain. Authentically-furnished rooms show how they and the garrison would have lived. The

Within the ancient walls of Peel Castle and cathedral on St Patrick's Isle are centuries of history.

spiral staircases may prove difficult for some visitors, but there is a shortened tour using normal staircases if you require it.

The castle dominates the town which with its narrow streets and medieval layout is a joy to explore. Almost opposite the castle entrance is the Old House of Keys, where for about 50 minutes you can become a member of the (now) elected house of the island's parliament and vote on subjects debated over the years as well as one yet to come! Tickets for these sessions have to be obtained from the Old Grammar School nearby, originally built as the town chapel of St Mary's in the first half of the 13th century and worth seeing for its *Story of Mann* displays. Across the harbour, the Nautical Museum has its own fascinating piece of the tale to relate in the shape of the historic open cutter *Peggy*, berthed in her boathouse with the club room above. The building is full of secret cupboards and exciting stories from 200 years ago –

Take your partners at the Grove Museum of Victorian Life, Ramsey.

yarns the staff are usually only too happy to tell you!

Still in the south, within easy reach of both Rushen Abbey and Castletown, is Cregneash. This was the first open-air museum in the British Isles and is very much a living village with a resident community. Certain of the buildings are kept for display purposes and those not needed for display are maintained

in their traditional form externally whilst being brought up to modern standards internally. The farm is part of the complex and is in general worked in the old ways and has period animals and crops, though if modern equipment is needed for a specific task it is used. The aim of this Manx National Heritage site is to show the village and its surrounds as they were about 100 years ago.

Industry rather than agriculture is the theme of the Great Laxey Wheel. The wheel, and the mines for which it was built, show the way of life of a different part of the community – men toiling far underground but joined by women and children in the surface tasks.

Different again in the *Story of Mann* is the Grove Museum of Victorian Life on the northern outskirts of Ramsey. In the 19th century this house was the home of the Gibb family and it retains all of their furniture and belongings. It opened as an attraction in 1979. The Gibb sisters who lived here latterly were keen bee keepers and there are displays reflecting this.

Back in the south, the Sound Restaurant and Visitor Centre close to Cregneash has been created to blend into the landscape and

Ancient castle, modern boats: Castletown.

give magnificent views and good facilities. Displays and toilets are available without necessarily patronising the restaurant, although the scenery and the wildlife, especially the seals, are likely to tempt you into staying longer than you originally intended.

Manx National Heritage is the island's National Trust, and access to all National Trust land is free and usually without restriction (except for dogs and shooting). Some ancient monument sites are available for public viewing but many are on private property and therefore prior permission is required. In recent years access to the important Braaid complex has been acquired and you can visit the remains of the Celtic and Viking homes which stood here.

The northern part of King Orry's grave at Laxey has long been readily accessible from the Ballaragh road, and more recently the purchase of the southern part of the burial site means that this too can be seen. Another

95 steps lead to the viewing platform of the Great Laxey Wheel.

The country life, Cregneash.

area of coast with access and parking is Fort Island on St Michael's Isle, Langness. The 16th-century artillery fort and the 11th-century chapel can be freely seen but not entered.

Recently acquired National Trust lands are at Niarbyl, whilst the lands at Spanish Head and the Maughold Brooghs have the coast path running through them and are relatively well known. Killabrega on the slopes of the Sulby Valley is perhaps less familiar to many.

Panoramic views at the Sound Restaurant.

Eary Cushlin in the south-west contains some of the most spectacular coastal scenery and provides access to Lag ny Keeilley, an ancient chapel, burial ground and hermitage.

There are many more sites to explore, not forgetting the Celtic and Scandinavian carved cross slabs which are in the guardianship of Manx National Heritage but in general are found at parish churches (and described where appropriate on the following pages about the island's churches).

The Manx Museum in Douglas is open Monday to Saturday throughout the year and admission is free. The House of Manannan is open 7 days a week all year round but there is a charge, as there is for all the other sites mentioned except the Old Grammar School and the Sound Visitor Centre. The charges vary and these sites are usually open from Good Friday till the last weekend in October, 7 days a week. The Sound Restaurant and Visitor Centre may open at other times at the discretion of the restaurant franchise holder.

KEEILLS
CHAPELS
AND CHURCHES

The traditionary ballad says, "That is how the first faith came to Mann, By Holy Patrick brought to us" – which should put it into the middle years of the 5th century.

However, the earliest monastic establishment in the Irish Sea area was set up at Whithorn by St Ninian some 50 years earlier. It is unlikely that such a community within sight of the island did not have an effect here and indeed in the 12th and 13th centuries Whithorn was the major pilgrimage destination for the island's religious. Some of the early church dedications and people mentioned in surviving stories also suggest a connection with South Wales. Other dedications show links with Iona and St Columba and his followers. At a later date Iona was part of the Kingdom of Mann and the Isles and some of the Norse Manx kings are buried there.

The Isle of Man was very firmly part of what is known as the Celtic Church which although its ritual differed from that of Rome had no central organisation of any kind and indeed looked to the Pope as universal leader.

Famous in Manx folklore – 12th-century St Trinian's.

St Mary's, Castletown.

There appear to have been perhaps as many as four or five monasteries on the island in this early period but the only one to leave any recognisable physical trace is Maughold.

A very early Christian site pre-dating chapels is St Patrick's Chair, which is a preaching site marked by a raised rectangle of stone surmounted by three standing stones, two of which are marked with simple line crosses.

A surprising proportion of the small earth-and-stone chapels (keeills) which served the community have however left some physical remains to see and visit. Most would have been surrounded by a small circular burial ground (rhullick) contained within an earth bank. Evidence for the burial grounds survives in a number of instances and in a very few cases the remains of a small hut for the visiting priest (or resident hermit) can also be seen.

Cabbal Pherick (Pherick means Patrick) has remains of a keeill, burial ground and

priest's house, but also shows the way that Celtic Christianity took over former pagan sites with its relationship to the waterfall of Spooyt Vane in Glen Mooar. Another showing this takeover is the keeill at Corrody, literally built into the centre of a Bronze Age burial mound.

A remote keeill with burial ground is keeill Vreeshey (Mary's Chapel) in the Corrany valley, where an inscribed stone was found linking it with Juan the Priest and the monastic/church site at Maughold. Another with good but very difficult access and set in the most magnificent coastal scenery is Lag ny Keeilley. This has a priest's house in addition to the burial ground, whilst the access path takes you past Chibbyr Vashtey (the Well of Baptism).

The rulings of the Synod of Whitby in 664 which should have marked the end of the Celtic Church seems to have had little effect. But on the Isle of Man reform came in the 12th century with influences from both

Ireland and the monks of Furness who founded Rushen Abbey.

The main visible change even then was the setting up of the parish structure and the building of parish churches. A number of parish churches still contain work of this period but all have been altered many times. They came in a variety of sizes but one basic style – long and narrow.

The original churches have a simple rectangular plan without change, other than a step in floor level, to mark the sanctuary and there are no aisles. Extra space was created later by constructing a gallery at the west end – used by the choir and the church band to provide what is now known as West Gallery Music. In the early to middle years of the 19th century the band was replaced by the organ. The access is normally from an external staircase.

These churches continued to be altered throughout the centuries. Old Kirk Braddan is a good example, while the roofless St Trinian's is perhaps the least changed, built in

the 12th century and altered in the 14th. By the time Bishop Wilson arrived in 1698 most of the churches were in a bad state of repair or too small for the island's increasing population, especially in the fast-developing towns. Bishop Wilson, like certain of the bishops who came later, instigated a major building programme.

A particularly strong programme was mounted in the 1830s by Bishop William Ward, who encouraged the use of 'named' architects from outside the island. The most prolific of these was the Hansom and Welch partnership in its various forms. Joseph Hansom was the man who designed and gave his name to the Hansom cab. They came to the island in connection with King William's College but were responsible for rebuilding Onchan, Kirk Michael and Ballaugh, although the old church here was not demolished. John Welch, the successor to the partnership, was also responsible for 'the triplets', the three multi-purpose churches of St Luke, St James (at Dalby) and St Stephen

keeills, **chapels** and **CHURCHES**

St Thomas's, Douglas, built 1846-49.

St Mark's church.

(at Sulby), although this last has been greatly altered since.

In 1844 the newly-appointed archdeacon, Joseph Christian Moore, had his cousin Ewan Christian alter his church at Andreas. Christian also designed St Thomas's in Douglas and Marown New Church. He was to become Architect to the Church Commissioners in England and his successor in this role was his pupil and son-in-law John Loughborough Pearson, architect of Truro Cathedral, who designed Braddan New Church and St Matthew, Douglas. In turn his successor was his pupil Caroe who designed St Ninian's, paid for with funds provided by Henry Bloom Noble, whose generosity to the island was celebrated in 2003.

In 1777 and again in 1781 John Wesley visited the Isle of Man, although others preaching his form of Christianity had already been working here. At the start converts met in the open or in house groups or rented properties.

Peel Chapel, sited just off the promenade and now a youth club, was the first purpose-built chapel on the island. It replaced the meeting room on the upper floor of the Summer House at Mount Morrison, of which only part of two walls forming the corner of the boundary wall now remains. There are tales of smugglers using the lower floor to store their goods whilst the Methodists sang their hymns upstairs.

Chapels spread across the island and were extended or replaced as congregations grew. By 1820 the Primitive Methodists had broken away from the Wesleyans and started to build their own chapels. The result was Methodist Chapels marching two by two throughout the island. The bigger chapels were galleried but of these only Trinity (formerly Rosemount) in Douglas remains largely unaltered. Kerrow Keeill is typical of the smaller early chapels but even this has been altered as can be seen by looking carefully at the front elevation.

Inside of St Mark's church.

keeills, **chapels** and **CHURCHES**

Old Kirk Braddan church probably dates from the 12th century.

The coming together again of the Wesleyans and the Primitives in 1932 along with reducing congregations has meant that many former chapels have now been sold and put to other uses. Other denominations have their chapels, the biggest group being those of the Roman Catholic Community where the church at Ramsey – Our Lady Star of the Sea and St Maughold, designed by Giles Gilbert Scott – is particularly outstanding. The oldest surviving Roman Catholic Church is Castletown, originally designed by Thomas Brine and having columns typical of his work.

Many of the churches and chapels have monuments 'decorating' their walls but by far the biggest, and best, collection is at Malew Parish Church. The policy for the safekeeping and display of the Celtic and Scandinavian style carved crosses is for them to be housed at the parish church at the parish in which they were found. The biggest collection of Celtic stones is at Maughold but other important early crosses can be seen at Braddan Old Church and Lonan Old Church, the latter having one of the very few such stones still standing in its original position.

The most important of the Viking age crosses are at Andreas, Bride, Jurby, Michael and Braddan. Some of the more fragile of the crosses are in the Manx Museum in Douglas, including perhaps the most important of them all – the Calf of Man Crucifix. One of the displays at Peel's House of Manannan allows some of the crosses to tell their stories.

Many of the churches and a few of the chapels have important stained glass, especially Ramsey Methodist, Ramsey Catholic Church and St Paul's and St Olave's, Ramsey. Lezayre, St John's and St Matthew's in Douglas are also important. However, the two Clarke of Dublin windows in the Roman Catholic Church at Castletown are outstanding. St Anthony's RC Church, Onchan – an interesting modern design – has an etched glass window in which Christ appears to be walking on the waters of Douglas Bay.

Each parish church and some of the Chapels of Ease have burial grounds, as does the Methodist Church at Peel, although this burial ground has long been closed. Historic figures in Manx churchyards include Trafalgar heroes at Arbory (Capt. John Quilliam), Bride (John Cowell) and Onchan (Lt. Lewis Buckle Reeves, one of the last surviving officers from *HMS Victory*). Also buried at Onchan are the parents-in-law of Capt. Bligh of *Bounty* fame. Other mariners of note are slave ship captains at Maughold (Hugh Crow) and Braddan (Quayle Fargher), whilst near the top entrance to Braddan lies the freed slave Samuel Ally.

The victims of the *Brig Lily* disaster – a ship which was wrecked and exploded at the Sound in 1852 – are buried in a mass grave at Rushen, and the 'hero' of all seafarers, Sir William Hillary (founder of the Royal National Lifeboat Institution) is buried beside the path at St George's, Douglas.

In a number of the burial grounds there are 'art noveau' headstones designed by the Manx artist Archibald Knox, whose metalwork designs for Liberty's of London are now avidly collected. His own is at Braddan new cemetery but others can be found at Douglas Borough, Lonan, Maughold and Old Marown. A number of the parishes also have war memorials designed by Knox.

Three other churches are worthy of note here because although relatively 'modern' they are of special interest in differing ways. St. Thomas, in Douglas, designed by Ewan Christian, has good glass and magnificent murals by John Miller Nicholson. The Royal Chapel of St John has a unique internal layout to accommodate the Legislature for the Tynwald Ceremony, and the interesting Minton floor tiles and its windows are a well-matched set with those in the nave depicting the patron saints of the island's ancient parishes. St German's, now the island's cathedral (the old cathedral is within the confines of Peel Castle) has good windows and panels in the Sanctuary painted by John Miller Nicholson. A display of Diocesan treasures is housed at the west end of the nave.

Some of the churches have leaflets or display panels for visitors and most of the parish churches, especially the ancient ones, and those with crosses, are open during the day. They give many and varied glimpses into the island's past – but they rely on the generosity of those who visit them to continue this role into the future.

*Now available from Lily Publications is an authoritative new book, **Churches of Mann**, featuring many large-format full-colour photographs and telling the story of the island's unique places of worship. See FURTHER READING on page 259.*

The 'new' St German's Cathedral, Peel.

FAIRIES
AND
OTHER FOLKLORE

If the British Isles is considered to be one of the most haunted and supernatural places in the world, then the Isle of Man can probably be thought of as the centre of this supernatural activity. Virtually every square mile of the island lays claim to its own tales of fairies and other unearthly creatures.

The Isle of Man has a wide and varied folklore tradition but the most famous and well-known aspect of Manx folklore is its fairy belief. Manx fairies, or Themselves as they are called by the Manx, are not the small pretty creatures with gossamer wings

illustrated in children's fairy tale books. Instead, Themselves are described as small human-like creatures, often three or four feet in height and dressed in blue or green with red peaked caps, who most definitely do not have wings.

Traditionally they are neither good nor bad and can be quite helpful or spiteful depending on how the mood takes them. They also take offence easily, which is why you should never talk about them directly or call them by name but only use terms such as Themselves or Mooiney Veggey (Manx

Gaelic for the Little Folk). Therefore, when crossing the Fairy Bridge on the main Douglas to Castletown road en route to and from the airport, it is always important to be extra polite and say hello to Themselves. It is uncertain how old this tradition actually is, but for several years locals and visitors alike have been very careful to observe it, and many have cautionary tales of what happens when you forget to say hello!

Tradition also has it that Themselves were particularly fond of hunting, feasting and fighting, with pitch battles between different bands of fairies. There are several sites on the island specifically identified with such fairy activity.

The Fairy Mound in Rushen, next to Rowany Golf Course, was considered to be the home of one of these fairy bands. A young man walking home late one night was 'took' by Themselves into the Fairy Mound where he witnessed a great fairy banquet. He managed to escape to tell his tale, taking with him a fairy cup as evidence of his adventures. Most are not so lucky and are doomed to stay permanently in the Fairy Kingdom or to

escape decades later, Rip Van Winkle style.

Another story of such a rare trophy relates to the Ballafletcher fairy cup given to the Fletcher family by the Lhiannan Shee (the 'peaceful spirit') of Ballafletcher. The Lhiannan Shee promised to protect the family and ensure no harm came to them as long as the cup remained unbroken and stayed within the family. The Fletcher family no longer lives at Ballafletcher, now known as Kirby, but the cup traditionally known as the Ballafletcher Fairy Cup still exists and can be seen on display at the Manx Museum in Douglas.

Fairy Hunts were considered to be a popular pursuit by Themselves, with various popular fairy hunting grounds being found around Douglas. A more physical relic of these nocturnal hunting parties is the 'Saddlestone' on the Saddlestone Road just outside Douglas. Here an apparently nondescript large stone protruding from a field wall is identified as being a saddle magically turned to stone.

The story is that the vicar of the parish found his horse tired and sweating every morning although it appeared that no one

West Baldwin reservoir – a picture of tranquillity. But beware of fairy mounds!

fairies **and** other **FOLKLORE**

had ridden it. Very early one morning, as he returned home from a late-night visit to a sick parishioner, he saw the reason why his horse was always exhausted. A group of fairies had ridden it all night and were taking the saddle off. When the fairies saw the vicar, they vanished in panic and horror and the saddle, which they had put on the wall, turned to stone! Maybe a more plausible explanation is that the stone was built into the wall to help people to mount their horses at the roadside – but the Fairy Saddlestone is the more popular and favoured version.

Another great fear and concern for the island's people was that Themselves took human babies and exchanged them for fairy changelings. As a result there were several ways to protect babies from being 'took'. The most powerful form of protection was to have a child baptised as soon as possible. Another was to sew vervain, the potent and powerful Manx herb, into the baby's clothes. If all else failed, it was critical to always put the iron tongs across the cradle if the child had to be left alone for even a moment – iron was considered a great defence against Themselves.

Fairies were believed to be particularly powerful and active at certain times of the year, one of the most dangerous being the end of winter and beginning of summer, May Eve. This was the time when the cattle, who had been kept inside all winter, were put back out on to summer pastures. It was also when cows began to produce milk again. Milk was an important part of the Manx rural economy because of its versatility – used as a drink and for making butter and bonnag (Manx soda bread). So for a subsistence crofting community, the difference between a cow producing milk and not producing milk could be the difference between respectable poverty and borderline starvation – and there was understandable anxiety that Themselves could stop the cows from milking or stop the butter from being made by tainting the milk.

Therefore every possible precaution was

Hunt the Wren, an age-old Boxing Day tradition.

taken on May Eve when Themselves were abroad. There were two main lines of defence. One was to spread primroses or other yellow flowers such as kingcups (the more powerful and effective Manx blutyn) on doorsteps and thresholds to stop evil spirits from crossing over; and the other was to make and put up over the doorway a crosh cuirn or rowan/mountain ash cross. The small crosh cuirn was made from two Rowan twigs formed into a cross shape and tied together with a length of handtwisted sheep's wool.

To make sure the cross was effective as a protective charm, no iron could be used in making it. So the twigs had to be broken by hand and not cut with a knife. To be extra sure of protection, the crosh cuirns were put up over the entrance to the cowshed and even tied to the cows' tails. People may not be so concerned now about protecting their cows from Themselves but many people on the island still put up crosh cuirns on May Eve. When visiting Cregneash Village Folk Museum, have a look inside the doorway of Harry Kelly's cottage and see a crosh cuirn

THE **ALL-ROUND** GUIDE TO THE **Isle** of **MAN**

already positioned to do its work!

The Isle of Man has more than one type of fairy. A solitary and hardworking but potentially bad-tempered Manx fairy is the Phynodderree – a large hairy shaggy house elf. The Phynodderree is renowned for being a good worker and helper to any Manx farmer lucky enough to have one. The only problem is that if the Phynodderree is offered a new set of clothes by a farmer as thanks and payment for all his hard work, he will be mortally offended by the gift and instantly disappear.

Another potential problem is that sometimes he takes his work far too seriously. Visitors to the island can see the mountain railway climbing to the top of Snaefell, but folklore tells of something far more alarming rushing around the mountain top. The Phynodderree was rounding up a flock of Manx Loaghtan sheep and, having easily caught 99 of them, proceeded to spend the rest of the long night on the slopes looking for the missing one. It took several hours but he finally made it, placing the last small Loaghtan back in the pen with the rest of the flock. Proud that he now had them all, the poor Phynodderree was dismayed to discover from the farmer that he only had 99 sheep and he had spent several hours trying to catch a mountain hare!

Not all Manx fairies are so hardworking or even mischievous, and one stands out as the most dangerous and terrifying of all – the buggane. This is the evil hobgoblin of the Manx fairy kingdom. Although there are various tales of bugganes around the island, the most famous is that associated with the roofless church of St Trinian's on the main road between Douglas and Peel.

The tale is told that several attempts were made to complete the church but that each time it neared the final stage, the buggane would appear and tear off the roof. As the fearsome reputation of the buggane grew and a new roof was put on the church, a bet was made by the local tailor, Timothy, that he

would stay in the church and make a pair of trousers regardless of what the buggane may or may not do.

As the tailor sewed, the buggane slowly emerged up through the church floor, uttering fearsome oaths. Undaunted, Timothy ignored the Buggane's threats and only when the last stitch was sewn did he flee from the church. The buggane tore the roof off, leaving the ruin you can see today, and chased the tailor all the way to St Ruinius (Old Marown) Church, where Timothy dived over the churchyard wall for safety. In his fury at being outsmarted, the buggane tore off his own head and threw it in vain at the tailor. Although the tailor was safe and the tale has a happy ending, St Trinian's Church is still roofless.

In addition to fairies and hobgoblins, the island has its own Black Dog – the Moddey Dhoo of Peel Castle. This is one of the oldest folk tales on the Isle of Man and was first published in 1732. The tale though is said to be older still and relates to a period in the 1600s when Peel Castle was a fortress with its own garrison of soldiers.

By all accounts, the soldiers on night guard duty had become accustomed to the fact that they were not alone and that they shared their guardroom with a spectral hound. One of them, under the influence of too much drink, announced that he was not afraid of the black dog. So when the castle keys needed to be returned to the Captain of the Guard, he was happy to do it on his own although his friends warned him strongly against it. Off he went, alone, followed by the Moddey Dhoo, which had left its usual resting place by the fireside.

Shortly afterwards, the guard's screams were heard echoing through the castle. Although he lived for three more days, the guard could not utter a single word or in any way describe what had frightened him, and the Moddey Dhoo was never seen again in Peel Castle.

Castle Rushen too has its supernatural side.

fairies **and** other **FOLKLORE**

There are stories of miles of underground passages, chambers and even magnificent mansions. The entrance to this mysterious underworld was apparently sealed up because all those who ventured down into the tunnels never returned, except for one brave soul who took the precaution of leaving behind him a trail of thread to lead him back out. This intrepid explorer, although courageous enough to travel through the underground passages, couldn't quite conjure up the nerve to enter the last mansion, where a great giant was asleep on a massive table. After making his retreat he was informed that his act of discretion rather than bravery had saved him – and so he lived to tell his tale.

Manx folklore can be witnessed as a living tradition, both on Tynwald Day (Old Midsummer's Day, July 5th) at St John's and when White Boys perform the traditional Christmas mummers' play around the streets of Peel.

Tynwald Day is the island's national day, when the Manx parliament holds an annual open-air sitting on Tynwald Hill for the reading aloud of all new laws. Part of this tradition is that rushes are strewn along the processional way as a symbolic tribute to Manannan, the mythical sea god and shape-shifting magician, who thanks to 21st-century technology is brought vividly to life in the House of Manannan heritage centre in Peel.

Christmas of course has its own special magic, and a variety of Manx festive customs are still practised. Traditionally, Christmas on the Isle of Man was never a single day's celebrations but rather twelve whole days (and nights) of festivities and merrymaking and was appropriately called 'Foolish Fortnight' (or Y Kegeesh Ommydagh in Manx).

The Christmas period would begin on Christmas Eve with the Oie'l Voirrey service, held in local parish churches decorated with seasonal hibbin as hullin (festoons of ivy and large branches of holly). After a short service, the clergymen would leave and the Oie'l

Voirrey would begin in earnest with the singing of carvals (Manx carols) late into the night or early hours of the morning. Surprisingly, although written and sung at Christmas most of the carvals are not about Christmas or the Nativity but about less seasonal themes such as sin and repentance, a particularly notorious one being the Carval ny Drogh Vraane or 'Carval about evil women'!

The Manx carvals were especially long, twenty to forty verses at least, and frequently the singing was not considered to be entertaining enough. As a result the parish clerk would act as Master of Ceremonies and try to ensure that the proceedings were not too unruly or riotous and that a certain degree of decorum was maintained. The young girls would go specially prepared with dried peas to fire at the bachelors. Pig tails would be routinely pulled and barracking of the singer would be considered standard practice. The parish clerk was also responsible for choosing who would sing and as a result would be strenuously lobbied by those wanting to sing their own carval. The clerk also had to ensure that no one sang for too long. So each singer was given a rush light (rush dipped in tallow), seemingly to provide light to sing by but also acting as a time limit. The service would carry on late into the night and it was not unknown for revellers to end up singing in the streets or along country lanes to greet the new dawn. Some would stop off at the public house for a traditional drink of hot ale flavoured with spices, ginger and pepper to prepare themselves for a long walk home.

Another essential part of a Manx Christmas was, and still is, the White Boys, who perform a mummers' play about St George and his battle with a series of saints – a greatly modified version of St George and the dragon. The characters wear white 'dresses' bedecked with all manner of ribbons, coloured papers, tinsel and matching tall cardboard hats, whilst the 'doctor' – who

A sure sign that it's Christmas! (The Millennium Way is a 26-mile footpath between Ramsey and Castletown.)

miraculously cures the dragon killed by St George – is dressed all in black. The 'doctor' collects contributions from the audience and also berates (and beats) them with an inflated pig's bladder on a stick if they approach too closely to the 'stage'.

The highlight of St Stephen's Day (otherwise known as Boxing Day) has for generations been Hunt the Wren, a very old custom once widespread throughout the British Isles, though its origins are unknown. The Manx ritual is one of many variations on the theme found throughout Europe and past antiquarians have attempted to trace its roots and symbolic meanings back to prehistoric times.

It was once a bloodthirsty ritual, gangs of youths scouring the countryside in search of a defenceless wren to trap and kill. Today an artificial bird is used. The wren became the centrepiece for a 'bush' – two wooden hoops set at right angles and placed on top of a pole and covered with ribbons and evergreens – carried from house to house in the hope that the singing of the Hunt the Wren song would be rewarded with money or treats. The song charts the demise of the poor wren as it is hunted, caught, cooked and eaten.

There are many suggestions as to why the wren should be singled out for such treatment. Some say it commemorates the martyrdom of St Stephen, others that the bird is the reincarnation of an enchantress who lured men to their death by drowning. The feathers of the wren are distributed amongst the 'wren' boys as a good luck charm, being particularly potent against witchcraft and to prevent a shipwreck (an important concern for Manx fishermen). The 'wren' is still 'hunted' every year by groups with a wren bush performing the traditional song and dance on St Stephen's morning.

The highlight of New Year's Eve on the Isle of Man is the Quaaltagh, a new year greeting similar to the Scottish First Footing, when groups of young men wander from house to house to bring good luck to each

fortunate (or possibly unfortunate) household. To ensure good luck the first person to cross the threshold after midnight should preferably be a dark-haired man bearing a small gift or token, and woe betide anyone whose first visitor is a red-headed splay-footed woman!

Several of the traditional New Year's Eve rituals related to much more sober concerns, such as trying to discover who in the family might die during the coming year. For each member of the household a thimble of salt was laid out on a plate, or an ivy leaf put into water; if overnight a pile of salt had collapsed or a leaf withered, it was bad news for that unlucky individual.

Similarly, ashes from the fire would be raked over the floor last thing at night and in the morning checked carefully for any trace of fairy footprints. The direction of the footprints was critical; toes to the door would indicate someone would die, but heel to the door and the family could expect a new addition during the year. Extra care then needed to be exercised in sweeping the floor so that everything went into the chiollagh (hearth) and the good luck wasn't accidentally brushed out of the house for the year.

Then there was the notion that on New Year's Day nothing could be lent, otherwise the lender would be doomed to lend all year. So, fearful of this, even if the fire itself went out in the hearth no one would lend either a flint or a burning turf (peat) to make a new fire.

The Isle of Man's rich and colourful folklore heritage is not just part of the Manx people's past but also their present and future. Maybe you don't normally believe in fairies – but on the Isle of Man it is better to be safe than sorry and to say hello to Themselves as you cross that bridge, just in case!

'THE TRADE'
INDUSTRY
AND COMMERCE

It is hardly surprising that the Isle of Man took its early development from its neighbours and surrounding cultures – namely the English, Irish, Scots and Welsh – but because of the island's unique status it suffered none of the legislative restrictions imposed by government in London.

Probably the earliest form of industry as we understand it evolved from the subsidence endeavours of crofters, who habitually farmed and fished. By the early part of the 17th century farming was the island's principal industry. In its wake it spawned many mills,

almost all being powered by horse or water. Remains of these mills can be seen in many remote places accessible from public rights of way. Most were corn mills but some were described as gorse mills, used for grinding and mashing gorse for animal feed.

The largest corn mills were at Castletown, Douglas and Laxey, almost all being water driven. There were very few windmills, which is surprising given the exposed position of the island. The remains of the largest windmill are at Castletown. All of the larger mill buildings remain, although the Nunnery

Mill at Douglas is now converted into offices. Only Laxey flour mill continues in use as a mill.

The real growth industry in the latter part of the 17th and early part of the 18th century was what has become known as 'the trade' – a euphemism for the noble art of smuggling. Fortunes were won and lost smuggling 'duty free' French wine and brandy into England. Lucrative profit was also to be had importing salt and goods from East India and China. The end for such activities came with the 'Mischief Act' of 1765.

By the start of the 19th century, woollen and cotton milling had found a small following in the island, the principle establishments being at Sulby, Laxey, St John's and the Douglas area. Traces of the buildings remain and place names such as Union Mills and Tynwald Mills give big clues as to their location. Remnants of the industry can be seen at St George's woollen mills at Laxey.

By far the most important of the mills in this particular line of business was Moore's mill at Cronkbourne on the outskirts of Douglas. The mill was the first truly mechanised factory and provided industrial workers' cottages nearby, along with electric light from the factory. The mill produced sailcloth of excellent quality and at one time held a contract to supply the British Admiralty and a suit of sails for SS *Great Britain*. However, the factory's eventual fate was that it became the island's largest laundry works.

From the 13th century fishing had existed as an industry alongside farming, reaching its height at the turn of the 19th century and encouraging other trades in its wake. Boatbuilding became a major industry in the principal towns and Peel was the fishing capital of the island, its boats produced by several local shipyards.

Qualtroughs of Castletown and Port St Mary built top-sail schooners which not only traded in the Irish Sea but also as far as the Baltic. At Ramsey the shipyard produced similar vessels, including some of the earliest iron-hulled square-rigged ships. The best known was *Euterpe*, launched in 1863 and later named *Star of India*.

It is claimed to be the world's oldest active ship and is preserved at the Maritime Museum of San Diego in California.

There were shipyards in Douglas both at the inner harbour and at Bath Place opposite the present Sea Terminal. John Winram's yard built the third vessel for the Isle of Man Steam Packet Company in 1842. It was named *King Orry* and although only 140 feet in length with a displacement of 433 tons, it operated winter and summer on the Liverpool route for 16 years.

Sail and rope makers started businesses in Douglas in support of this new industry. Messrs Quiggin and Co had a ropewalk at their yard in Lake Road, roughly located where the rear aisle of the Tesco supermarket is at present; their rope was much in demand in the port of Liverpool because of its excellent quality. There were ropewalks in the most unusual places, for example in Woodbourne Lane which at the time was beyond the upper limits of the town. There were also net makers at Peel and numerous chandleries in all the major ports.

During the same period mining on the island became a force to be reckoned with. It had been known since the 13th century that lead and silver deposits existed on the island, but it wasn't until the middle of the 19th century that mining became a serious industry – and the dominant one at that. Trial shafts and exploration for lode-bearing veins were enthusiastically pursued, eventually centring on Laxey, Foxdale and to a lesser extent Port Erin where ore had been extracted through addits and shallow shafts for many years.

The mineral wealth of the island in relation to its size was outstanding during the latter half of the 19th century. Between 1845 and 1900 no less than 233,292 tons of lead ore, 215,397 tons of zinc ore and 150 tons of silver were produced with smaller amounts of iron and copper. The value of the ore shipped from Laxey Mines in 1876 reached £90,000, with the value of ore produced from the Foxdale group of mines regularly reaching half that figure.

Foxdale had the most extensive workings with at one time up to twelve shafts involved. The three main shafts were Bawdens Shaft, Potts Shaft and Beckwiths Shaft, the latter being the deepest and reaching 320 fathoms. Some surface remains can still be seen at Foxdale.

Just to the west of the Shoulder Road leading to the Round Table Cross Roads there are visible remains of three more mines – Cross Vein, Dixons and Beckwiths, the latter being the most westerly of the mines in the Foxdale group and easily distinguished by the leaning brick chimney which forms a familiar landmark. At its peak 350 people were employed at Foxdale including women and children. All of the mines were hard rock mines, the upper levels in slate, the lower sections in granite and the main problem being water.

Conditions were much the same at Laxey, where the problems with water became much greater as the mines were driven deeper underground. The earliest records of mining at Laxey date from 1781. By the time the mine reached its zenith there were seven main shafts, all of which were connected underground and by 1854 were all operated by the Great Laxey Mining Company.

This was the same year in which the Great Laxey Wheel was built to pump water from the mines, from a depth of 200 fathoms. The wheel, designed by engineer Robert Casement, is now the focal point in the telling of the *Story of Mann*. The Laxey mines produced significant quantities of zinc blende and although production of lead ore was less than at Foxdale, the quality was exceptional and contributed to some of the finest silver in the British Isles.

The oldest group of mines was at Port Erin

A monument to Foxdale's extensive old mine workings.

and operated latterly by the Bradda Mining Company. Although it is believed that these veins were worked in the 13th century, it wasn't until 1869 that the enterprise was significant. Shafts were sunk to a depth of 72 fathoms but their location, so close to the sea, meant that flooding was a constant problem, leading eventually to an early demise. Surface remains can be seen almost at sea level at Bradda Head.

By 1929 the mining industry of the Isle of Man had ceased due to world competition and other factors which made it no longer profitable to extract the ore.

One other extractive industry involved quarrying for building stone. There are many scars around the island which hold testimony to this activity. In Douglas there are two large industrial sites built in what remains of two quarries from which most of the stone was won for the building of lower Douglas and the older houses on the promenade.

Summerhill Quarry nestles behind the horse tramway stables and was the source for most of the houses on the nearby sections of the promenade. At the other end of town the Douglas Head Quarries, long since defunct, form the backdrop to the inner harbour.

There were many similar quarries near to the other towns, still easily discernable. At Peel some attempt was made to obtain roofing slate but the poor quality of the country rock meant that the slates were both large and very coarse. Some better slate for roofing was won in the Sulby Valley and at Glen Rushen where levels and inclines are visible on the hillside. Large slate lintels were obtained from the cliffs at Spanish Head near Port Erin from what can only be described as a most dangerous location.

At Billown, in the south of the island, limestone has been worked for many years and still is to a limited degree. Remains of some of the oldest limekilns can be found here.

In 1713 the first highway act was introduced, putting the onus on landowners to repair highways. This saw the start of many small parish quarries for the purpose of winning roadstone. As traffic increased and the horse and cart eventually gave way to the motor vehicle, the need for a harder stone became apparent and after 1923 the production of roadstone in the form of granite was concentrated on four main quarries on the island – Oatland in Santon, Glenduff in Lezayre, The Dhoon in Maughold and Poortown near Peel. The latter is still the island's main source of roadstone, supplemented by production from South Barrule at the site of an earlier spar and micra quarry.

The majority of these industries fell into decline and their workers sought employment elsewhere. In the case of the miners many took their skills across the Atlantic to the New World but for many others unemployment became the stark reality.

The saviour was the tourism industry,

already established in 1850 but at its climax at the start of the 20th century. It generated many small tourism-related businesses, notably manufacturers of seaside rock, confectionery, beer and mineral water. The brewing industry also blossomed. Two breweries survived into the 20th century, one at Castletown and the other in Douglas. Okells brewery is a thriving business today, producing several types of beer but in new premises on the outskirts of Douglas.

Tourism was a huge employer, but when the Depression struck a severe blow to the north of England, from where the majority of the island's visitors came, the shockwaves were felt on the Isle of Man. Two world wars followed. Later came the advent of package holidays to the sun and suddenly there was another cloud over traditional British seaside destinations.

The Manx Government responded by attracting light industry to the island and the manufacture of high-precision parts for the aeronautical industry resulted in significant new employment. But something more was needed to fill the gap – and the answer was a long-term plan to capitalise on the Isle of Man's advantageous tax laws. As a result, offshore banking, finance and insurance have presented an attractive proposition to investors and a profitable business for the Manx economy. The strategy has worked and today the Isle of Man enjoys virtually full employment.

NORTHERN'
LIGHTS

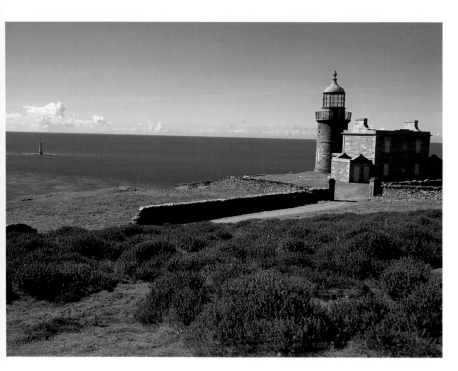

L ighthouses were born out of the need to protect the lives of those in peril on the sea – yet the great fascination of these often brilliant feats of engineering goes far deeper than the vital function they perform.

Towering above treacherous shorelines and from remote rocks far out in the ocean, these beacons of reassurance inhabit some of the least hospitable places on earth and stand up against the most hostile conditions nature can contrive. Even in the 21st century, this triumph over the elements appeals greatly to our imaginations and sense of wonder. Tales of the men who built them and those who served in them until the switch to automatic operation are woven into the very fabric of

Britain's rich maritime heritage.

Today there is more interest in lighthouses than there has ever been, with many groups dedicated to researching and preserving this heritage for younger and future generations. The first lighthouses of the Isle of Man were built in the early 19th century and their history, and that of subsequent island lights, is very well recorded.

Isle of Man lighthouses owe their origin to a United Kingdom Act of Parliament of 1786 and the establishment in Edinburgh of the Commissioners for Northern Lighthouses. Initially the Commissioners proposed the construction of four lighthouses around the Scottish coastline, and in 1818 built two on the Isle of Man – the island's first – at the

The 'pepper pot' lights, Castletown harbour.

Calf of Man and the Point of Ayre

Known today as the Northern Lighthouse Board, this body now controls 84 major lighthouses (whose lights have a range exceeding 15 nautical miles) and 112 minor lights which mark the coastlines around Scotland, including the islands, and the Isle of Man. Prior to automation the lighthouses were manned by up to four keepers, but with the switch to new technology they are now monitored from the Board's Edinburgh headquarters.

In the early 19th century, funding for the lighthouses came from a levy on shipping. Dues were calculated on the basis of the number of lighthouses passed in any one journey and collected on arrival in port. Dues varied according to tonnage and whether vessels were from a home or foreign port, with concessions for smaller craft and fishing boats.

The Northern Lighthouse Board is steeped in history. It established engineers such as the brilliant young Robert Stevenson, who was only 19 years old at the time of his appointment and became a pioneer in lighthouse construction. Thus began a 130-year association between the Board and the Stevenson family, Robert's descendants succeeding him in the position of engineer for several generations and continuing his outstanding contribution to lighthouse history.

The Board's first real interest in building lighthouses on the Isle of Man was sparked by Robert Stevenson's visit to the island in 1801. He inspected the two harbour lights at Ramsey and Castletown but viewed them

northern **LIGHTS**

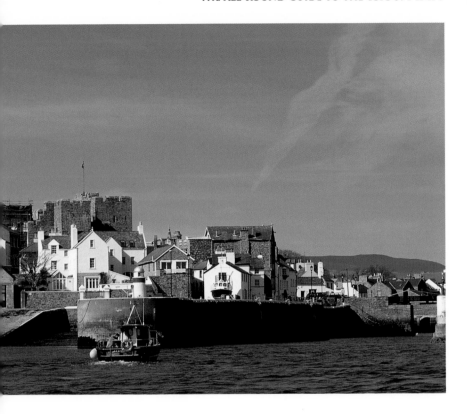

with little consequence. However, he described the lighthouse at Douglas, erected by the local harbour trustees, as 'an elegant structure erected upon that famous pier'.

During his visit Stevenson met William Scott, Receiver General of Customs, who persuaded him to look at the Calf of Man and Langness Point – both of them sites where previous requests for lighthouses had gone unheeded. Stevenson was of the opinion that if anywhere in the British Isles needed a lighthouse, it was the Calf of Man. But it was not until 1815 that a second UK Act of Parliament gave powers to the Commissioners for Northern Lights to erect lighthouses on the Isle of Man.

Point of Ayre lighthouse was completed on 1st November 1818, followed by two lights on the Calf of Man on 1st February 1819.

Over the next 100 years further lighthouses were built at Douglas, Langness, Maughold and on Chicken Rock, which marks a dangerous reef close to the Calf.

The last lighthouse built by the Board on the Isle of Man is the light which replaced the original two on the Calf, erected in 1968 and still in use. The buildings which housed the two lights of 1819 are now in the care of Manx National Heritage and well worth seeing.

The original Point of Ayre lighthouse also remains operational and is the most northerly building on the Isle of Man. It's just 18 miles across this treacherous stretch of water to Burrow Head on southern Scotland's Galloway coast, the hills of which are clearly visible on a fine day. The lighthouse's distinctive red and white tower dominates the

Winkie, the secondary light at the Ayres.

low-lying landscape, erosion of the coastline having claimed much of the foreshore.

Within the lighthouse grounds, hugging close to the tower, are the flat-roofed houses which for many decades were home to two families of keepers but now serve as holiday accommodation. In front of the tower is the disused plant room. Along the shore to the east are two other buildings. One, now rather derelict, used to house the foghorn. The other, built in the late 19th century, is a small secondary lighthouse known affectionately by mariners as Winkie.

Travelling clockwise round the coast, the next lighthouse is at Maughold Head in the north-east. Built in 1914, it stands 212 feet above sea level and is another excellent example of Stevenson family design. Immediately to the north is the sweep of Ramsey Bay and to the south are the cliffs of Bulgham Bay and the small coastal village of Laxey. The mountains and coastline of Cumbria can be seen when weather permits.

Before the lighthouse was built its function was performed by a simple light on the low-lying Whitestone Bank, a sandbank to the east of Point of Ayre, aided from 1848 onwards by a Trinity House lightship at Bahama Bank, 4 miles south-east of the Point. But complaints of the Whitestone light's unreliability throughout the latter years of the 18th century gave engineer D. Alan Stevenson the task of designing the new and overdue lighthouse for Maughold Head. The tower is 70 feet high and the whole structure stands alone, perched halfway up the vertical face of the headland. The keepers' houses are 128 steps above the lighthouse and command spectacular views.

Estimates for the work amounted to £11,000. Construction commenced in 1911 and was completed early in 1914, the Trinity House lightship at Bahama Bank withdrawn from service soon after.

Maughold Head was a good station to work. The three keepers and their families enjoyed modern accommodation and with Ramsey only three miles away were well served by shops, schools and doctors. But the lighthouse hasn't been without its share of drama. On the morning of 12th November 1915 a raging gale forced the Norwegian-registered barque *Sigrid* to shelter in Ramsey Bay, but a change of wind direction caused it to break anchor. Soon after 9.00 am, principal keeper William Quine reported that the vessel was in imminent danger of striking the shore – a prediction which huge seas wasted no time in bringing about. Fortunately, despite the appalling conditions, the crew of ten were able to take to the ship's lifeboat and make the beach safely at Port Moar, just to the south of the lighthouse.

A more bizarre incident in lighthouse history occurred on 20th March 1947. An R.A.F. Spitfire returning to the nearby airfield at Jurby in bad fog hit the keepers' houses, causing extensive damage. The pilot was killed but nobody at the station was injured. Records show that the property repairs cost

Laxey harbour.

£711.11s.6d.

Maughold lighthouse, automated in the early 1990s, still uses its original lens and equipment. The huge lens revolves 24 hours a day and the light gives three white flashes every thirty seconds. To get the best view from land you need to travel into Maughold village centre and take the narrow track around the edge of the graveyard and continue up the hill for a further 300 yards or so. The lighthouse is well hidden until you take the left turning, up the rise, immediately before the lighthouse gates, but there is no access to the grounds as the keepers' quarters are now private houses.

Moving south down the east coast brings you to Douglas Head lighthouse, which is not easily accessed. There are no roads leading to the light and only two steep paths take you directly to it. Originally all its supplies were delivered by boat from the harbour to Port Skillion, a short journey. The lighthouse grounds included keeper accommodation but

The Ayres lighthouse.

no gardens because of the difficult terrain.

Today you can walk to Port Skillion and on to the lighthouse along South Quay and up the track past the gas works by the Battery Pier. The lighthouse isn't open to visitors and the houses are in private ownership, but steps lead up to the top of Douglas Head and give you magnificent views over the bay and beyond.

The long history of a lighthouse guiding seafarers into Douglas goes back to 1671. Records show that various lights and beacons were erected at the harbour entrance, an early one of which is described as a great lantern displaying two lights.

During the 18th century, as Douglas developed, the Harbour Commissioners built a pier with a brick lighthouse at the entrance to the port. In the summer of 1787 fierce easterly gales swept away part of the pier and the lighthouse with it. In 1793 a sum of £24,000 was provided from public funds to build a new stone pier. Called the Red Pier, it was well over 500 feet long and extended into the bay to provide much-needed shelter. It was completed in 1801, but three years into its construction a 34-foot tower was erected at its end, the light visible six miles out to sea and greatly increasing safety for ships heading into Douglas.

In 1826 Sir William Hillary, resident of Douglas and founder of the Royal National Lifeboat Institution, proposed the building of a 'Great Central Harbour' with a lighthouse. Although this never materialised, the current Battery Pier and its lighthouse, completed in 1879, is based on Hillary's original idea but to a smaller design, and is now protected from the seaward side by a larger breakwater built in the 1980s.

In 1832, six years after Hillary's proposal, the Isle of Man Harbour Commissioners built Douglas Head lighthouse. In 1857 they handed over control of it to the Commissioners of Northern Lighthouses, to whom the annual running costs of £200 were insignificant in comparison with the

Chicken Rock lighthouse.

1845 surplus of £4,000 they had accrued from dues collected in respect of Manx lights under their control. Following the takeover it was proposed to extend the station's living quarters to accommodate two resident keepers and their families, but by the late 1880s the buildings were reported to be in need of a great deal of repair and engineer Stevenson advised that the old buildings, including the tower, should be removed and rebuilt to a more convenient plan.

This task was duly completed in October 1892. The new Douglas Head lighthouse became a very popular tourist attraction and in the summer of 1895 an average of 74 people every day paid to see it.

Throughout the 20th century the station changed little in outward appearance. The revolving light has a candle power of 738,461, one white light flashing every ten seconds. It was automated in 1986.

Next stop on this clockwise tour of the Isle of Man coastline is Langness in the extreme south-east. This low-lying two-mile peninsula forms natural havens in the shape of Castletown and Derbyhaven bays, and the lighthouse stands at the peninsula's southern tip.

Despite its wildlife and tranquil scenic beauty, Langness has claimed the lives and vessels of many unsuspecting mariners over the centuries. In 1811 the British Government built the unlit Herring Tower to the seaward side in the centre of the peninsula, but it was of limited help to shipping, and wrecks continued to pile up.

In 1850 the Harbour Commissioners used the old 13th-century fort of Fort Island to place a beacon at the northern end of Langness. Initially it was lit only during the herring season to guide the fishing fleet safely back into Castletown, but pressure from the local community soon saw the light operating during hours of darkness all year round. As a result, the number of shipping casualties fell considerably and demonstrated the need for a lighthouse.

But it was not until 1st December 1880 that the Langness lighthouse was finally built and operational. The layout remains much as it was then: the 50-foot tower in the centre of a courtyard with three keepers' houses, workshops and gas plant room (for the foghorn) surrounding it in the two-and-a-half-acre complex. The light had a power of 9,000 candles with a sequence of one flashing white light every five seconds. The light at Fort Island was discontinued in 1883.

On 12th December 1933, a fire in the Langness light room destroyed the lamps. Gilmour, the keeper on duty at the time, claimed he was in the toilet when the fire broke out.

In 1937 new apparatus was installed, boosting the light power to 200,000 candles and its character changing from a one-second flash every five seconds to a one-third second flash every ten seconds. In more recent times the configuration has been changed to two flashes every thirty seconds.

In the summer of 1996, Langness became

Langness lighthouse started service in 1880 and in 1996 was the last of the island's lights to be automated.

northern **LIGHTS**

Douglas harbour.

above the other, on high cliffs overlooking Chicken Rock, which is one and half miles out to sea. The light tower on Chicken Rock itself was not built until 1875.

Stevenson incorporated many unusual architectural features which are unaltered today. Close by the lower light are the remains of the smithy, a stable and an assortment of other buildings used for stores.

Originally, four light keepers and their families lived on the Calf of Man. Life was pretty basic – no shops, school, church or doctor – but they made this their home. Census information suggests that the Calf's total resident population in 1820 was fifteen people. And then, an unforeseen problem: the higher of the two lights was all too frequently rendered useless by the constant menace of fog. In 1866 the Commissioners for Northern Lighthouses recommended that a new tower should be built on Chicken Rock as a matter of urgency.

Thus began the process of replacing the

the last of the island's lighthouses maintained by the Northern Lighthouse Board to turn to automatic operation.

On the opposite end of the south coast, off the south-west tip of the island, is the Calf of Man, where the rewards for lighthouse historians are probably unsurpassed anywhere. The modern lighthouse of 1968, originally occupied by three resident keepers, sits neatly between its 19th-century predecessors and is the most powerful light in the Irish Sea area.

The building of Robert Stevenson's two lighthouses, unique examples of great construction engineering, began in 1817, at one time employing more than 300 men who toiled in all weathers without adequate shelter. By 1st February 1819 the lights were illuminated for the first time, the higher tower standing at 375 feet above high water and the lower tower at 282 feet. The lights could be seen from 24 and 22 miles' distance respectively.

The two lights were built in line, one

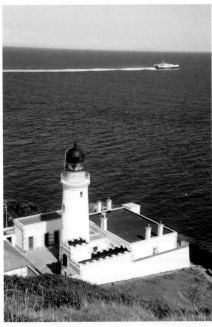

The Douglas Head station was completed in 1892 and soon became a shining light as a tourist attraction.

lighthouses on the Calf of Man. But it was seven years before David and Thomas Stevenson had their light built on Chicken Rock – a granite tower 150 feet high, built on a pinnacle of rock with only 4,000 square feet exposed at low water, and located in extreme isolation. The cost of building it soared £20,000 over the £46,000 estimate. Tide and weather conditions created enormous difficulties in landing on the rock and construction work could only be carried out on site during calm summer months. And even then it was restricted to five-hour periods between tides before the rock was underwater again.

Thirty-five skilled artisans toiled on Chicken Rock during the construction. Granite stone was imported from Dalbeatie in Scotland, dressed and shaped into dovetail blocks, assembled together course by course at the Port St Mary workyard, and shipped out to Chicken Rock for construction. This method of building was developed by Robert Stevenson at the Bell Rock lighthouse off the east coast of Scotland in the 1830s.

The first 32 feet of the Chicken Rock tower were built of solid granite masonry. A bronze access ladder climbs up the outside of the tower, leading to the entrance door. From the entrance there are seven storeys to the lantern machinery room and then to the lantern itself..

On 1st January 1875 the new light on Chicken Rock was exhibited for the first time and the two lights on the Calf of Man extinguished.

Three keepers lived on the rock at all times – a principal and two assistants – with one relief keeper living ashore on rotation. Life on the rock was barely comfortable, let alone luxurious. The duty keepers' accommodation consisted of two rooms with twin bunks, a kitchen and living room. Naturally, all the rooms were circular and no more than ten feet in diameter. So much for the romantic notion of the adventurous lot of a lighthouse keeper!

The most traumatic event at Chicken Rock lighthouse was a ferocious fire which broke out in the kitchen area on 23rd December 1960. The only means of escape for the three keepers was to climb up to the lantern room and out on to the balcony. From here they had to descend to the rock 150 feet below using the safety rope kept in the light room. Everything seemed to be against them. The weather was poor, the sea rough and it would not be long before the next high tide covered the rock

The lifeboats of Port Erin and Port St Mary were launched and many attempts made to approach the burning lighthouse, but rough seas made rescue impossible. It was four and a half hours before all three keepers were safely evacuated. Following the fire, the light was converted to propane gas-powered automatic operation, eventually becoming solar powered in 1999.

Today, inspection visits to the keeperless lighthouse are made by helicopter. Landings on Chicken Rock are not possible, but in summer – time, weather and visit numbers permitting – the boatmen operating from Port Erin take their passengers around it.

It was the near-disastrous fire of 1960 which led to the building of the 1968 lighthouse and fog signal station on the Calf of Man. Several years went into the planning and during its construction 870 tons of materials were moved to the Calf by helicopter – a method calculated to preserve the Calf's delicate eco-system and minimise the disturbance to wildlife. By the summer of 1968 the new lighthouse was ready for service, with accommodation for four keepers, each having his own bedroom. Another luxury was the golf course which the resident keepers made themselves!

Unfortunately, the architecture of the whole complex is typical of the 1960s and completely out of character with its environment and the natural beauty which surrounds it. The lighthouse was switched to automatic operation in March 1995.

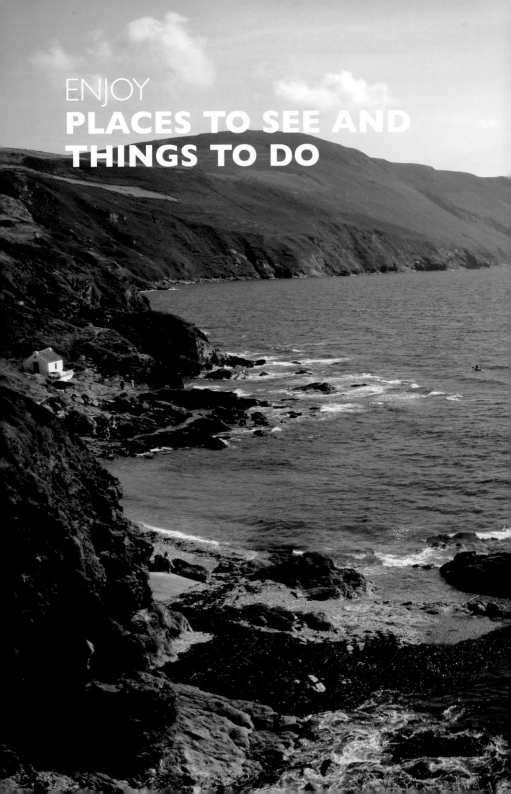

ENJOY
**PLACES TO SEE AND
THINGS TO DO**

There are not enough superlatives to conjure up the true magic of Niarbyl – a very special place framed by green hills, big skies and spirited seas.

WHERE
TO GO AND
WHAT TO SEE

The following A-Z listing is a brief introduction and guide to many of the Isle of Man's best known and frequently visited natural and man-made attractions.

ALL ABOARD!

One of the great joys of exploring the Isle of Man – particularly for children and families – is to experience the extraordinary network of Victorian railways and trams which is still so vital to the island's public transport system.

You can travel all the way from Port Erin in the south-west to Ramsey in the north-east – a journey of about 33 miles – by a combination of steam and electric railways which meet roughly halfway at Douglas. You also have the option to stop off en route at Laxey and take the 5-mile electric mountain railway to the top of Snaefell. Not forgetting a 2-mile canter along Douglas promenade by horsedrawn tram!

It was the tourist boom of the latter half of the 19th century which inspired the creation of this surviving rail network, which is now well into its second century of operation and, amazingly, still using much of the original

Enjoy your holiday along these lines

Steam Railway

Manx Electric Railway

Snaefell Mountain Railway

Make a present of the past and discover the Isle of Man by rail.

Steam your way south by train to Port Erin on a 15½ mile journey that takes you through town and village to sea and sand. And where you can delve further into the past at the Steam Railway Museum.

Sit back and relax on a 75-minute ride by electric tram as you pass through quiet countryside and around rugged coastlines on a trip all the way from Douglas to Ramsey in the north.

Or climb aboard the British Isles' oldest electric mountain railway as you slowly wind your way around Snaefell Mountain that reaches a lofty 2036 feet.

Altogether, you won't find a more enjoyable route around the Island.

For a free timetable including great deals on tickets and details about special events call 01624 662525 or visit the Welcome Centre at the Sea Terminal, Douglas.

Great savings with Island Explorer Tickets
1 Day, 3 Day, & 7 Day available.
Giving unlimited travel on the Island's Buses, Steam Railway, Manx Electric Railway, Snaefell Mountain Railway and Horse Trams.

Isle of Man
Raɪlways
Raaɪoyn-yɪarn vannɪn

Operated by the Dept. of Tourism & Leisure

Visit www.gov.im/tourism or call (01624) 662525
email: heritagerailways@gov.im

Another world, another time. The steam railway at Port Soderick.

equipment, rolling stock and motive power.

At one time both Douglas and Ramsey were connected by rail to Peel on the west coast, as described in the walks section of this guide. For more information about railways and trams, see their individual headings and the separate chapter describing a journey on the coast-hugging Manx Electric Railway.

The Isle of Man's public transport system is not served exclusively by rail, of course. In fact, there are many more parts of the island accessible by bus than there are by train or tram.

ANCIENT SITES & MONUMENTS

Many of the island's ancient monuments stand on privately-owned ground and can only be viewed with prior permission, but among the freely-accessible sites are Balladoole (remains dating from prehistoric to Viking times) near Castletown, Cronk ny Merriu (Iron Age promontory fort) at Port Grenaugh between Douglas and Derbyhaven, The Braaid (Iron Age and Norse settlement) west of Douglas, St Michael's Isle (12th-century chapel and 16th-century fort) at

Langness, Mull Hill (a circle of Neolithic burial chambers) near Cregneash, King Orry's Grave at Laxey, 14th-century Monks Bridge at Ballasalla and the well-preserved Neolithic chambered tomb of Cashtal yn Ard near Glen Mona, overlooking the parish of Maughold.

Throughout the island there are more than 200 decorated stone crosses of the type which have served as grave markers and memorial stones on the Isle of Man since the 5th century. Most of them remain in the churches and the churchyard cross shelters of their parish of origin, but cast copies of all the stones are housed in the Manx Museum in Douglas as a permanent record.

BASKING SHARKS

The world's second biggest fish, sometimes exceeding 35 feet in length, these giants of the ocean are regular visitors to Isle of Man waters. For more information see the chapter The Wild Isle.

CAMERA OBSCURA

Acquired by the Isle of Man government in the 1990s and reopened in 2005 after major restoration, the Great Union Camera

Obscura on Douglas Head, overlooking the harbour and town, was built for the Victorian tourism boom and is one of only four now remaining in the British Isles. Through a series of mirrors and lenses it gives spectacular views over Douglas.

CASTLES

The Isle of Man has two historic castles – one a ruin and the other in remarkably good state of preservation.

The latter is Castle Rushen, which gave its name to Castletown. It is one of Europe's best-preserved medieval fortresses, its origins dating from the 12th century with the fortification of a strategic site to guard the entrance to the Silverburn River. The oldest part of the castle, believed to have been built during the time of Magnus, the last Viking King of Mann, who died here in 1265, is the keep – a central stone tower standing in an inner courtyard. The castle was developed by successive rulers for a further 300 years, being surrendered to Parliamentary forces during the English Civil War. In more recent times the castle has served as a centre of administration, a mint, a law court and a prison, and today it is a major visitor attraction, showing detailed displays which authentically recreate castle life as it was for the kings and lords of Mann.

Peel Castle stands on St Patrick's Isle, which in the 6th century was established as a centre of Manx Christianity and survived in this role until the arrival of the pagan Norse Vikings at the end of the 8th century. In the 11th century it became the ruling seat of the Norse Kingdom of Mann and the Isles. A major programme of excavation conducted in the 1980s revealed much about the site's prime importance, and Viking jewellery and other finds are on display in the Manx Museum in Douglas. The story of St Patrick's Isle is introduced in the nearby House of Manannan, Peel's other great heritage attraction, and by means of an electronic aid Manannan himself will give you an exciting personal tour of the castle.

CHURCHES & RELIGIOUS HERITAGE

From the cathedral in Peel to the Royal Chapel in St John's, the Isle of Man is richly endowed with ancient and modern sites to visit, as detailed in the chapter Keeills, Chapels and Churches and also in the

Privileged: Peel is blessed with a magnificent setting.

definitive new book of the same title now available from Lily Publications.

The two most developed and active visitor attractions dedicated to telling the story of the island's religious heritage are Rushen Abbey in Ballasalla (see page XX) and St Patrick's Isle, which is the site of Peel Castle and the ruins of the original medieval German Cathedral. The history and religious significance of St Patrick's Isle can be accessed via Peel's nearby House of Manhattan heritage centre and the Manx Museum in Douglas.

COACH TOURS

In summer months you can take your seat for a round-island excursion and other coach tours.

ELECTRIC RAILWAY

The Manx Electric Railway runs for almost 18 miles between Douglas and Ramsey, much of the route enjoying magnificent views along the east coast. At Laxey, roughly midway, you can transfer to the Snaefell Mountain Railway.

In operation since 1893, the Manx Electric Railway has the two oldest working tramcars in the world. With a 3-feet gauge double track, it is also the longest vintage narrow-gauge line in the British Isles.

A journey from Douglas to Ramsey and the sights and places of interest en route are described in the chapter All Aboard the Manx Electric Railway.

ENTERTAINMENT

As you'd expect, the capital Douglas is the focus of island entertainment. The Villa Marina and Gaiety Theatre Complex presents a colourful year-round programme of great live shows and cinema to suit all tastes, and hosts a variety of major events, dance and other functions. Douglas also has its fair share of popular nightspots, including lively pubs, clubs, discos and attractions such as tenpin bowling.

Other important centres are internationally-renowned Erin Arts Centre in Port Erin and Peel's Centenary Centre. And in Ramsey, Mooragh Park hosts a variety of summer concerts and special events. For the bigger picture see the chapter On With the Show.

EVENTS

The Isle of Man's annual calendar of events is not only a celebration of Manx culture, heritage and traditions but also a lively programme of sport, games, fun and challenges – not all of them serious! Although typically including major festivals for TT racing, walking, food, darts, bowling and more, plus favourites such as the colourful and ever-popular Round the Island Yacht Race and the hilarious World Tin Bath Championships, the programme varies from year to year. See Useful Information at the back of this guide for details of how to keep up to date with what's on and where.

FARM & ANIMAL ATTRACTIONS

One of the biggest attractions for children of all ages is Curraghs Wildlife Park in the north. Within its 26 acres are more than 100 species of birds and animals from wetland areas around the world, along with nature and butterfly trails and the island's smallest passenger-carrying railway – the very popular Orchid Line.

Another welcoming Isle of Man family attraction is Moaney Mooar Open Farm & Tea Room, where kids can make friends with farm animals and small pets. The Mann Cat Sanctuary at Santon, in the south, and the Home of Rest for Old Horses near Douglas – the retirement destination for the tram-pulling shires – are also pleased to welcome visitors.

FILM & TV LOCATIONS

Since 1995, the Isle of Man's magnificent scenery and unspoilt natural environment

Streets cars to desire. The Manx Electric Railway at Port Jack.

have established the island as a rare and desirable location for producers of film and television, with more than 80 productions credited to date. These have included Miss Potter, Stormbreaker, Island At War, Tom Brown's Schooldays, Waking Ned, The Brylcreem Boys, The Tichborne Claimant, The Tamworth Two and many more. For details of how to download a free movie locations map, see Useful Information at the back of this guide.

FUN & FROLICS

When it comes to keeping kids amused and entertained, what the Isle of Man lacks in theme parks it more than makes up for with the sheer variety of other possibilities.

Water-based activities are well catered for with beaches at Peel, Port Erin and Port St Mary, the pools complex at the National Sports Centre (Douglas), the boating pool at Silverdale (Ballasalla, near Castletown), the lake at Mooragh Park (Ramsey), and a variety of swimming pools such as   Castletown's.

Just north of Douglas is Onchan Park & Stadium, overlooking Douglas Bay. There's great fun to be had here too – motorboats, karting, squash, tennis, stock car racing, mini golf, flat and crown green bowling and more. Another park with lots of facilities and attractions is Noble's Park in Douglas, and for toddlers the Villa Marina has a safe play area.

Also in the capital is 10-pin Superbowl, and around the island there are opportunities to combine fun with learning at attractions such as the Manx Museum, House of Manannan and Curraghs Wildlife Park. Other popular family activities include walking, cycling, pony trekking, quad biking, sailing and pleasure cruises.

GLENS

From the Victorians to the many generations of holidaymakers since, these havens of peace and tranquillity have been high on the list of the Isle of Man's most visited attractions, several glens achieving fame for their spectacular waterfalls.

Seventeen designated national glens across the island are owned and protected by the Manx government and preserved in their natural state. In the east these glens are Summerhill, Groudle, Molly Quirk's, Laxey, Port Soderick and Ballaglass; in the south, Colby and Silverdale; in the north, Elfin, Ballaglass, Dhoon, Tholt-y-Will (Sulby), Bishopscourt and Glen Wyllin; and in the west, Glen Maye, Glen Helen and Glen Mooar. For more information see the chapter The Nature of the Landscape.

HORSE TRAMS

Horsepower has been keeping trams on the move along Douglas promenade since 1876. The horses are specially bred for the task and their working conditions are enviable: a two-hour shift per day in the summer season (with the rest of the year off to enjoy the grazing) and a Douglas Corporation pension scheme which on retirement guarantees permanent residence and good care at the Home of Rest for Old Horses. The home, located at Richmond Hill on the Douglas-Castletown bus route, also welcomes families and children and has facilities for the disabled and ample car parking.

A compliment of 42 horses and 23 tramcars operates the summer-only service, the route running for nearly 2 miles between the Derby Castle depot at one end of the promenade and the Sea Terminal at the other. The trams are the oldest in the world. On display in the depot is a restored Douglas electric bogie tramcar – the only one outside San Francisco still in existence.

MINIATURE RAILWAYS

Unlike the island's other railways, the Groudle Glen and the Orchid Line were created purely as leisure attractions and are not part of the public transport system.

Lovingly restored to its former glory by the volunteers and supporters who run it, the Groudle Glen Railway is a marvellous little reminder of the feats achieved by Britain's

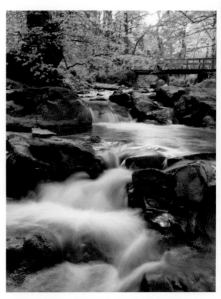

A gem of a glen, one of many treasured since the Victorian era.

great railway builders. The 2-feet gauge line just to the north of Douglas climbs up out of the glen's lower reaches and winds along the very edge of the hillside through trees, gorse, bracken and heather to the clifftop terminus – a distance of about three quarters of a mile. The views are fabulous. The railway celebrated its centenary in 1996, and the meticulously-restored carriages are still pulled by Sea Lion – the original 1896 steam engine. Opening hours are limited to certain times in summer and at Christmas only – you'll need to check with the Welcome Centre in Douglas.

On a smaller scale still – and great fun for children of all ages – is the Orchid Line in Curraghs Wildlife Park. The track gauge is just three and a half inches, making this one of the tiniest passenger-carrying railways anywhere in the world.

MINING HERITAGE

In the 19th century, the lead mines at Laxey and Foxdale were highly productive

Hard act to follow: a promenade horse tram struts past the Gaiety Theatre.

and though the industry ceased in the early 20th century when it was no longer profitable, the island's rich mining heritage is still very evident. Visitor attractions which reveal much about the Isle of Man's industrial archaeology include the Great Laxey Wheel, the Mines Heritage Trail, the restored surface section of the Laxey Mines Railway and the Snaefell Mine waterwheel. See also under Laxey on page XX.

MOUNTAIN RAILWAY

Completed in 1895, the Snaefell Mountain Railway is the only electric mountain railway in the British Isles. The distance from base camp (Laxey station) to the summit (or more precisely, to within 46 feet of the summit) is almost 5 miles, up gradients as steep as 1 in 12, and the gauge of the track is three feet six inches.

The leisurely ascent up the side of Laxey Glen is slow and gradual, with changing views of Robert Casement's huge waterpump wheel Lady Isabella. The double line crosses

the TT course at the Bungalow station and embarks on the long, final climb to more than 2,000 feet above sea level.

Journey's end is marked by the licensed Summit Cafe – as revitalising as the mountain air and amazing views. On a clear day you can see the island spreading below you in all directions and, beyond, England, Scotland, Ireland and Wales.

The construction of the Snaefell Mountain Railway took just seven months. The task was aided by the steam locomotive Caledonia, which was despatched by sea from Ramsey to Laxey harbour and then moved on baulks and rollers through the village to Laxey station. The track width of three and a half feet for the new mountain railway had been chosen to accommodate a central Fell rail – a braking device for the electric tramcars when descending steep gradients. However, the much heavier Caledonia was not equipped with the caliper brakes needed to grip the rail and so had to steam up and down the mountain in its somewhat hazardous daily work dependent entirely on the hand and steam brakes.

The effort and vision required to build the Snaefell Mountain Railway have been rewarded many times over – as anyone who has ever travelled on it will tell you.

MUSEUMS & ART GALLERIES

The chapter Manx Heritage and the Story of Mann gives more detailed information about many of the following.

Erin Arts Centre, Port Erin. Regular exhibitions are held at this important venue for the visual and performing arts.

Grove Museum of Victorian Life, Ramsey. A Victorian time capsule of fine period furnishings in an elegant country house set in lovely gardens. A Story of Mann attraction.

House of Manannan, Peel. See Manannan and hear his own gripping story of how the early Manx Celts and Viking settlers shaped the island's history. This interactive heritage centre uses audio, video and state-of-the-art display techniques to inform and entertain. A *Story of Mann* attraction.

Jurby Transport Museum. Created by the Manx Transport Trust, this new museum on the redeveloping Jurby airfield opened at Easter 2010 and is dedicated to the island's road transport heritage, particularly buses. The Trust's aim is to salvage, preserve and display as many vehicles as possible, and visitors will be able to see old buses and the like being restored on site.

Kipper Factory & Museum, Peel. See a working demonstration of how herring are prepared and oak-smoked to produce delicious Manx kippers – a tradition dating back to 1770.

Leece Museum, Peel. The story of Peel as revealed in a unique collection of old photographs.

Manx Aviation Museum. Located next to Ronaldsway Airport, the museum records Manx wartime and civil aviation history.

Manx Museum & Art Gallery, Douglas. The excellent award-winning museum opens the pages of the Story of Mann and presents 10,000 years of the island's history through a vast collection of

This perfect partnership of safe harbour and friendly fortress can only be Castletown.

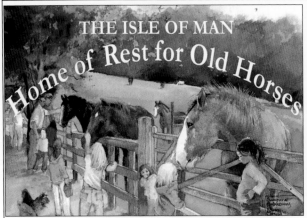

THE ISLE OF MAN
Home of Rest for Old Horses

Visit the wonderful Retirement Home for the Ex-Douglas Tram Horses along with all their friends. Set in over 90 acres of glorious countryside which is so peaceful and tranquil. We have an Adoption Scheme for all our horses and donkeys and there are over 50 to choose from! Visit our newly refurbished Gift Shop and enjoy our home baking in our new Tea Rooms. Afternoon Teas and Children's Parties are a speciality.

"BULRHENNY" RICHMOND HILL, DOUGLAS TEL: 01624 674594, PARTIES TEL: 07624 463198 (JILL)

OPEN MONDAY TO FRIDAY 10AM-4PM, MID MAY TO MID SEPTEMBER

Only 3 miles from Douglas on A5 Castletown Road & on bus route

The home is a registered Charity No. 620. Run entirely on voluntary contributions.

FACILITIES FOR THE DISABLED, COACH PARTIES WELCOME BY ARRANGEMENT

ADMISSION FREE

studio Craftworks

POTTERY PAINTING • SILVER CLAY JEWELLERY • WORKSHOPS • BIRTHDAY PARTIES

Paint your own pottery at Craftworks Studio, a fully equipped ceramic studio situated in the beautiful surroundings of Silverdale Glen.

Follow the signs to Silverdale from Ballasalla, near Castletown.

Fun for the whole family with lots of bisque to choose from. All pieces are glazed and fired on the premises.

Learn to make silver jewellery at one of our regular workshops. Silver Fingerprint Jewellery made to order.

Opening times:

During School Term:
Wednesday - Saturday 10:30 - 5:30
Sunday - 12:30 - 5:30

During School Holidays:
Monday - Saturday 10:30 - 5:30
Sunday - 12:30 - 5:30

The perfect place for birthday parties for all ages!

Telephone Martin on: 01624 823244
or Mobile 07624 407543
Craftworks Studio, Silverdale Glen,
Ballasalla, Isle of Man IM9 3DS
e-mail: craftworks_studio@manx.net
www.craftworks-studio.co.uk

Seen here at Derbyhaven, *Karina* is a cruise experience not to be missed.

artefacts. The art gallery is dedicated to works either featuring the Isle of Man or created by Manx artists. The museum shop displays many books and souvenirs, including jewellery fashioned in the style of Manxman Archibald Knox.

Manx Transport Museum, Peel.

Located in the office of the former brickworks on a site now used by Peel power station, this is the Isle of Man's smallest museum – about 60 square metres in all. It houses artefacts representing all forms of Manx transport, including a P50 – the world's smallest road-legal car, made in Peel in 1964 – and features historical movie clips, photos and collectibles.

Museum of the Manx Regiment.

Delve into the Isle of Man's military history at this museum in Tromode, near Douglas.

National Folk Museum, Cregneash.

This authentic village of thatched whitewashed cottages, a popular film location, still uses traditional farming methods and shows how 19th-century Manx crofters lived and worked. It is also the home of the fascinating Harry Kelly's Cottage. Britain's first ever open-air museum, Cregneash is a Story of Mann attraction.

Nautical Museum, Castletown. This small museum (another Story of Mann attraction) is dedicated to the amazing story of Peggy – an historic 18th-century vessel involved in local smuggling but walled up in her boathouse and undiscovered for a hundred years. The National Maritime Museum in Greenwich has listed this vessel as a ship of historic significance, meriting preservation.

The Old Grammar School, Castletown. Built as a chapel in about 1200, this small whitewashed building changed its role many times over the centuries. It was used as a school from 1570 and is best known for the Academic School – the forerunner of King William's College – and the Grammar School, which closed in 1930. Now restored, it is a Story of Mann attraction.

The Old House of Keys, Castletown. This restored 1820 building was once the assembly and debating chamber for part of the Manx Parliament. It gives an insight into the island's unique political heritage and is a Story of Mann attraction. For more information, and to find out how you can participate in a live debate, see page XX.

Railway Museum, Port Erin. This small

museum of railway memorabilia is located in the station building. Port Erin is the southern terminus of the Isle of Man Steam Railway.

Sayle Gallery & Arcade, Douglas. Named in memory of popular Manx artist Norman Sayle (1926-2007), the gallery is located within the Villa Marina & Gaiety Theatre Complex.

PARKS & GARDENS

Children love parks for the opportunity to let off steam while adults are often content to simply relax and appreciate the peace, quiet and colour of gardens created by experts. The Isle of Man has designs on keeping everyone happy.

For fun and activities, there are pleasure parks in Douglas (Noble's) and Onchan, and the attractions at Silverdale Glen near Ballasalla include the very popular Craftworks, where youngsters can create their own prized piece of art or craftwork based on local Manx designs.

Even bigger on activities is Ramsey's Mooragh Park. It boasts a 12-acre boating lake – ideal for beginners to learn the ropes in canoeing and sailing – and 40 acres of parkland. Bowling and crazy golf are other options on offer.

As for gardens of the horticultural variety, it's hard to beat those at Laxey, laid out on the old washing floors of the mines, or the beautiful setting of historic St John's. The village's Tynwald National Park & Arboretum contains many species of exotic trees, and the ducks and pond make this an ideal picnic spot in summer. Close by, at Tynwald Mills Centre, you can also enjoy the Manx Wild Flower Garden.

Lining the promenade in Douglas are the capital's famous sunken gardens. A riot of colour in spring and summer, the gardens often reflect the theme of notable anniversaries and other important occasions and are designed and planted accordingly.

PLEASURE CRUISES

What's an island holiday without venturing out on to the sea? At harbours all round the Isle of Man coastline you can board a fishing or pleasure boat for a bit of sporting action or a very leisurely cruise.

Karina, a distinctive sight in the summer season, will take you from Douglas to a choice of destinations – Laxey, Port Soderick, Derbyhaven and around Douglas Bay.

Pleasure cruises also operate from Ramsey, Peel, Port St Mary and Port Erin, the latter two serving the Calf of Man island nature reserve in summer (conditions and visitor numbers permitting).

SEALS

These appealing marine mammals are resident in island waters and frequently seen on rocks close to shore, as described under Wildlife & Nature Reserves and in the chapter The Wild Isle.

SHOPPING

The emergence of Douglas as an important international offshore banking and commercial centre is reflected in the town's redevelopment and increased number of designer retail outlets. There are also two shopping centres – the Strand and the more recent Tower House galleria, built round a large central atrium – plus three supermarkets, including the island's own Shoprite, which also has stores in Onchan, Ramsey, Peel, Port Erin and Castletown.

Away from the capital, a notable new development for upmarket shopping is Callow's Yard in Castletown. Each of the island's towns is also well served by local shops, and the Isle of Man is increasingly known for its number and variety of antique shops.

The same is true of specialist arts and crafts studios and outlets. Some of the best examples are Tholtan in Sulby Glen, Ballabrara Arts and Gansey Pottery (both in

Port St Mary), Courtyard Crafts (Port Erin) and the Fabric Centre in Peel. Also in Peel is Celtic Gold, which specialises in Celtic Manx and Archibald Knox jewellery, as well as producing Manx, Scottish and Irish kilts. And if you're a fan of auctions, Friday is the day and Ramsey is the place.

Laxey is very well known for the genuine Manx tweeds produced at St George's Woollen Mills. But perhaps the biggest shopping surprise of all is to be found at the Tynwald Mills Centre – an attractive selection of shops sharing the old mill buildings in the very pleasant setting of St John's, a few miles inland from Peel. Food, fashions, furniture, housewares, gifts, garden products and pet products are all on sale here in a very cosy and relaxed environment.

STEAM RAILWAY

The sense of wonder evoked by the sight of a living, hissing, fire-eating steam locomotive is timeless and hypnotic – as you can discover simply by standing on the station platform in Douglas or Port Erin and enjoying the magic of the Isle of Man Steam Railway.

The unique cocktail of sights, sounds and smells is as exciting to today's kids as it has been to generations before them. Thomas and the Magic Railroad was filmed on the island – and you could say that the title and the location were made for each other.

Opened in 1874, this is the oldest of the Isle of Man's surviving railways and the longest narrow-gauge (3-feet) steam line in the British Isles. The restored Beyer-Peacock 2-4-0 locomotives date back to this time. But far from nearing the end of the line, the railway has been granted a new lease of life since the turn of the millennium and is enjoying all the benefits of the largest reinvestment in renewal, improvement and maintenance since the railway was built.

In July and August, the peak months of the holiday season, there are 7 return trains a day, each leisurely one-way journey snaking

Stress-free shopping: you have it made at Tynwald Mills, St John's.

through some of the island's prettiest countryside in about an hour. The station at Port Erin has a cafe and a museum of railway memorabilia. The Douglas terminus also has a cafe.

VISITOR CENTRES

There are four dedicated visitor centres on the Isle of Man, each concerned with aspects of Manx natural beauty, wildlife or geology.

Scarlett Visitor Centre near Castletown explains how volcanic activity created the spectacular rock formations at Scarlett about 250 million years ago. Along with a nature trail, the refurbished centre gives an insight into the area's local flora and dramatic old limestone workings.

Also in the south is the Sound Visitor Centre and Restaurant near Cregneash. A panoramic window looks out across the tidal waters of the Sound to the Calf of Man. Niarbyl in the west also has a new visitor centre and cafe.

Close to the island's most northerly outpost – the Point of Ayre – is the Ayres Visitor Centre. Run by Manx Wildlife Trust, it explains the significance of the Ayres National Nature Reserve and its unique variety of habitats and sensitive ecosystem, comprising shingle beach, dunes, lichen heath, dune slacks, conifer plantation and gorse scrub.

WILDLIFE & NATURE RESERVES

Basking sharks, seals, hen harriers, choughs, gannets, mountain hares, wallabies – on the Isle of Man you can see them all, and in the wild at that. Then there are the more exotic bird and animal inhabitants of Curraghs Wildlife Park and the rare flora to be found in the island's many and varied nature reserves.

Basking sharks are attracted to the waters of the south and west coasts from about mid-summer onwards and have been regular visitors for more than two decades. They feed just below the surface on microscopic plants and animals and are not difficult to spot – particularly if you take a boat trip to observe them at close quarters. There are several places where you're likely to spot seals, notably the Sound in the south and the Ayres in the north.

Manx Wildlife Trust has 20 nature reserves, including Close Sartfield in the north – the largest winter hen harrier roost in Western Europe. Details of the reserves are available at the Trust shop in Tynwald Mills Centre, St John's, as are the seeds of native Manx wild flowers to grow in your own garden.

The Calf of Man is also a nature reserve and bird sanctuary, under the management of Manx National Heritage. A little over 600 acres in size, the island has been an official British Bird Observatory since 1962. A small flock of Manx Loaghtan sheep is kept here. This rare native breed is distinctive for its rams, which have four or even six horns. Grey seals can be seen all year round in the surrounding waters. Summer boat trips run to the Calf from Port St Mary and Port Erin, but visitor numbers have to be limited because of the island's sensitive environment.

For more detailed information about Manx birds and wildlife, see the chapter The Wild Isle.

THINGS TO DO
AND
WHERE TO FIND THEM

Whether you want to participate or spectate, the Isle of Man's combination of first-class facilities and idyllic surroundings gives you many ways to pursue your sporting and leisure interests and activities.

BOWLS

Bowling of all kinds is very well catered for, including annual festivals. There are venues in Douglas (crown green and ten-pin), Onchan Park (crown and flat green), the National Sports Centre (indoor flat green and short mat), and crown greens in Port Erin, Port St Mary, Castletown, Peel and Ramsey.

CYCLING & MOUNTAIN BIKING

From family groups to committed cyclists and mountain bikers, the Isle of Man's beautiful coast and countryside and varied terrain are a sheer delight for everyone on two wheels. To help you explore the island there are six designated cycle trails, described and shown in detail on pages 241-250.

DIVING

Based at Port St Mary, Isle of Man Diving

Golf at Ramsey.

Manx Fishing: a very popular way to cast all cares aside.

Holidays promise you some of the best diving in the British Isles – a combination of great natural beauty, diverse marine life and a fascinating variety of wrecks. The weekly and long-weekend packages includes 4-star accommodation, and a wide choice of courses is available.

Experienced divers making their own arrangements to visit the Isle of Man should note that many of the wrecks are protected by the wreck laws and some are owned by local people or sub-aqua clubs and should not be dived without permission.

FESTIVALS OF SPORT

The Isle of Man's action-packed calendar of annual events is never short of exciting sporting festivals and tournaments (as well as less serious competitive events such as tin

Bowls at Castletown.

bath and Viking longship racing) and typically includes yacht racing, soccer, rugby, table tennis, walking, marathon and fell running, darts, motorsport, motorcycle racing, angling, hockey, crown green and flat green bowling, drag racing and street kart racing.

FISHING

No wonder anglers are hooked on the Isle of Man: two annual festivals, more than twenty great locations for sea angling (conger eel, wrasse, ray, tope, cod and mackerel), a dozen rivers and streams (rainbow and brown trout and migratory sea trout and salmon), and five reservoirs (rainbow and brown trout). Rivers and reservoirs, good until the end of September and October respectively, require licences but these are widely available on the island. Late summer and autumn are the ideal time to land salmon and sea trout.

A challenge for experienced sea anglers is the Point of Ayre, where fast-flowing tides and the Gulf Stream call for every ounce of strength and concentration, though the rewards can be fabulous. For details of boat hire and offshore fishing grounds, contact the Welcome Centre in Douglas.

GOLF

The Isle of Man is something of a golfers' paradise. In a week you can play all nine courses, particularly as each is open to visiting players, and the game is very much part of

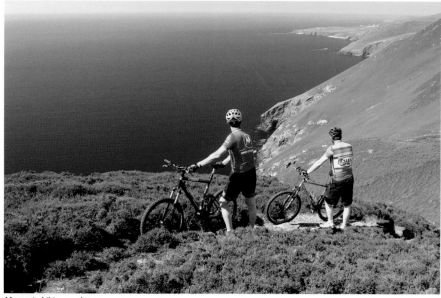

Mountain biking on the west coast.

the Manx way of life. Queues are rarely a problem here and the mild climate makes it a year-round sport.

The links course at Castletown was used for the 1979 PGA cup matches against the USA. It was laid out by golfing legend Mackenzie Ross in the late 1920s and early 1930s and provides some of the best links golf anywhere in the British Isles. The infamous 17th calls for a 185-yard drive across a gaping sea gully. King Edward Bay at Onchan has magnificent views across Douglas Bay, although the 6th tee at Port St Mary (the island's only 9-hole course, designed by 1920 British Open Champion George Duncan) boasts one of the finest views of all.

HEALTH, BEAUTY & FITNESS

If you want to address mind, body and spirit, and engage in personal luxuries which hectic lifestyles too often forbid, the Isle of Man is the perfect place to indulge yourself. Opportunities include beauty salons, stylists, well-equipped venues such as the National Sports Centre, Mount Murray's total Fitness

Club and the Hilton Health Club. A new experience for many people awaits you at Brightlife – a leading centre for holistic learning, stress therapy, yoga, reflexology and other aspects of personal care and development.

KAYAKING

A sea kayak is unbeatable for exploring the island's coastline and taking you into otherwise inaccessible coves and bays and close to grey seals, dolphins, basking sharks and other marine wildlife. Tuition is available from Adventurous Experiences and the Venture Centre.

NATIONAL SPORTS CENTRE

This is the flagship of the island's sports and leisure facilities, incorporating a first-class watersports complex. You can make quite a splash here: as well as the 25-metre competition pool, there are leisure pools and fun features such as bubble tub, flow pool, jets and geysers, water cannon, mushroom sprays and a toddlers' slide.

There's also a fitness zone and health suite, a 5-rink indoor flat green bowling hall, a secondary sports hall, 6 competition-standard squash courts, an athletics stadium and astroturf pitch, and a licensed cafe.

Other sports and leisure facilities can be found at two large municipal parks and at Onchan Park & Stadium.

Noble's Park in Douglas has an 18-hole mini golf course, tennis courts, bowling greens and a children's play area, while Mooragh Park in Ramsey is best known for its 12-acre boating lake – ideal for beginners to learn the ropes in canoeing and sailing – and also has a bowling green, mini golf, tennis courts, BMX track and children's playground. Onchan Park, just north of Douglas, has tennis courts, a bowling green, pitch'n'putt and a children's playground.

OUTDOOR PURSUITS

There's probably no better way to appreciate the Isle of Man's natural attributes than through its great outdoors. Maughold's multi-activity Venture Centre on the north-east coast offers an impressive range of

See the Manx countryside with Quad Bike Trail Rides.

activities and professional tuition starting, alphabetically speaking, with abseiling, archery and the assault course and going right through to raft building, rock climbing and supervised activity days for children – with lots more in between.

The island's other dedicated centre for outdoor pursuits and extreme sports is Adventurous Experiences, specialising in sea kayaking and offering British Canoe Union courses for absolute beginners and upwards. Other activities include coasteering.

PONY TREKKING & RIDING

Whether you're new to the saddle or an experienced rider, seeing the world from horseback gives you a unique perspective. Isle of Man establishments such as Abbeylands Equestrian Centre and GGH Equestrian Centre cater for all abilities and take you from the quiet lanes of Manx coast and countryside to the island's more challenging and expansive open moorlands and high hills.

QUAD BIKING

Quad Bike Trail Rides are a fabulous and fun way to enjoy the great outdoors. Full instruction, protective clothing and home-made cakes and tea are all part of the deal.

SAILING & WATERSPORTS

One of the big attractions for sailing

Carting at Jurby.

Horse Riding.

Niarbyl.

enthusiasts is the Isle of Man's varied conditions – the relative calm of Ramsey and Douglas bays for novices, and the more rugged north and south coasts for those sailors who relish a challenge and the chance to put their experience to the test.

Cruising, racing and dinghy sailing are all very popular and the island has six sailing clubs. Port St Mary is home to the Isle of Man Yacht Club and is the main sailing centre. The star event of the sailing calendar is the Round the Island Yacht Race, supported by numerous competitions throughout the year.

The abundance of safe harbours also makes the Isle of Man a regular stopping-off point for vessels crossing the Irish Sea. Harbours information and telephone numbers are included at the back of this guide.

As for watersports, surfing in Gansey Bay is really taking off in a big way and Derbyhaven on the Langness peninsula is an ideal spot for windsurfing.

TT & MOTORCYCLE RACING

The Isle of Man is famous around the world for its annual Tourist Trophy races. For more information see *Wheels, Wigs and Other Events*.

WALKING

The Isle of Man Walking Festival was introduced in 2004 and was so successful that there are now two festivals a year - in summer and autumn. This guide details 14 island walks including the 95-mile coast path (broken down into seven sections) and a selection of easy but interesting town walks. If you really want to discover the Isle of Man, on foot is the perfect way to do it.

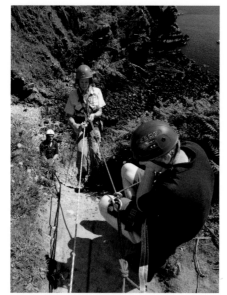

Abseiling with the Venture Centre.

ON
WITH
THE SHOW

There can't be too many holiday destinations where one year you might be lucky enough to catch a piece of the action as the scene for a new movie is being shot on location in front of you, and the next year you come back and go to the cinema and there it is – the finished thing on the big screen before your very eyes.

Yet it's entirely possible on the Isle of Man. Since 1995, film and TV production have become part of the island's long tradition of outstanding achievement in the performing and visual arts. And putting on a show and providing great seasonal entertainment is not only a necessity for the island's tourism coffers – it's at the very heart of Manx life and culture.

For film buffs who are interested in discovering the island locations that regularly make the shooting list, Isle of Man Film produces a movie map which can be downloaded free from the website. The map points you to places such as Castletown, Niarbyl and the Sound, though on screen the movie men would have you believe that you're in Cornwall, Ireland, the Brecon

on **with** the **SHOW**

Beacons or even the Caribbean!

The Broadway Cinema in Douglas is part of the Villa Marina & Gaiety Theatre Complex – the island's biggest name in entertainment, enjoying a seafront location on the capital's long and wide promenade.

The Gaiety Theatre and Opera House was created by master theatre architect Frank Matcham (1854-1920) and opened in 1900. Thanks to an authentic and painstaking 10-year restoration, completed and celebrated in 2000 – the theatre's centenary year – the Gaiety stands proud as one of the finest surviving examples in Matcham's portfolio. Over a 34-year period he worked his magic on at least 150 theatres, mainly in England and Wales but also in Scotland and Ireland. Today, only about 25 Matchams survive in the British Isles, his other most famous and enduring achievements including London's Palladium and the restored Coliseum. The colourful and entertaining story of the Gaiety's restoration is told in another book from Lily Publications, *Saving the Gaiety*, and you can see behind the scenes at the theatre by joining a Gaiety guided tour.

The new Villa Marina – the other half of the Villa Marina & Gaiety Theatre Complex – has enjoyed a rebirth of its own. It opened in 2004 after major refurbishment and redevelopment of the tired and jaded old original, which although well past its best by the time of closure had successfully entertained massive holiday crowds over many decades.

Particularly striking is the new Villa's centrepiece – the octagonal Royal Hall and its elegant high ceiling – and outside are beautiful landscaped parkland gardens, linked to the Gaiety by the promenade's Colonnade Walk.

Above the main entrance to the Villa Marina is a commemorative bronze plaque of Henry Bloom Noble (1816-1903), one of the island's most generous benefactors, who gave so much back to the town after making a fortune in the boom years of Victorian

Horse tram at Douglas

tourism. The land on which the Villa Marina stands was once Noble's 8-acre estate. The plaque is the work of Manxman Bryan Kneale, who also created the *Three Legs of Mann* sculpture at Ronaldsway Airport.

The Villa Marina & Gaiety Theatre Complex caters for the visual as well as the performing arts. It is home to the Sayle Gallery & Arcade, named in memory of the late Manx artist Norman Sayle (1926-2007). Just a short walk away is the Manx Museum's National Art Gallery, where lovers of fine art and design can appreciate works by Manxman Archibald Knox (1864-1933), whose creations famously included jewellery and decorative wares for Liberty's of London.

The future of creative arts and crafts on the Isle of Man would seem to be in good hands. For almost forty years the Isle of Man Arts Council has vigorously supported the work of local amateurs, professionals and visiting artists. And get 'em while they're young is a strong driving force behind much of this work, school-based workshops teaching dance, drama, creative writing and crafts, with the further encouragement of free tickets for

The striking Villa Marina and part of the gardens and colonnade which link it to the nearby Gaiety Theatre.

school children to attend matinee performances by visiting companies.

Although the Villa Marina & Gaiety Theatre Complex is vigorously promoted as the hub of year-round Isle of Man entertainment, another very notable venue is Erin Arts Centre, founded by John Bethell in the lovely resort of Port Erin in 1971 as a centre for music and theatre. Run almost entirely by volunteers, and known for its fine acoustics, it now enjoys international recognition and presents an impressive variety of prestigious events, including the Mananan International Festivals, Lionel Tertis International Viola Festival & Competition and Barbirolli International Oboe Festival & Competition. The Sir James Mellon Gallery, opened in 1994, is another of the Centre's valuable assets.

Also on the Isle of Man entertainment map is the Centenary Centre in Peel, well patronised for its lively and varied programme – from pantomime and young Manx bands to performances by celebrated international stars.

And then there's the year-round programme of island events, typically embracing a colourful mix of Celtic music and dance, festivals, theatre, jazz and a feast of sport and games.

WHEELS
WIGS
AND OTHER EVENTS

The Isle of Man's rich Celtic and Viking heritage, along with much more recent traditions such as the TT Festival, have created a calendar of annual events full of interest, colour and variety – a feast of culture and entertainment, particularly in the months from spring through to late summer.

TT RACING: HOW FOUR WHEELS BECAME TWO

The world's only surviving motorsport event to be run on a long circuit of public roads, Isle of Man TT racing celebrated a remarkable centenary in June 2007 as fans, spectators and competitors from the world over converged on the famous Mountain Course to savour the high excitement and party atmosphere of TT Festival Fortnight.

At 37.73 miles per lap, this legendary circuit is still acknowledged as the ultimate test of rider skill and machine durability. For many competitors it is the fulfilment of a lifetime's ambition to race on it, while for others it is simply being here that matters. Whatever their motivation, to compete on

On some sections of the TT Mountain Course, speeds of up to 200 mph are clocked.

the gruelling course requires absolute concentration, an almost photographic memory of the circuit, and the ability for riders to become one with their machines.

Men such as Stanley Woods, Geoff Duke, Mike Hailwood, John Surtees, Steve Hislop and Joey Dunlop are among the legends who have tasted TT success, and anyone who competes in either the TT itself or the amateur Grand Prix races has to be just that little bit 'special' – and, as some would say, just that little bit crazy.

To watch the racing costs nothing, as there's no ticket to buy or admission to pay. Regular spectators tend to have their own favourite vantage points, the best being those that enable you to move around during the races, and all the festival action is supplemented by entertainment such as vintage and custom bike shows, sprint racing, extreme stunt riding and displays by the Red Arrows aerobatic team.

To trace the beginnings of Manx TT racing, you have to go back to the last years of the 19th century and a wealthy American living in Paris. James Gordon Bennett, son of

the owner of the *New York Herald*, had gone to the French capital to establish a continental edition of the newspaper. He quickly embraced the European way of life and particularly the passion for automobiles.

The French were already elevating the status of the horseless carriage to something far more exciting than a rich man's toy. In the summer of 1895 they staged a road race from Paris to Bordeaux and back to Paris – a distance of 727 miles. It was the first of several such contests in that decade, and Bennett wanted a piece of the action, not least to promote this thrilling new sport to his fellow countrymen back home.

In 1900 he instituted his first competitive event – the Gordon Bennett Cup Race, open to countries which had national automobile clubs. His sponsorship over the next 5-year period was to play a significant role in the development of international motor racing.

In Britain, a speed limit of 14 mph meant that such foolhardiness on public highways was a non-starter, and the Automobile Club of Great Britain and Ireland cast envious eyes across the Channel to the achievements of their continental cousins and the emerging superiority of their cars and drivers.

Undaunted, the great English racing driver and motoring entrepreneur S.F. Edge, representing Ireland, drove his much-improved Napier to victory in the 1902 race – the only starter to complete the 351-mile Paris–Innsbruck course. As it was down to the winning nation to host the following year's event, the Emerald Isle seized the opportunity and passed new legislation to permit racing on public roads.

The 1903 race duly took place in County Kildare, over a distance of 327 miles, and was won by the German driver Jenatzy. Despite the failure of the British team, and the prohibitive speed limit (by now increased to 20 mph), interest in the sport in Britain was very much on the up. For the sake of national pride and the future development of the British automobile industry, one man believed he could redress the balance. Julian Orde, cousin of Lord Raglan and later to be knighted, had an ace up his sleeve. That ace was Raglan himself – Governor of the Isle of Man.

Orde reasoned correctly that this small island nation, with its own parliament and a fledgling tourist industry, was ideally placed to host the eliminating trials to decide the British entries for the 1904 and 1905 Cup races. To permit such road racing on the Isle of Man, Tynwald passed the Road Closure Act, which remains in force to this day.

On 10th May 1904, the Gordon Bennett Cup Eliminating Trials began on the island and paved the way for a long tradition of Manx motor car and motorcycle racing. The teams competed in three separate events – a hill climb, speed trials on Douglas promenade, and a high-speed reliability trial over five laps of a 51-mile course.

This automobile spectacular was a great success and repeated a year later for the 1905 eliminating trials. But this was to be the last of the Gordon Bennett Cup Races, and the Automobile Club of Great Britain and Ireland (forerunner of the RAC) decided to fill the void by introducing its own Tourist Trophy races to aid development of touring cars for the benefit of ordinary motorists.

It was also in 1905 that the Auto Cycle Club (later to become the Auto Cycle Union) held eliminating trials on the Isle of

Action from Southern 100 races, held on the Billown road circuit near Castletown.

Man for the International Cup event in France. This race event too was short lived and so the Club followed the lead of the cars and in 1907 launched its own Tourist Trophy motorcycle races. The winner's trophy – a silver statuette of Mercury poised on a winged wheel – is the same in every detail as the trophy awarded today to the winning rider in the Senior TT Race. In 2007 this was John McGuinness – his 12th TT victory overall and his 3rd Senior.

Who in 1907 could have believed that this pioneering event would not only go on to achieve global cult status, but also endure for more than a century?

MANX ROAD RACING AND MOTORSPORT FASTFACTS

- The winners of the first TT motorcycle races (1907) averaged under 40 mph. The current lap record is more than 130 mph, the biggest bikes hitting 200 mph on the straights.

- The TT circuit is known as the Mountain Course and on each lap (37.73 miles) riders have to negotiate towns, villages, railway tracks, river bridges, hairpin bends and more than 220 corners.

- The Prep-TT Classic and TT Festival Fortnight kick-start a whole series of summer motorsport events on   the Isle of Man.

- Manx Grand Prix: motorcycle event for amateur riders keen to experience and master the difficult Mountain Course. It is held in late summer.

- Southern 100 series: motorcycle racing on the 4.25-mile Billown road circuit near Castletown.

- Steam Packet Road Races: sponsored motorcycle racing on the Southern 100 circuit.

- Manx National Two-Day Trial: the biggest event of its kind in Britain, staged in some of the island's remotest places. Around 300 competitors test their ability to control a motorcycle on the most extreme terrain,

including rocks, gullies and slithery mud.

- Manx motorsport also includes motorcycle meetings at Jurby airfield and Jurby South road circuit, motocross, beach cross, long-distance Enduros off-road motorcycle competitions, car rallies (Rally Isle of Man, RBS International Manx Rally and the Manx Classic), karting at Jurby airfield and the Peel Kart Racing Grand Prix, and summer stock car racing on the 400-yard oval stadium track at Onchan Raceway – the Island's smallest motor racing circuit.

- The fascinating history of the TT is recorded and presented at the Manx Museum

A PROUD NATION'S VERY SPECIAL DAY

- In an age of global uncertainty, insecurity and massive change, it's remarkable that the Isle of Man's system of self-government survives intact more than 1,000 years after it was established here by Norse rulers – the longest continuous parliament in the world.

- Tynwald is government for and by the people. Every July in the village of St John's the Manx celebrate Tynwald Day with a colourful open-air event. This great festive occasion combines the pomp, ceremony and traditional proceedings conducted from Tynwald Hill with all the colour and excitement of a fair and other entertainment. It's a public celebration of national culture and identity but accessible to everyone, visitors included.

TYNWALD FASTFACTS

- Tynwald is the Isle of Man Parliament, believed to date back to the 10th century or even earlier and first held at a place called Thing-vollr (Parliament field) from which the word Tynwald is derived.

- On Tynwald Day (held on July 5th except when this falls on a weekend), Parliament meets publicly in the open air and all the law passed during the legislative year is announced in Manx and English.

Tynwald Day – keeping the long tradition alive.

- The traditional site at St John's is an ancient one, close to Norse burial grounds. Four-tier Tynwald Hill is artificial, reputedly covered by sods of turf from every one of the island's parishes.
- Tynwald is the only parliament in the world with three chambers – Tynwald Court (and its branches), the House of Keys and the Legislative Council.
- The House of Keys consists of 24 popularly elected members representing the island's 15 constituencies. There is no parliamentary party system, the majority of the members being independent. So decision making is by consensus, promoting political stability.
- Each year a Junior Tynwald is held, at which sixth-form students (16-18) take the role of members of Tynwald and hold a mock sitting at the court.
- The Tynwald Millennium was celebrated in 1979.
- Apart from this national level of government, the Isle of Man also has a system of democratically-elected local government.

- Head of State of the Isle of Man, by virtue of the title Lord of Mann, is Her Majesty Queen Elizabeth II. She is represented on the island by a Lieutenant Governor but on occasions, attends in person as the Tynwald Day guest of honour.
- In 1765 the Isle of Man came under the full control of the British Crown as a Crown Dependency, the island's current status. As such it is not part of the UK, Great Britain or EU and has its own parliament, taxation system, flag, currency and language.
- Since 1765 the Isle of Man has gradually developed to become largely self-governing, the UK now only providing defence and foreign relations, for which the island pays an annual fee.
- The Isle of Man has no representations in either the UK or EU parliaments, but free movement of manufactured goods and agricultural products between the EU and the island is conducted under a special protocol.

A **TASTE**
OF MANX HOSPITALITY

Over the centuries, the Manx population has depended heavily on the fruits provided by land and sea to put food on the table. Farming and fishing were the traditional staple industries. But in a changing world which even touches these independent shores, finance and insurance now top the economic menu as the island's main breadwinners.

This shift in fortunes means that today eating out on the Isle of Man promises more choice than ever before – a veritable feast of taste sensations. Now you can enjoy the best of fresh local produce, dishes and seafood alongside a banquet of popular international cuisine.

Although agriculture has slipped overall in the island's income rankings, farming is still very healthy. There are around 450 commercial farms. Their meats, dairy products and cereals are much in demand, both on and off island, and flower exports are blooming.

The quality of Manx beef and pork is exceptional and consistent. But the biggest success story is the native breed of Loaghtan lamb. Awarded the prestigious and coveted EU Protected Designation of Origin status, the dark meat has a distinctive flavour and significantly less fat and cholesterol than conventional lamb.

The long tradition of cheesemaking on the island dates back to the Viking era. The variety of mature full-flavoured cheddars includes oak smoked and black peppercorn and you can now buy them off island at many UK supermarkets, particularly in the festive season.

The Manx sea fisheries fleet is now less than a hundred strong, about half of which are smaller part-time vessels. Quota restrictions mean that the catch is focused mainly on shellfish, and the island's twelve-mile territorial waters are patrolled by a fisheries boat.

Most of the shellfish is processed on the island prior to export, but fresh crab, lobster, scallops and fish are served up daily in many Isle of Man restaurants. There are two varieties of scallop – small but delicious queenies in summer and larger king scallops in winter.

Globally, the most famous Manx offering of all is the humble but delicious kipper, still in year-round demand despite the decline in the island's fishing industry. At its height in the 1870s and 1880s the fleet provided the daily bread for one in every five of the population.

Isle of Man kippers are still prepared in the traditional time-honoured way – an art which is becoming increasingly rare. The herring are gutted, soaked in brine and smoked over oak chippings for exactly the length of time required to create that very distinctive flavour. Eating kippers with butter or marmalade, as they often are, is a sheer delight to the taste buds.

Other food producers on the Isle of Man make heather honey, Manx preserves, chocolate, ice cream, pate (kipper and crab are specialities) and mineral water. There are also three breweries and a distillery. Home-made Manx offerings you may come across on your travels round the island are bonnag (made with soured milk and sultanas or other dried fruit) and blaeberry pie.

EATING OUT

Available from the Welcome Centre is Douglas is *The Taste Directory* – a guide to the

Street cafe, Douglas.

a **taste** of manx **HOSPITALITY**

Isle of Man's restaurants, pubs, wine bars, cafes and tea rooms. The following also gives a broad idea of the many eating options you can enjoy, catering for all tastes and budgets – cafes to carveries, fast food to fine restaurants, steaks to vegetarian.

The emergence of Douglas as a major centre of international banking and commerce means an international choice of restaurants – Italian, French, Spanish, Cuban, Indian and Chinese serve as good examples. Fashionable wine and tapas bars sit alongside friendly pubs and hotels and other eating places promising a warm Manx welcome.

Many country and village pubs such as the Highlander Inn at Greeba and The Waterfall at Glen Maye are particularly well known for their menus and hospitality. And Manx National Heritage can satisfy your hunger as well as your thirst for knowledge with the Bay Room Restaurant at the Manx Museum (Douglas), tea rooms at Cregneash, Conservatory Restaurant at the Grove Museum of Victorian Life (Ramsey), the restaurant with spectacular views at the Sound Visitor Centre, the cafe and visitor centre at Niarbyl and the new Abbey Restaurant at Rushen Abbey (Ballasalla).

DR OKELL AND THE SCIENCE OF BEER MAKING

Beers bearing the Okells label rank amongst the best in Britain and they've been produced on the Isle of Man since 1850.

Owned by Heron & Brearley, the business was started by a man whose profession was more akin to scars than bars. Dr William Okell, a surgeon from Cheshire, opened his first brewery at Castle Hill in Douglas.

Within twenty years or so, after buying up many of the island's pubs – a considerable number of which had brewed their own beer until then – he was unable to meet the demand of his outlets and he set about the task of building not just a new brewery, but a model brewery based on his own ideas using advanced scientific principles. His

handwritten book, which is now one of Heron & Brearley's most treasured possessions, described in great detail the brewing process, the ideal equipment to use and the specifications for his new brewery.

When it was built in 1874 at Glen Falcon – in those days a greenfield site on the edge of Douglas – he called it the Falcon Steam Brewery. He opted to use steam to boil the brewery coppers rather than the more usual and accepted direct coal fire because he calculated it would cause less charring and caramelisation of the sugars during the boiling process. He figured correctly that this in turn would eliminate any unwanted burnt flavouring and give the final beer a much cleaner and superior taste.

It speaks volumes for Dr Okell's forward thinking that the brewery far outlived him and stayed in production until 18th August 1994, when the last brew was mashed – and for the best possible reason. The time had come to move the business on to yet another advanced new production plant, at Kewaigue on the outskirts of Douglas.

This separately produces both ale and lager. The ale facility was built first and went into full production in August 1994, lager brewing commencing in September 1995.

The brewery's capacity is 20,000 barrels – 10,000 each of ale and lager. The core production consists of Okells Bitter, Okells Mild and Cooil Lager, complemented by a range of seasonal and special beers under the popular Celtic Knot brand.

Production is highly automated, most of the brewing process controlled by programmable logic controllers and computers. If yu have a passion for, and understanding of, the technicalities of brewing you may be interested to know that the majority of the ale production is cask conditioned, the brewhouse consisting of a mash conversion vessel, lauter tun, copper and whirlpool. The brew length is 60 barrels.

The copper is of unusual design, having a vapour condenser to prevent steam and any aromas escaping into the outside air. It is also

Castletown.

heated by an external heater – not uncommon in itself, but in this case utilising a very rare wide gap plate and frame heat exchanger. The fermentation facility for ales consists of four 60-barrel fermenters and one 30-barrel.

The lager facility comprises three 120-barrel conical fermenters and six 120-barrel maturation vessels. There are also two 120-barrel bright tanks to feed the kegging plant. A well-equipped laboratory backs up the quality control and production functions.

No doubt Dr Okell himself would approve of such advanced technology – particularly as Okells Bitter has since become the winner of at least one prestigious International Brewing Award.

EVERYTHING YOU EVER WANTED TO KNOW ABOUT KIPPERS

■ Kippers, eaten the world over, are smoked herring: split, gutted, cleaned, soaked in a brine mixture, hung on racks in kilns and smoked according to their size and oil content.

Not a pub in sight – but a long walk on a west coast beach is a very agreeable way to work up a thirst.

Kipper House, Peel

■ The origin of the kippering process is uncertain, but some believe it was inspired by split-smoked finnan haddock processing.

■ In the 19th century the staple Manx diet was spuds and herring – mashed potato on a wooden platter with herring and butter, eaten with fingers and no cutlery! In the 1840s almost 12 million herring a year were on local tables.

■ Herring live for about 20 years in the North Irish Sea. June to August is the best time to catch them as their oil content is at maximum before spawning – after which they are unsuitable for kippering.

■ Kippers are rich in nutrition. Oil-rich fish (which also includes mackerel and sardines) are unique in supplying the special Omega-3 polyunsaturated fats proven to help reduce cholesterol levels. They are also an important source of vitamins A & D, calcium, iodine, flourine and protein.

■ Cooking kippers is quick and easy: boiled in water for 5-6 minutes, microwaved in 2-3 minutes or grilled for 5-6 minutes.

■ Vacuum-sealed kippers can be kept in a fridge for up to 10 days. Loose kippers will keep in a fridge for 4-5 days. Both vacuum-sealed and loose kippers will keep in a deep freeze for up to 18 months.

■ The home of Manx kippers is Peel. Devereau's was established in 1884 and in 1972 Peter Canipa, having worked for the company since the age of 13, bought the small kipper curing factory and shop. Today it is a Canipa family business with two shops and a factory four times the size of the original.

■ Deverau's kippers are available from the factory shop in Mill Road, Peel, the shop in Castle Street, Douglas, or online at www.isleofmankippers.com

Isle of Man Meat

Locally produced fine dining

Thanks for choosing Manx

For advice on meat or to pick up your free recipe cards just pop into your local shop

EXPLORING
ON FOOT, BY ROAD OR BY RAIL

Looking north from the Calf of Man.

THIS
ISLAND'S
MADE FOR WALKING

It doesn't matter whether you're a dedicated or an occasional walker – if you love fresh air and beautiful surroundings, the Isle of Man is a truly invigorating experience. As well as the wonderful variety and richness of the landscape, stepping out to explore offers you a rewarding choice of options. You can simply go where the fancy takes you – countryside, beaches, clifftops, glens, high hills – or use this section of the guide to help you conquer and enjoy some of the island's designated waymarked trails.

FOURTEEN TOP WALKS

The walks described in the following pages touch each end of the spectrum – from the challenging long-distance coast path to much more leisurely circular town walks. The first route covered, broken down into seven manageable sections, is the 95-mile coast path itself, Raad ny Foillan – the Road of the Gull.

Following this are the Heritage Trail (11.5 miles), the Millennium Way (26 miles), the Foxdale Line (just 2.5 miles along disused railway lines) and four town walks – in Douglas, Castletown, Peel and Ramsey.

THE COAST PATH

The Road of the Gull opened in 1986 and embraces most of the island's dramatic coastal paths, but also takes in unusual rural walks and the vast beach walks of the northern alluvial plain. The total length of 95 miles is approximate and varies according to the options you take along the way.

Serious walkers, using overnight accommodation at the main towns en route, can manage the coast path at a comfortable pace over a week's holiday. Purely for the purposes of this guide it is assumed that you will be (a) walking it in sections, (b) using public transport each day to get you to the start and to return from the finish of the walk, and (c) based at accommodation in Douglas (though bus and train links are good wherever you stay.) Options (for half-day or even shorter walks) are highlighted in italics where appropriate.

MANX PLACE NAMES

Many of the island's place names are in Manx Gaelic, or a corrupted form of it, and often describe very aptly either the shape or some other feature of the place. Others describe the origins of the place in relation to the family name of the historical owner. The remaining names have their origins in Norse and date from the Viking period. Where appropriate the English translation is given in the text to add interest and a better understanding of the Manx name.

WHAT TO WEAR

For reasons of safety and comfort you should always wear suitable shoes or, preferably, walking boots. This is particularly important on cliff paths where wet grass can be very slippery and catch out even the most experienced walkers. As for clothing, it is sensible to bear in mind that although you will never be far from civilisation, exposed coastal areas are sometimes subject to rapid

this **island's** made for **WALKING**

Looking south from South Barrule.

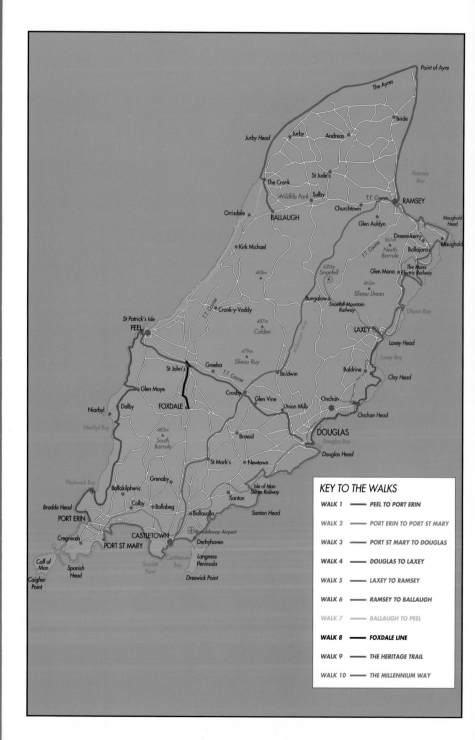

KEY TO THE WALKS

WALK 1	———	PEEL TO PORT ERIN
WALK 2	———	PORT ERIN TO PORT ST MARY
WALK 3	———	PORT ST MARY TO DOUGLAS
WALK 4	———	DOUGLAS TO LAXEY
WALK 5	———	LAXEY TO RAMSEY
WALK 6	———	RAMSEY TO BALLAUGH
WALK 7	———	BALLAUGH TO PEEL
WALK 8	———	FOXDALE LINE
WALK 9	———	THE HERITAGE TRAIL
WALK 10	———	THE MILLENNIUM WAY

changes in the weather and if unprepared you can easily get caught out before reaching shelter.

MAPS

The Isle of Man Public Rights of Way Map, published by the island's Department of Local Government and Environment, contains a wealth of information essential to serious walkers. Ordnance Survey's 1:50,000 Landranger map 95 is also well worth obtaining, whether you're walking, motoring, cycling or exploring the Isle of Man by any other means.

RAAD NY FOILLAN: THE ROAD OF THE GULL

The seven sections into which this guide divides the 95-mile coast path (signposted along its route by a gull symbol) are as follows. The walk time indicated against each section is a guideline only and reflects the terrain, places and points of interest en route.

1: Peel to Port Erin (13 miles, 7 hours)

COAST PATH SECTION I

PEEL TO PORT ERIN (13 MILES, 7 HOURS)

Take public transport to Peel and alight at the House of Manannan – the site of the former railway station and a Manx National Heritage attraction which tells part of the *Story of Mann*.

The walk starts from here. There are options to take two half-day walks, one from Peel to Glen Maye and return, and the other from Port Erin around Bradda. Begin by walking alongside the harbour to the bridge at its head. Cross the bridge and head towards the castle. After a short distance, follow the broad track up the hill, being careful to take the grassy track sharp left at the corner as the castle comes into view. You will soon see that there are two distinct parts to the hill which dominates Peel. The first, which you have just passed, is Peel Hill and the next part is Corrin's Hill, surmounted by Corrin's Tower.

From the saddle between the two hills you can either carry straight on to the summit of Corrin's Hill, or take the path to the right that follows the old horse tramroad to the quarry on the back of Corrin's Hill. The latter is by far the more spectacular but the path is close to the cliff edge in places so care is needed, particularly with young children – and this caution applies to many places on the walk.

Either option will bring you to the same spot, overlooking the south-west coast of the island. Niarbyl (literally meaning the tail –

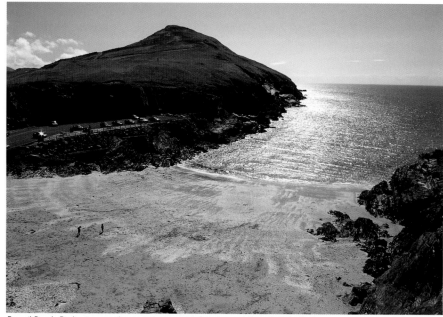

Peveril Beach, Peel – its name has associations with Scott's novel Peveril of the Peak.

from the tail of rocks stretching out to sea) is clearly visible. Cronk ny Irree Laa (hill of the dawn) dominates the skyline above and the hills stretch south to Fleshwick (green creek) and Bradda, with the Calf of Man just appearing in the far distance.

The path now becomes a real cliff path but is easy to follow as it skirts the various bays and inlets. Look for Traie Cabbag (cabbage shore – so named after the wild cabbage that grows here) and the unusual rock known as the Bonnet Rock, which is surrounded by water at most states of the tide. You will see why it has this local name when you find it. Now, as you approach Glen Maye (yellow glen) you have another choice. The path reverts to the coast road here for a short distance. You can follow the path down to the mouth of the glen as you round the headland and take the path up the opposite side of the glen to join the main road. Alternatively, carry on down into the glen and follow the lower path, stopping to admire the waterfall before climbing the steps to the main road.

There is an opportunity here to break for lunch at Glen Maye before returning by public transport or walking back to Peel along the main road – the first of the two half-day walk options referred to on page 165. Turn right, follow the road down the hill and climb the other side to continue south parallel to, and in sight of, the coast all the way to Dalby (glen farm).

To continue the main walk, turn right in the village and walk along the road leading to Niarbyl, right down to the sea. Look for the path to the left alongside the small cottage which once belonged to popular music hall artiste Florrie Forde (a regular summer performer in Douglas from 1900-1937) and follow the signs directing you up the path and along the top of the cliff. After a short distance the signposting directs you down steep steps to the shore Traaie Vane (white beach). Walk along the shore and cross the stream, where in winter the small waterfall can be spectacular. Look for the tall trees behind the beach hut and follow the broad track up again and away from the shore. Signposting takes you to the top of the cliff and a view south, and a steady climb joins a broad path on Manx National Heritage property that takes you south above Feustal (precipice) towards Cronk ny Irrey Laa.

Cross the stone wall over the wooden stile. The path is on the top of a cliff and should be treated with extreme care, swinging inland to cross a stream and wall above Gob ny Ushtey (headland of the waterfall, although the literal translation means beak of the water – the early Manx often described headlands as looking like the bill or beak of a bird and so the description came into common use).

From here strike uphill past the old farmhouse at Eary Cushlin (Cosnahan's shieling), now an outdoor pursuits centre. Continue uphill, following the signs all the way to the top of Cronk ny Irrey Laa. There are spectacular views all the way up the climb and when you reach the summit you will be at the highest point on the coastal path. Take time out to admire the view back over Niarbyl towards Peel with Corrin's Tower visible in the distance.

Now make your way down towards the Sloc (or Slough, meaning pit or hollow) over open moorland. Flocks of chough frequent this area and they are quite distinctive birds – easily recognisable as members of the crow family but with bright red beaks and legs which contrast sharply with their black plumage. Choughs are increasingly rare in much of Britain, the Isle of Man being one of their last refuges.

At the Sloc you will leave the moorland very briefly to use the road, rejoining the moorland almost immediately by the picnic site on the other side of the boundary wall. Here as so often with the coastal path you are faced with a choice – the easy wide track to the left, or the path to the right which favours more experienced walkers and takes you to the summit of Lhiattee ny Bienee

(literally meaning summit on the side), commanding excellent views back towards Cronk ny Irrey Laa and the big bay below.

Next, take the wide track and follow it to Surby (a Norse word – 'Saurbyr' meaning moorland farm), where it joins a surfaced road. At Surby turn right and follow the road to Fleshwick (green creek) down the east side of the valley.

As you approach the end of the valley look for the signs on the left of the road, just after the farm, which will lead you over a stile to start a really steep climb to the top of Bradda. Take your time climbing the path and admire the views behind you of the coast all the way up to Niarbyl and across the valley to Fleshwick. Once you are over the top of this climb, the view down the coast to the Sound opens out in front of you.

The descent into Port Erin is easy and you will pass Milner's Tower on your way. Here again you are faced with a number of alternative paths. Take the one following the coast through Bradda Glen and on to the upper promenade at Port Erin. Walk into the village and follow the signs to the railway station and bus depot, from where you will have a choice of transport back to Douglas.

The second optional half-day walk – from Port Erin around Bradda – starts from the railway station as described in the following.

From the station cross the road into Bridson Street past the Cherry Orchard Hotel. Turn right into Bay View Road, left up Harrison Street and on to a public right of way, which takes you across Rowany Golf Course. Be aware of golfers and the possibility of wayward balls, but the path is clearly marked and the views are good.

Keep heading for the valley ahead, avoiding the junctions with other paths, and eventually emerge at Honna Hill, crossing through an old stone-built stile in the boundary wall. Turn left and head up the hill to the top. Look for the sign marking the Ernie Broadbent Walk off to the right. Follow this narrow road down the west side of the

A breathtaking view, looking south to the Sound and the Calf of Man.

Fleshwick valley until joining the surfaced road to Fleshwick beach just past the farm. Turn left and look for the signs showing where Raad ny Foillan leaves the road a little distance further on, and where the longer walk from Peel joins.

There is time to walk down to the beach at Fleshwick and admire the views up the coast towards Niarbyl from sea level. The cliffs below the Carnanes sloping down to the sea are dramatic from here, and you can see where the high-level path from the Sloc descends to Fleshwick and why it is for more experienced walkers.

COAST PATH SECTION 2

PORT ERIN TO PORT ST MARY (6 MILES, 4 HOURS)

This is perhaps the most beautiful of all the island walks, whatever the weather and time of year. You should allow about four hours to give yourself enough time to take in the terrific views. The starting point is Port Erin station. An option is to get to Port Erin by first travelling to the Sound (where there is a café and car park) and taking in the village of Cregneash – a folk museum which is part of the *Story of Mann* and well worth seeing. The road from the Sound leads you to the village, from where the Darragh Road (place where oak trees grow) takes you into Port Erin.

From the station, turn left along Station Road and make your way down to the lower promenade and follow the sweep of the bay to the former Marine Biological Station near the lifeboat station. You will have to look very carefully for the start of this next section of the coast path, as it begins from behind an electrical sub station! But once you've found it, the path is easy to follow. Climb the rough steps cut in the cliff to the stile in the wall. Follow the path along the wall and up above Kione ny Garee (literally meaning the end of the thicket), where throughout the year fulmars nest on the north-facing shaded cliffs.

The path levels out above Bay Fine and

you have a good view back towards Port Erin and Bradda Head before descending towards Aldrick (old people's creek). On the way, look out for an unusual finger of rock known as Jacob's Rock. Ahead is the Calf of Man, the Sound, Kitterland and Thousla Rock. You can often see fast-flowing waters as the powerful tides rip and race through here, and if it's at all stormy you'll be treated to spectacular seas and views. An excellent viewpoint is provided by the wide panoramic window of the Manx National Heritage café and visitor centre at the Sound – not only a warm retreat in one of the Isle of Man's wildest places but also welcoming for its choice of hot meals, snacks and refreshments.

Crossing Manx National Heritage land, the path skirts around Burroo Ned (nest hill) and you will see the back of Spanish Head above Baie ny Breechyn (bay of the breeches – so named because it resembles a pair of blue trousers laid out on the sea!).

Pass through a gate and cross a small stream to commence the very steep assault on the back of Cronk Mooar (big hill, although its

Steaming through the countryside near Port Erin.

local name of Cronk y Feeagh, meaning hill of the raven, is more appropriate as ravens do nest here). This is the southernmost hill in the island – not very high but you will know it's a hill after you've made the climb!

Pause at the top and take in the views all round over the Sound and the Calf. If you're lucky and the wind's in the right direction, you may hear the baying of common seals as they bask on the Cletts (rocks) on the Calf immediately opposite this point. The path now starts to drop, still skirting the cliff edge and then turning north to start its run up the east coast. The path is very close to the edge above Black Head, so take great care, especially if you have children with you.

The path now starts to fall quickly towards Bay Stakka (a corruption of Baie yn Stackey, referring to the stack of Sugar Loaf Rock) which it skirts and then climbs to the Chasms, which are on the right. Again the path is exposed at this point so tread carefully. Then cross the wall on the substantial stile

and head towards the derelict Chasms Café. Go through the wooden gate and follow the waymarked route alongside the wall on your left. This should avoid having to cross any of the Chasms – deep clefts in the rock and quite an unusual phenomenon. Be careful to descend the path beside the wall on your left all the way to a metal kissing gate above Cashtal Kione ny Goagyn (meaning the castle of chasms' head) or Sugar Loaf Rock as it is more popularly known because of its unusual shape. It is inhabited by colonies of guillemots, kittiwakes, fulmars and the occasional razorbill and puffin, and this is perhaps the most spectacular view of the rock, providing you have a good head for heights.

The path crosses the next field diagonally, heading for a gap in the stone wall opposite. Before leaving the cliff edge you can just catch a glimpse of 'the anvil', or as it is sometimes called 'the pulpit rock', which is a rock standing clear of the cliff in the small bay behind the Sugar Loaf.

Follow the well-defined path between walls, leading eventually to a surfaced road to Glenchass (an English corruption of Glion Shast meaning sedge glen) and Port St Mary. At Glenchass take the right fork in the road and follow it downhill for a short distance, looking for a sign on the right to take you to the shoreline at Perwick (harbour creek). The route follows the beach at Perwick and Traie Coon (narrow beach) before swinging up a zigzag path from the stony shoreline to join the path beside the golf course and on to Port St Mary promenade. Walk along the sea wall, passing the disused limekiln and past the breakwater into Lime Street and the inner harbour. Port St Mary remains largely unspoilt but the harbour is now occupied by pleasure craft rather than commercial fishing boats.

Turn left at the end of Lime Street and then right to follow the lower promenade and join the Cain Karran elevated walkway, which gives an impressive entrance into Chapel Bay – without doubt one of the island's prettiest and most sheltered bays. Walk up into the village, where you'll find a variety of places to eat and a bus to take you back to Douglas.

COAST PATH SECTION 3

PORT ST MARY TO DOUGLAS (15 MILES, 8 HOURS)

If you're arriving at Port St Mary by bus, get off at the harbour. If you're travelling by train, it's only a short walk from the station to the village.

Start this section by rejoining the path along Port St Mary's lower promenade and Gansey Point to Bay ny Carrickey (bay of the rock), following the coast road to Fishers Hill for approximately one mile. You will pass the gatehouses and boundary wall to Kentraugh House, and where there's a break in the windswept trees that form the boundary you may just catch a glimpse of this fine mansion. Continue along the sea wall and take the right fork at the bottom of Fishers Hill to follow the single-track surfaced road almost

Volcanic activity shaped the landscape around Castletown.

this **island's** made for **WALKING**

on the shoreline to Poyll Vaaish (literally meaning the pool of death; the name's origin is obscure but one likely explanation is that a slaughter house associated with the farm drained into one of the many sea pools).

The whole area teems with birdlife, particularly herons fishing patiently in the rock pools and on the edge of the water, competing with curlews and oystercatchers. The path continues through the farm buildings at Poyll Vaaish and round the low headland beside the quarry from which the black marble for the steps of St Paul's Cathedral in London was reputedly obtained. Cross the stone stile over the wall on to the grassy headland at Scarlett (cormorant's cleft). The path follows the edge of the fields and skirts the rocks, which change dramatically, showing their volcanic origin and culminating in Scarlett Stack – a volcanic plug to a vent long since extinct. The broken, jagged rocks are the remains of an ancient lava flow. The rock changes from basalt to limestone as you now join a surfaced road once again and approach Castletown, which you will see straight ahead.

Enter the town square and turn right to skirt Castle Rushen, passing the police station. Turn immediate right again, then left over the footbridge to cross the harbour. Turn right into Douglas Street and past the Nautical Museum, which together with the castle is part of the *Story of Mann*. Continue along Douglas Street and Bowling Green Road to join the main road to Douglas.

Unfortunately, new runway extensions at Ronaldsway Airport mean that part of the original route of the coastal path from here towards Douglas no longer exists. You now have to walk along the main road past the airport as far as Ballasalla, turning left towards Balthane industrial estate and following the road until it turns left at the airport boundary and on to the entrance of the lime quarry. Look out for the stile to the right and cross it to follow an old road to Santon Gorge.

The path follows the gorge inland, crossing the river over the footbridge and returning to the coast down the other side of the gorge. A raised boardwalk now makes it much easier to cross this very wet and boggy section. The path eventually climbs away from the river and follows the top of the gorge amongst shoulder-high gorse before joining the coast again.

Once at the coast the path is easy to follow along the top of the cliffs. You will be rewarded with good views all the way to Douglas.

The next bay you come to is Port Soldrick (sunny creek). Just where the path turns inland to drop down to the shoreline, you will see large caves in the opposite headland, with a view of the coast north towards Santon Head. After travelling along the beach for a short distance, climb back on to the path as it takes you higher still to continue along the cliff top.

The next inlet is Port Grenaugh. Again, after reaching the shoreline, climb up the other side of the bay. Look for the promontory fort and Viking settlement at Cronk ny Merrui (literally the hill of the

Port Soderick – a popular beach resort in its Victorian heyday.

dead people) on the right as you climb. Continuing along the coast you will pass Purt Veg (little port) and Santon Head before starting the climb up to Ballanhowe, where the path goes inland once again. The single-track road crosses the line of the steam railway before joining the Old Castletown Road. Turning right, follow the road for a little over a mile, but take care as there is no footway.

Descending Crogga Hill (from the Norse Króká meaning winding river), you will pass Crogga House and its decorative lake before seeing a waymarker directing you down towards Port Soderick (which has the same meaning as Soldrick – sunny or south-facing creek) and passing under the line of the steam railway.

Keep to the road and take the left fork

along Marine Drive, where the coast path follows the route of the former Marine Drive tramway all the way to Douglas. Proceed along the coast, passing the inlet at Keristal. Note the change again in the rock formations, the contorted strata here in fragmented slate and clearly visible in the cliffs all around you. Problems over the years with rock falling from the cliff faces, plus a major landslide in 1977, mean that as a through road Marine Drive has been closed to traffic for quite a time – but take care, as both ends of the drive are still accessible to cars and motorbikes as well as to walkers and sightseers.

The sight of the old toll gatehouse at the end of Marine Drive means that you're almost in Douglas, confirmed by the panorama of the whole bay spread out before

Marine Drive – stunning views near Douglas Head.

you as you round the corner. The coast path now descends the steps between the lighthouse and the Camera Obscura (a restored Victorian attraction) to the breakwater, passing the Lifeboat House. The Douglas Lifeboat is appropriately named *Sir William Hillary* in honour of the Douglas resident who in 1824 was hugely influential in the creation of what was to become the Royal National Lifeboat Institution.

COAST PATH SECTION 4

DOUGLAS TO LAXEY (9 MILES, 4 HOURS)

This is a good half-day walk and Laxey has a lot to show you, including a fine choice of places to lunch and the fascinating Laxey Wheel and mines area – an important part of the island's rich industrial past.

Start at the Sea Terminal at the southern end of Douglas's impressively wide and sweeping 2-mile Loch Promenade. The prom was built in the 1870s to enclose part of the foreshore and to extend the lower part of

what was then the island's newly-appointed capital. Some of the original Victorian facade is now giving way to modern development as the changing face of Douglas continues to take shape, but enough survives to give you more than a flavour of Victorian grandeur as you make your way north along the bracing and spacious seafront.

On the opposite side of the promenade note the attractive elevations of the Sefton Hotel and the Gaiety Theatre. The church to the left and set back off the prom was completed in 1849 and dedicated to St Thomas, the patron saint of architecture. It was designed by Ewan Christian R.I.B.A., who was of Manx descent and Architect to the Church Commissioners, noted particularly for his work at Carlisle Cathedral.

The construction of the church was by local contractor Richard Cowle. It was built to serve the needs of an expanding town, and the arrival of the tourist development along Loch Promenade led to its being referred to as 'the visitors' church'. In 1912, a fire in the tower destroyed the bells, as well as the organ made and installed in 1886 by William Hill of London. The fire damage was repaired and a new peal of bells installed five months later. At the same time the organ was repaired and enlarged, and today recitals and concerts are a regular feature of church life.

As you continue towards the northern end of the crescent-shaped promenade, where stands the terminus of the unique Douglas Bay Horse Tramway, you'll see more evidence of redevelopment. The horse trams are a summer-only attraction and date from 1876. Here also is the southern terminus of the Manx Electric Railway, which has been running north to Ramsey since operation commenced in 1895. Both the horse trams and the railway still use original equipment and, unsurprisingly, they are a mecca for transport buffs from all over the world.

Continuing past Port Jack and around the loop of Seaview Road, you'll soon see why it is so named, overlooking Douglas Bay. Look for the coast path waymarker directing you

along the cliff top and almost through the front gardens of the houses here. The path joins the road again at Lag Birragh (literally the sharp pointed hollow – referring to the rocks below) and continues along King Edward Road to Groudle (narrow glen), where you should follow the narrow road down to the shore by the holiday homes. Cross the river by the footbridge and climb up the path to cross the Groudle Glen Railway. A popular Victorian novelty and attraction, the restored railway is now operated by enthusiasts at various though limited times during summer months and for Santa specials.

Follow the path upwards and on to a narrow surfaced single-track road. Look for the waymarker directing you across the fields to Garwick, and also for the signpost to Lonan Old Church – well worth a detour, not least to see the stone Celtic wheel cross in the grounds.

Walk through the fields to the point where the path joins Clay Head Road, which you

Ferries of the Steam Packet at Douglas.

This commemorative statue of popular TT champion Steve Hislop stands at Onchan Head.

must follow towards Baldrine. Look for the waymarker directing you to Garwick, and follow the fishermen's path to the shore and climbing immediately all the way back up the other side of the glen. Follow the signs to join the main road again.

Turn right at the top and continue towards Laxey on the main road beside the tramway (there's no pavement so be careful). Reaching Fairy Cottage presents you with an option – as long as you know the state of the tide! At low water you can take another fishermen's path down to the beach and walk to Laxey harbour the very pretty way. Alternatively, stay on the coast path and continue down Old Laxey Hill into Old Laxey and the harbour. Follow Glen Road to Laxey village and up the hill under the church to the centre of the village. Christ Church Laxey is situated in what must be a unique setting for any church and its history is entwined with the mining history of Laxey. The village was a very busy place in the mid 1800s as a direct result of mining. The population had increased significantly, and with the temptation of public houses on the doorstep the need for a place of worship within the village was long overdue.

In fact, the Laxey Mining Company and

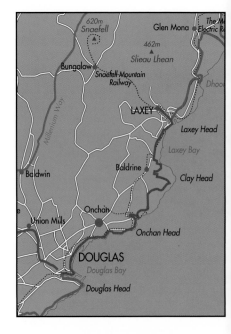

one of its principal shareholders, G.W. Dumbell, were instrumental in promoting a church. Built largely by the miners themselves, right in the middle of the village on land which was formerly part of the garden of the Mines Captain's House, it was designed by architect Ewan Christian. Early

Wonderful rolling countryside near Laxey.

It's a long climb up that winding staircase to the top of the Great Laxey Wheel – but the views are worth it.

English in style, it has an interesting scissorbeam roof and simple internal decor and it merits spending a little time here. Take lunch in the village and complete this leisurely day's coastal walk with a visit to the Great Laxey Wheel & Mines Trail – yet another chapter in the Manx National Heritage *Story of Mann*.

In fact, Laxey now boasts not one but two restored waterwheels. The wheel once used at the Snaefell mine, situated further up the valley, has been painstakingly rebuilt by local enthusiasts and is displayed in the mines' former washing floors – the same location in which (in summer) you can see and travel on a restored section of the Laxey mines tramway and its authentic replica locomotives of the 1870s.

At the end of the walk, return to the station and take the tram back to Douglas.

COAST PATH SECTION 5

LAXEY TO RAMSEY (12 MILES, 6 HOURS)

From Douglas, travel by bus or electric railway to Laxey station and you're ready to resume your conquest of the coast path. Start by taking the path alongside the station building and down to Captain's Hill. Turn right to join Glen Road opposite St George's Woollen Mills and make your way to the harbour. Note the large factory-type building on the opposite side of the river – built to generate the power for the Laxey section of the Manx Electric Railway.

At the junction by the harbour bridge, look to the opposite side of the road for the coast path waymarker. It directs you up an old packhorse road to Ballaragh (of doubtful origin but best seen as derived from Balley arragh, meaning farm of the spectre or apparition). Continue up through Ballaragh to the top of the hill and the views towards Maughold Head and east across the Irish Sea to Cumbria and the Lake District.

The road curves away from the coast but look for the waymarker on the corner, pointing you over the fence and diagonally down through the fields. Cross the road and the railway track and continue on the footpath until it joins the Dhoon Glen Loop Road. Cross one stile on to the road and then immediately back over the adjacent stile to follow the track down to sea level again. It is worth the effort even though this is another of those down-and-back-up-again detours.

The path skirts Dhoon Glen and you will catch a glimpse of the wheelcase of the Dhoon Rhennie Mine (Dhoon is probably derived from an Irish word meaning fort and rhenny is a ferny place), which extracted lead and zinc but was not productive and eventually abandoned. Then the mouth of the glen opens up and you will have a view of the headland of Kion e Hennin (Kione ny eaynin – headland of the cliff; Kione literally means beak or bill of a bird but by common usage has come to mean headland). Its area, and immediately behind the headland was a granite boss which for years was quarried for its pink granite.

The path drops to the shore and then returns behind the picnic table. Follow the path within the glen, climbing past the island's most spectacular waterfall, comprising three falls emptying into a pool beside the path. A further steep climb will take you back to the point where you began this detour. Turn right, back on to the Dhoon Loop Road and follow it over the railway back to the main road, where you turn right. Almost immediately turn right again and at the bottom of the hill take yet another right turn, making sure you follow the right fork by the ford and the single-track road down to Cornaa (an ancient treen name meaning land division).

You are now back at sea level again, but

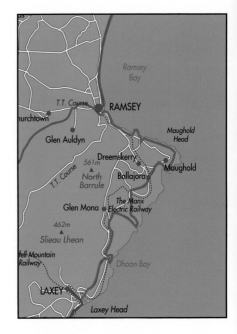

this time with a difference. Behind the shingle bank is a saltmarsh with an attendant variety of birdlife.

The path crosses the river and follows an unsurfaced road known as Benussi's lane all the way up the right-hand side of the valley, heading inland. Cross the railway again, and the main road, to continue up the Raad ny Quakerin (the Quakers' road), noting the Quakers' burial ground at the summit.

Descending through Ballajora (farm of the strangers), you'll enjoy a view of Maughold Head and the lighthouse. At the bottom of the hill look for the signs taking you right to Port Mooar (the great harbour). Follow the path round the coast through the tall grass to Gob ny Rona (headland of the seals) where you may very well see some of these marine mammals. At Dhyrnane, before climbing away from the shore, you'll pass derelict workings from an iron ore mine.

Now cross fields past a lime kiln to join the road to the lighthouse, turning right for a short distance before turning left on to Maughold Brooghs. Follow the path over the

this **island's** made for **WALKING**

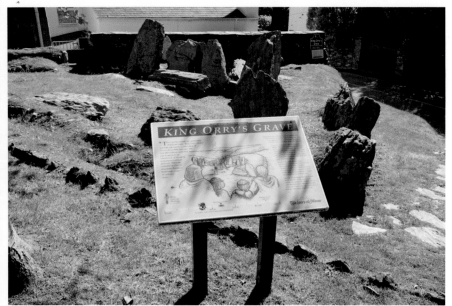

King Orry's Grave near Laxey – but did King Orry ever exist?

headland through more old mine workings at Gob Ago (literally edge headland) before joining the road again and turning right towards Ramsey.

Not for the first time, you have a choice of routes: carrying on into Ramsey along the main road or, if the tide is out, going down the slip at Port e Vullen (harbour of the mill) to the shore and following the cliff path around the headland at Tableland to rejoin the road again a little further on.

Either way, it is back up to the main road, passing Belle Vue railway halt and all the way down into Ramsey. At Ballure (Balley euar meaning yew tree estate or farm) you could make a detour into Ballure Glen and on to Ramsey along the beach, but this option is only possible at low water. Once in Ramsey, proceed along the promenade and the harbour. At the end of the promenade is the church of St Maughold and Our Lady Star of the Sea, built in 1900 and designed by Giles Gilbert Scott.

This marks the end of the Laxey-Ramsey section of the coast path, and you can return to Douglas by bus or electric railway from the station in Waterloo Road.

COAST PATH SECTION 6

RAMSEY TO BALLAUGH (18 MILES, 8 HOURS)

Now for something completely different! This section of the Isle of Man coast path embraces the northern alluvial plain – a flatter, gentler landscape compared with the rest of the island, the Bride Hills topping a modest 300 feet.

However, the walk is very dependent on tidal conditions and should not be undertaken when the tide is rising. The ideal time to start is shortly after high water, although there are alternatives which avoid the risk areas.

The starting point is Ramsey station – the northern terminus of the Manx Electric Railway, and also close to the bus station. To proceed, make your way from the station to the harbour, follow the quayside and cross the stone arched bridge at the harbour's head. Turn right into North Shore Road to Mooragh Promenade (Mooragh meaning waste land by the sea) and then left, following the promenade as far as the Vollan. The state of the tide will determine which way you go from here. If the tide's out it's possible to walk all the way to the Point of Ayre – the most northerly place on the Isle of Man – along the shingle beach. But if the tide's in, the only option is to walk up the hill, turn right and follow the road to the village of Bride and onward from there to the Point of Ayre.

Of geological interest is the fact that the cliffs of this part of the island are composed of sand. The high cliffs at Shellag (the original Norse name means seal creek or bay) are quite dramatic – deformed glacial deposits – but because of erosion the bay no longer exists. As you continue along the shore it is clear to see that the whole area is subject to storm erosion.

If you've taken the road to Bride and onwards, you will pick up the coast path

again at the Phurt (port) north of Shellag Point. Follow the raised beach and the glacial formation of the northern plain which is clearly evident. The whole of the Ayres was formed by alluvial deposit and here the terrain changes yet again with shingle underfoot all the way around the northernmost tip of the island.

The lighthouse which marks the Point of Ayre was designed by Robert Stevenson for the Commissioners of Northern Lights and built in 1818. The shingle is constantly on the move, as can be seen by the smaller lighthouse added 72 years after the original and now automated, controlled from a remote central station.

Continuing along the coast on the shoreline is heavy going underfoot but worth it for the wild natural beauty to seaward, with birdlife in abundance. Look for gannets, whose spectacular dive-bombing action, black-tipped vivid white wings and highly distinctive blue bills set them apart. As you make your way along the beach it's probable that you'll be followed by curious seals and

Rich farmland near the remote Point of Ayre.

constantly leapfrogged by flocks of oystercatchers – a wonderful sight in flight.

Passing Rue Point and Blue Point, where the rifle range and the old coastguard lookout are located, will put sand back underfoot. The whole of the northern plain has been drained by successive generations to reclaim many acres of fertile agricultural land. The last major undertaking was the formation of a lengthy drainage channel which discharges at the Lhen (Lhen Mooar – meaning great ditch). You'll know when you reach it, as the Lhen Trench discharges across the shore and wading is the only way to get across – so it's boots off and round the neck.

As you approach Jurby Head, the sand cliffs are back with a vengeance and continue almost to Peel. If the tide's well out at Jurby Head look for the remains of the trawler *Passages*, which was driven ashore in 1929 in a north-west gale, the crew rescued by the rocket brigade of the day.

After passing Jurby Head you approach the Killane (from the Scandinavian kjarrland, meaning brushwood land), where another drainage ditch discharges to the sea. Shortly after this, look for the signs where the Ballaugh shore road joins the shoreline at the Cronk.

Leave the shore and walk to the village of Ballaugh, passing the old parish church of St Mary de Ballaugh. Dating from the middle of the 18th century, it is noted for its leaning gate pillars. Old photographs and other sources suggest that the pillars must have been in this condition for a hundred years or more.

Walking towards Ballaugh, you can admire the backdrop of the western hills and see the tower of the 'new' parish church. Work on the church commenced in May 1830. The old church was considered too small and, as the village community grew, too far from the centre of the population it was supposed to serve – even though it was no more than a mile away!

Designed by Hanson and Welch, the

Winkie, the secondary lighthouse on the beach at the Point of Ayre.

Looking towards Snaefell from the green and pleasant landscape near Bride.

church is built in local stone in a style unique for the island. The tall lancet-type windows and intervening buttresses to the nave, and the ornate pinnacles, make it quite distinctive.

You will arrive in the centre of the village opposite the public house and beside Ballaugh Bridge – a famous landmark along the TT course.

COAST PATH SECTION 7

BALLAUGH TO PEEL (13 MILES, 5 HOURS)

To complete your anti-clockwise conquest of the Isle of Man coast path, here's a walk which is easy going all the way. It begins from the centre of the village, beside Ballaugh Bridge. Leave the village by Station Road and proceed to the Cronk, passing the two churches described in Section 6. On the way you will pass the Dollagh (a corruption of Doufloch, meaning black lake), a name rooted in the fact that in much earlier times, a great deal of the northern plain was flooded, the

land dominated by several large lakes. No visible signs of these lakes remain, except in periods of heavy rainfall, when remnants appear here and there. Other places such as Ellan Rhenny (ferny island) and Ellan Bane (white island), and even the parish name of Ballaugh (a corruption of Balley ny Loughey – lake farm), give a clue to what this area was like in those days long gone.

At the Cronk turn left and follow the Bollyn Road (Boayl ein – spot of the birds) as far as the Orrisdale Road. There are good views of the western hills which form the backdrop to Bishopscourt, the ancient seat of the Bishop of Sodor and Mann but now a private residence. Turn right at the junction with the Orrisdale Road and follow the road through Orrisdale (from the Scandinavian Orrastŏr, meaning estate of the moorfowl).

At the corner after the farm look for the signpost leading to the shore at Glen Trunk. Go through the gate and follow the wide grassy track to the shore, past one of the island's best-preserved lime kilns.

Once on the shore you will be able to see Peel in the distance. Turn left and walk along the shore, flanked by steep sand cliffs, and note how these are also subject to erosion. For this reason it is advisable to steer a wide berth when walking underneath them.

This is an interesting spot for bird lovers. You're likely to be in the company of oystercatchers, herring gulls and black-backed gulls. Curlews, living on the slopes of the western hills, graze the foreshore in flocks and ringed plover and the occasional chough are often seen in these parts.

As you approach Glen Wyllin (glen of the mill) you will spot sea defence works on the foreshore – an attempt to slow down the rate of erosion. Beyond these, a little further along the shoreline, look for the waymarkers directing you off the shore at Glen Mooar (the great glen).

Leave the shore here and make your way up the narrow surfaced road to the main coast road. Look across the road and you will see a waymarker directing you into the glen. Follow the path as far as the stone pier – one of two piers which once carried the railway across the glen on lattice steel girders. Climb the roughly-cut steps up the side of the embankment to join the disused railway track. This now forms part of the coast path and will take you to the old station at St Germain's Halt, 3 miles away.

Once on the track, look back and this elevated position will show you just how severe the erosion of the sand cliffs is at this point. In places it will not be long before the coast road is threatened.

There are a couple of farm crossings before you approach a rock cutting and the road overbridge at Skerisdale (or more correctly Skeresstaðr from the Norse meaning rocky farm). The railway now runs closer to the sea than the road does and you can imagine just how dramatic a journey it must have been as the train clung to the cliffs and spanned the glens on viaducts and embankments.

Leaving the cutting, the track bed emerges on to an embankment at Glion Cam (the winding glen), opening up views of Peel and the castle on St Patrick's Isle in the distance. The coast road can be seen to the left and above, winding around the head of the glen – hence the local name of the Devil's Elbow.

Half a mile further on, in a shallow cutting which is sometimes quite wet and muddy, the path emerges into the open and really does cling to the cliff. This section, known as the 'donkey bank', suffered continuous settlement problems when the railway was operating, and these are evident as you proceed. Below, as you cross the second of the embankments, you can also see rocks on the shoreline at Gob y Deigan. From here on in the physical features of the coast change yet again – from the sand cliffs to slate and to red sandstone as you get nearer to Peel.

The path continues on the track bed for a further mile, crossing yet another glen on an embankment at Glion Booigh (the dirty

Wonderfully wild – but northern sections of the west coast
are being eroded by the sea.

Peel's attractive new marina and revitalised waterfront.

glen). It's worth stopping on the embankment to look down at the trees growing in this glen. There's a great variety, with some surprises, and in many ways it is one of the most unspoilt corners of the island and only really appreciated from this location.

The path now curves left to join the coast road at the site of the former St. Germain's Halt, the old station building and gatehouse just about recognisable as such. Leave the track here and follow the road for a short distance downhill and round the corner at the bottom. Look for the waymarker on the right and go through the kissing gate to join the headland path. The path climbs rough-cut steps and reaches a promontory above Cass Struan (stream end). Stop and look north back along the route you've just walked and you'll see the sand cliffs stretching all the way north to the prominent white outline of Jurby Church and Jurby Head in the distance. Now look down below where you're

standing and you'll see the sandstone (referred to earlier) which outcrops here in a glorious burst of russet red.

The path continues to Peel along the headland above Traie Fogog (or more correctly Traie Feoghaig – meaning periwinkle shore), commanding probably the best views over Peel and the castle. Continue on the headland path and descend into the town and the promenade. There are several places to take refreshment and any of the roads off the prom leads to the town centre and the bus station for return to Douglas.

If you've completed all seven sections of Raad ny Foillan, you'll have to admit it's been an adventure. Congratulations – and here's to the next time!

THE HERITAGE TRAIL

DOUGLAS TO PEEL (10.5 MILES, 4 HOURS)

This easy and leisurely walk along a disused

narrow-gauge railway follows the route of the first line which connected Douglas to Peel. When the railway was built in 1873, the Isle of Man Railway Co. had a simple wooden building as its station. But by 1892 it had developed at such a pace that the company had built a new station to rival many of the mainline stations in the British Isles – so where better to start the walk than in the station forecourt, close to Athol Street and the heart of Douglas's business community.

Unfortunately, the first half mile or so of the original line has been extensively built over, so you have to make a detour before joining the line at the Quarterbridge. But as you leave the station, look at the impressive Victorian clock tower, which gives a good idea of the grandeur of the station architecture when it was built.

From the station turn left up Bank Hill and left again into Peel Road. The shops you pass on the left were also built by the enterprising railway company. Continue to the junction with Pulrose Road and turn left over the bridge – built in 1938 to replace an earlier level crossing on the line you'll be

joining a little further on. Note the bridge's two arches. The intention was to construct a double track, but it was an ambition never realised. You'll also be able to make out the route of the track bed as it threads its way behind the development in this area, which has taken place over the last twenty-five years.

Continue on towards the power station and turn right immediately before the bridge over the Douglas River. Follow the pathway behind the Bowl, part of the King George V playing fields. The whole area was reclaimed using waste from the spoil heaps at the Foxdale mines. The Isle of Man Railway locomotive No.15 *Caledonia* was used almost exclusively to haul thousands of tons of material here between 1935 and 1939.

The path takes you to the confluence of the River Dhoo (black river) and the River Glass (green river), and now you can see how the name of the town of Douglas evolved. Follow the right fork alongside the Glass and cross it by the bridge, which leads to the National Sports Centre. Follow the river for a short distance past the rear of the grandstand and join the railway track behind the office

The Millennium Monument and Oakwood at Ballafletcher, Braddan, where every primary school pupil on the island has

building. This is where the railway crossed the river on a skew lattice girder bridge.

Now you can start the walk in earnest. A little way along the old track bed you'll reach the site of the level crossing which took the railway over the Castletown Road. Note the crossing keeper's gatehouse on the left, but take care crossing the very busy road because visibility is restricted.

All of the island's disused railways are now service corridors for gas, electricity, water and telephones, and nearly all are public rights of way and over time have been improved for walkers. In 1989 this line was the most complete in terms of the overall scheme and was designated the Heritage Trail. It is now also a designated cycle way. The next section of the track bed serves an access road for vehicles to the inside of the TT course when the main road is closed for racing. Continue behind Quarterbridge Lodge and walk between the stone boundary walls. On the from acorns collected in Worcestershire woodlands.

left you will see Kirby Estate and possibly catch sight of grey herons, which roost here and range the river. The name Kirby is Scandinavian in origin and means church farm.

As you pass under the road you're approaching the site of what was formerly Braddan Halt. This was used in connection with Open Air Sunday Services at Braddan parish church, shortly coming into view to the left. It was not uncommon to see 10-

coach trains on this short special service from Douglas and hundreds of visitors getting off at the halt, which had no platform, and walking up the steps by the bridge and up Vicarage Road to the fields behind the new parish church.

Carry straight on along the old track bed, which from here on is more recognisable as a disused railway. The River Dhoo, which has never been very far away from you, is now beside the railway. Approaching Union Mills the line curves left after crossing the river on a steel girder bridge. This replaced an earlier stone-built structure which gave rise to flooding in the early years of the railway. A small wayside halt existed here originally to serve a horseracing course at the Strang.

Now, with industry left behind, the scenery becomes more attractive. It's hard to believe that even as late as 1960 there was little or no industrial development between Pulrose Bridge and Union Mills!

Entering Union Mills station through the tall trees which have grown with the railway, you are now 2.5 miles from Douglas. Early photographs show almost no cover at all. Successive station masters took tremendous pride in the station, which became noted for its wonderful rhododendron and floral displays.

The station was on the curve and had a very long passing loop, added some time after 1906. On the left you will see the single platform serving the station. Look for the name of the manufacturer of the non-slip paving slabs which form the edge of the platform. Also on the left, before you reach the platform, there's a roadway accessing the station area. There was a short trailing siding here serving goods traffic and a cattle dock. The wooden station building was situated on the right just before the line passed under the road.

Part of the development of the Heritage Trail has been the inclusion of picnic tables and information boards. Here at Union Mills there is also a static display of a Gibbins breakdown crane – one of two operated by the railway – on a small section of track. Dating from 1893, it was hand operated and had a lifting capacity of 8 tons.

Immediately after crossing the River Dhoo yet again (the original steel structure was removed when the line was being dismantled), continue past a small industrial area where the remaining parts of the old Union Mills are still in use. The name evolved because a corn mill and a woollen mill built on the site by William Kelly both drew water for their machinery from the same dam.

The mills were big employers for this area in the early part of the 19th century. Later they were owned by the Dalrymple family, who continued to operate them until the end of the century. Dalrymple Maitland was a director of the railway and locomotive No. 11 was named after him.

Now cross the Trollaby stream (possibly meaning the stream of the trolls) and enter open country as the line sweeps into the central valley of the island. The River Dhoo is still on your left and you can see remnants of the curragh (bog) between the river and the railway. Much of the central valley was like this, with wet boggy land, water meadows and willow growing in what was in effect the flood plain of the river. Henry Vignoles, who surveyed the area for the line, chose a route which skirted the valley floor and just managed to keep above the water table.

The line passes Glen Lough (literally Lake Glen) and runs straight for a short distance to cross the road at Closemooar (great enclosure), just after milepost 4. The crossing keeper's gatehouse still survives and is on the left before the crossing.

There was a short cutting here and the line ran straight towards Marown Church, with Greeba Mountain dominating the view. The track bed here has also been surfaced to allow access to the nearby sewage works, so beware of lorries! The track bed passes behind the parish church and swings left, entering more of the curragh land before approaching another level crossing, where the gatehouse still remains.

Cross the road and enter the playing fields. This was the site of Crosby station, some 4.75 miles from Douglas. Nothing remains to give a clue as to what was here. There was a passing loop and the facing point for this was positioned just before the level crossing, where two tracks crossed the road. This meant that when trains passed here the road was

Marown Old Church dates from the 12th century.

obstructed for longer than usual. If the second train was late the gates would often be opened in between the passing operation. There was a typical IMR wooden station building, painted green and cream, on the right at the point where you entered the playing fields. Just beyond that was a wooden goods shed served by a siding off the passing loop, with a further short siding to a cattle dock, the whole of which was partly screened by a wooden boarded fence.

You are now much closer to Greeba (an obscure Scandinavian word meaning peak) and the hills on both sides are closing in on the railway. You are still climbing and haven't yet reached the summit. On the hill on the left above the Highway Depot you can see the old school which served the parish of Marown.

Leaving the playing fields, you are soon back on the old track bed. Straight ahead is Creg y Whallian (rock of the whelp) with

Cooilingill Farm (low nook) on the hillside. You will just be able to see the edge of Archallagan Plantation to the left on the skyline. The River Dhoo has its source in the centre of the plantation before tumbling down the hill below Cooilingel and joining the Greeba River on your left.

The line, now 5 miles out of Douglas, swings right with Greeba and Slieau Ruy (red mountain) straight ahead. As you approach and cross the track leading to Cooilingel Farm, you are into the true remaining curragh of the central valley. This was an accommodation crossing and the gates were always open to the railway. Walk over another short bridge which crosses the Greeba river and continue close under Creg y Whallian. This is the narrowest part of the valley and very near to the summit of the line.

The next level crossing over the Rhenny road (boayl y rhennee – place of the fern)

The Royal Chapel of St John and the Processional Way to Tynwald Hill – the focus of Manx national day celebrations in July.

was also an accommodation crossing. The house with the unusual farm buildings on the right is Northop (another Scandinavian word meaning north village). Here is another chance to look at Greeba before the curragh closes in and you pass through a very wet area which was the site of an early settlement. You emerge approaching the Ballacurry Road, another unmanned crossing. The summit of the line, at 185 feet, was marked by the small stream after the Ballacurry Road. The Greeba sports field is on your right, just visible through the trees. This is the site of an accident in 1909 when the locomotive *Derby* (No. 2), acting as pilot engine on a late train running to Peel, had the misfortune to hit a fallen tree. It was completely derailed and toppled on to its side – the second accident in which it was involved (but more of that shortly).

As you pass through Greeba the curragh is still visible in places, but over the years drainage work and farming activity have reclaimed a large portion of it. The wooded hill ahead is Slieau Whallian, although its true summit is further to your left. The hill dominates the village of St John's, and it is up its flank that the Foxdale Railway climbed the gradient of 1 in 49 to the mines. This is the point from where the Isle of Man Railway Co. at one time proposed to build a branch line to Foxdale. It would have gone off to the left, climbing the side of the hill above Kenna (Aodha's hill – Aodha being a name of Irish descent).

Next you cross the Kenna Road, which was yet another unmanned accommodation crossing. After a shallow reverse curve under the trees, the track runs straight all the way to St John's.

Now Slieau Whallian is much closer and you can see the gatehouse for the keeper at the Curragh Road level crossing. The track bed has been surfaced here and an additional road built to serve the adjacent amenity site. Cross the road and the stile on to the right-hand track – the original route of the railway

– and pass under the bridge which carried the Foxdale Railway over the Peel line. The bridge is covered with ivy but you can see the brick arch springing from the stone abutments.

You are now approaching the site of St John's station. It grew from very modest beginnings to become the 'Crewe Junction' of the island railways. In its final form the line was single, passing under the bridge and running for a short distance parallel to a three-line steel carriage shed on the right.

There was a fourth carriage siding in the open on the far side of the shed. A small signalbox stood in the middle of the grassed area to your right. Here the line split into two, each with a passing loop and served by a single low platform, just one brick high, placed between them. This is where the Ramsey line and the Peel line divided. At each end of the central platform was a water tank supported on a brick structure.

St John's was served by a simple wooden station building situated on the left near the road (the site now part of a housing development). It had a small waiting room, ticket office and station master's office and was never developed or replaced by more impressive facilities despite the relative importance of the station.

Two lines crossed the road on a gated level crossing, the Peel line on the left and the Ramsey line on the right.

To continue the walk you have to make a slight detour from the original route, as the bridges over the river beside the Mart have been removed. Cross the road and go through the gate opposite, leading to the sewage works, and rejoin the track alongside them.

Walking down from the road you can see an interesting red brick building behind the hedge on your right. This was the terminus of the Foxdale Railway and was a grand building compared with the IMR's modest station at St John's.

Passing through the gated stile puts you back on clear track bed again. The two lines were still running parallel here, the line to Peel on the left and to Ramsey on the right. As you approach the two bridges crossing the River Neb at Ballaleece (Leece's farm), you will see the Ramsey line start to rise alongside you in order to pass over the Peel road as it swings away to the right.

The Peel line makes a gradual descent from the river crossing before levelling out on the ancient flood plain of the Neb (the meaning of the river's name is obscure). The river, having looped around to the left towards the Patrick Road and joined with the Foxdale river since the bridge at Ballaleece, is now back alongside the railway on the approach to Shenharra (meaning Old Ballaharra, possibly referring to an ancient earthwork).

The river meanders away to the left as you approach the cutting at Ballawyllin (Byllinge's farm), which was a notorious spot in winter for snow. The cutting is through the tail of what appears to be a moraine, deposited at the time of the retreating ice sheet in the last ice age.

Through the crossing at Ballawyllin you can now see the true flood plain extending out towards Patrick, and the full extent of Peel Hill and Corrin's Hill, surmounted by Corrin's tower. Further to the left are the Creggans (literally rocky place but describing the small rocky outcrop), forming the southern boundary to Knockaloe (Caley or Allowe's hill), the site of a First World War internment camp. A branch of the railway was built to serve the camp and shortly you will see where it joined the Peel line. The line ran straight for a short distance before skirting the sand cliffs of Ballatersen (part of the old Bishop's Barony but literally meaning farm of the crozier), now the location of Peel's golf course.

You'll see that the railway passed through the last remnants of the curragh and if you're particularly observant you might spot the remains of some of the drainage channels dug in the 1940s as a winter employment scheme in a further attempt to drain this area.

The line now ran beneath the cliffs and through boggy ground again – terrain which caused big problems throughout the entire lifetime of the railway. You can get some idea of the nature of the ground as you pass close under the sand cliffs. The willow catkins are a sight to behold in spring and the area abounds with the yellow heads of wild iris.

A little further on and the river is once more back alongside the railway and slowed by a dam built for the Glenfaba Mill (a mixture of English and Manx; it should be Myllin Glenfaba, meaning Mill in the glen of the Neb). The pond is known locally as the 'red dub', and you can see where the mill race was taken off the dam and under the track on its way to the mill. The name for the area, which also gives its name to the weir, is the Congary (rabbit warren).

Before reaching the mill you'll cross a small stream by means of a footbridge. Pay particular attention to the widening of the track bed just after the bridge. This is where the branch railway to Knockaloe Internment Camp left the Peel line by means of a trailing point from this direction. You can just make out the line of the branch as it curved round to cross the river on a wooden trestle bridge to climb for a little over a mile, at a gradient of 1 in 20, to the village of Patrick and Knockaloe.

Next on the right is the Glenfaba Mill. Some indication of what it was like can be gleaned from the size and shape of the building. The waterwheels remain and the overflow from them would have discharged under the track into the river. In fact the railway occupied the original river bed here, the river re-aligned to accommodate it. The railway passed under the Patrick Road and alongside the river, which was also diverted here to allow the line to run through this natural gorge on a gentle curve. It was here, in 1874, that the ill-fated locomotive *Derby* suffered the first of its two major accidents.

Following heavy rain, the embankment gave way and the loco tumbled into the river.

It was the first train of the day and although the driver saw that the track had been washed away he was unable to stop. He and the fireman both fell with the engine but were uninjured, as was the only passenger who fortunately occupied one of the coaches which remained on the track. The railway was temporarily diverted on a reverse curve to the right, almost on the original line of the river, while the present retaining wall was built on the original alignment.

Follow the railway through the remaining fields of Glenfaba farm as you enter Peel, through the back door past the old power station on the left. On your right are the Total Oils storage depot and the new Peel power station. When the railway was running the first buildings encountered would be the brick kilns and tall chimneys of the Glenfaba Brick Company – no doubt aesthetically more pleasing than the concrete chimney now occupying the site.

Straight ahead on the left-hand side of the track is one of Peel's original kipper houses, now operated as a working museum and worth a visit. The modern kipper houses are in the fish yard on the right. The railway finally arrived at Peel station by a level crossing over Mill Road where Peel Heritage Trust have a small transport museum in the old brickworks office.

The station site had been reclaimed from the harbour bed. The water tank, station building and goods shed are all that remain of the station itself, the last two buildings having been incorporated into the House of Manannan heritage centre, which now occupies the site. Behind the water tank there was a small engine shed and on the right a cattle loading dock and the goods shed. This had a loading bay into Mill Road which can still be seen. The station, having undergone several changes throughout its life, ended with four roads and a run-around loop served by a long platform.

The Creek Hotel – originally the Railway Hotel – is a good place to stop for well-earned refreshment. The railway ceased operation between Douglas and Peel in 1972 after five years of uncertainty. The rails had been lifted and sold for scrap before the Isle of Man Government stepped in and purchased everything, which fortunately included the now-thriving Port Erin line of the Isle of Man Steam Railway.

THE MILLENNIUM WAY

RAMSEY TO CASTLETOWN (26 MILES)

This can be undertaken as a full-day walk or as two walks breaking at Crosby. The Millennium Way was the first long-distance path to be introduced on the Isle of Man as part of the celebrations associated with 1,000 years of independent government. Opened in Easter 1979, it is based on the ridgeway used by the Norse kings to travel from their ancient landing place on the Sulby River near Skyhill to their fortress on the southern plain. The road is recorded in the *Chronicles of Mann and the Isles* - the first written record of island life, produced by the monks of Rushen Abbey.

NORTHERN SECTION: 14 MILES

Take a bus or tram to Ramsey and make your way from the station to the harbour, which is a short distance along Parliament Street and down Post Office Lane opposite the Courthouse. Turn left at the harbour and follow it to the junction with Bowring Road. Note the shipyard on the opposite side of the harbour which was built on the site of a former salt works.

Cross the road at the top of the harbour and look for the public footpath sign leading to Pooyldhooie (pool of the black ford), where a nature reserve has been constructed on what used to be the town tip. It is now a very pleasant walk and a credit to the local commissioners and the volunteers who have carried out the work.

The path emerges by the Whitebridge, which crosses the Sulby River, and this must

The bleak but hauntingly beautiful Windy Corner – a north-east landmark of the legendary TT Mountain Course.

have been the most likely place for the Vikings to have made their safe harbour. At the time of their invasions and subsequent settlement the island was a very different place and the Sulby was by far the biggest river. Here they could sail their longships at least a mile and a half from the open sea and moor them in a sheltered lagoon – something which was not possible anywhere else on the island.

Walk up Gardeners Lane to the main road and turn right for a short distance, looking for the distinctive waymarkers for the Millennium Way, striking off to the left over the bulk of Skyhill (the Norse named it Skógarfjall – the wooded hill). Follow the path up through the plantation, which was the site of a battle in 1079 when Godred

Crovan overcame the native Manx and assumed kingship of the island.

From the plantation the track opens out on the level near some rugged flat-topped pine trees at Park ny Earkan (pasture of the lapwing). Stop and look back over the northern plain, formed by the outwash from the retreating ice sheet at the end of the last ice age. The Point of Ayre is in the far distance.

Carry on to the top mountain gate and enter the open moorland. The track is still discernible and there are waymarkers which you follow to a very wet boggy area. Cross by means of the planked walkway and be careful to follow the waymarkers off to the right, heading for a cairn on the skyline in the saddle between Slieau Managh (mountain of the monks) and Snaefell (snow mountain).

The original kings' road veered off to the left here and followed the line of the mountain road for some distance, travelling around the east flank of Snaefell. The Millennium Way favours the west flank to keep away from the traffic on the mountain road and at the same time introduces you to some of the more inaccessible places in the island.

Pass the cairn and carry on over the saddle a short distance to join the mountain wall above Block Eary Reservoir (from blakkärg meaning black shieling). Follow the mountain wall where it turns steeply down below the massive bulk of Snaefell. Cross the wall at the bottom by the stile and over the river. The way strikes off steeply from the river and at

right-angles to it. It can be wet here at all times of year but only for a short distance. As you climb it is worth looking back across the valley at the route you have just walked. You should just be able to make out the shape of some circular mounds. These are the shielings where the young men used to live with their animals on the mountain pasture during the summer months – another remnant of a past way of life and the best example of such structures on the island.

Follow the waymarkers across the mountain until you pick up a stone wall and sod dyke which is part of a large earthwork known as Cleigh yn Arragh (stone rampart). Follow this until you reach a forestry department track and then the Tholt y Will Road.

Sulby Reservoir – 6 years in the making and holds 1,000 million gallons of water!

Cross the road at the signpost and strike diagonally down the mountainside towards the mountain ahead, which is Beinn y Phott (very loosely interpreted as turf peak). At the bottom of the valley cross the river by means of an old stone bridge, built and used by the miners who operated the mine a short distance upstream. The stone structure you can see is the remains of the wheelcase of the waterwheel. The mine closed in 1867.

Climb up on the left-hand bank of the gulley, being careful at the top to take the left-hand fork, and head for the signpost which you should be able to see on the Brandywell Road. This is where the Millennium Way joins the route of the old ridgeway again. Cross the road and follow the track over the saddle between Beinn y Phott and Carraghyn (meaning scabby, with reference to its stoney top) as far as the mountain gate giving access to a rough track, which you follow for almost two miles. As

you skirt the shoulder of Carraghyn, the views open up over the Baldwins and on towards Douglas in the distance.

The track starts to drop down at Cronk Keeill Abban (the hill of St Abban's church) where an old keeill was located near an ancient Tynwald site on your right. At St Luke's Church, built as a chapel of ease to Kirk Braddan, join a surfaced road taking you downhill into West Baldwin.

At West Baldwin, cross the bridge and the road to follow the signs up a track through Ballagrawe (Balla ny Groa – farm of the cotes or coops) and across the fields of Ballalough (farm of the lakes). After passing the farm, cross the stone stile and follow the lane for a short distance before crossing a ladder stile. Follow the waymarkers across two fields on the eastern flank of Greeba.

There are superb views to the left over Douglas as you head for the saddle between Greeba and Cronk ny Moghlane or

Mucaillyn (hill of the sows) and the signpost on the skyline. After the next stile there is a diversion around the edge of the field before reaching the narrow road leading to Cronk Brec (hill of many colours – literally piebald). You must now make a left and right to follow a rough stone track down to Ballaharry. Just before you reach the cottages, look to the right and the sign pointing to an ancient monument. This is the site of the remains of Keeill Vreshey (the church of St Bridget) and is an example of early Celtic Christianity. There were many such sites on the island.

At Ballaharry the track joins a surfaced road which takes you into Crosby village at the crossroads with the main Douglas to Peel highway. Here you can finish the walk and return to Douglas by public transport – or if you have the energy, carry on along the southern section to Castletown.

SOUTHERN SECTION: 12 MILES

The southern section of the Millennium Way is totally different in character, and the old ridgeway passed to your left to cross between the Mount and Slieau Chiarn (the Lord's mountain). It has been incorporated into the present road network, and in order to keep the walk more attractive the Way takes a slightly different but parallel route.

The start of this section is tough. Make your way down Old Church Road, formerly Station Road when the railway was in operation. You will see where the railway crossed the road as you pass the distinctive small crossing keeper's house. Then it is a stiff climb up School Hill, passing the old school built in 1874. Its bleak location may seem a little strange when you look around and see where the centre of population is now. When it was built, however, the school was in the centre of the parish serving numerous remote farmsteads as well as the village. The same factors applied to the old parish church which you will pass at the top of the hill. The church is dedicated to St Runius and dates from the 12th century, although the remains

of a keeill dating from the 7th century can be seen on the site.

Continue along the road under the avenue of trees towards the Garth crossroads. Look out for the ancient monument sign on the right as you start to climb the next hill. It directs you to the site of St Patrick's Chair - a small group of stones which according to tradition is the spot where St Patrick first preached and intoduced Christianity to the Isle of Man.

Carry straight on over the crossroads, passing Ballanicholas and drop down the hill to Campbells Bridge, which marks the boundary between the parishes of Marown and Malew. Stop at the bridge, spanning the Santon River, to read the interesting plaque. Look over the bridge and you may just be able to make out the remains of old mine workings.

Continue on past Shenvalley (old farm) and in the distance you will be able to see the tower of the church at St Mark's. The church is a good landmark and you will need to turn left and then right at St Mark's and around the old schoolhouse. The church, school and adjoining houses were built in the 18th century at the instigation of Bishop Hildesley as a chapel of ease to Malew parish church. You need to be careful here and look for the waymarker beside the old parsonage. The path follows the lane beside the parsonage to the Awin Ruy (red river) and crosses it on an old stone slab. The path meanders through the fields of Upper and Lower Ballagarey (farm of the river thicket), crossing hedges through kissing gates and eventually arriving at a surfaced road.

Cross the road and follow the waymarkers through two fields before entering Ballamodha Mooar farmyard and following the farm road through Ballamodha Beg to its junction with the Ballamodha Road (Ballamodha meaning farm of the dog, Mooar meaning big, and Beg little).

Turn left and walk along the road for approximately a mile, taking care as there is no footpath. The Ballamodha straight was used in the past for hill climb and reliability trials when the motor car was in its infancy.

Continue to the bottom of Silverburn Hill and at the Atholl Bridge turn left to Silverdale and walk on the path alongside the river. Approaching Silverdale you will come to a children's playground, boating lake and cafe. The boating lake gives the clue as to the function of the old building adjoining the cafe. Creg Mill was one of two built by the monks of Rushen Abbey, and the lake powered the waterwheel. The little waterwheel which now turns the children's carousel is worth more than a passing glance as it came from the Foxdale Mines when they closed.

Continuing downstream you pass Ballasalla Ochre & Umber Works – an old industrial site now converted into a private residence. The company was a substantial one and had warehousing in Castletown, from where shipments were made. The north quay still carries the name Umber Quay.

Leaving the wooded glen you emerge through a gate at Monks Bridge, dating from the late 14th century and probably the oldest bridge in the island, built by the monks of Rushen Abbey.

Approaching the site of the abbey, look left to the opposite side of the river to Abbey Mill, now converted to private apartments. It was a substantial mill with an internal waterwheel and gives an indication of the importance of the abbey. The whole area of the abbey has been acquired by Manx National Heritage and archaeological research is further revealing the unfolding *Story of Mann*.

Follow the boundary wall of the abbey to the right and walk around the perimeter – on the way you may be able to catch the odd glimpse of abbey remains through a gate. Cross the road and almost opposite, the waymarkers direct you down a narrow lane and then left to the river again. The Way follows the river into Castletown on a pleasant walk through river meadows. Cross the river on a wooden bridge, continuing on the other side nearer to the steam railway. Look for the weir that took water from the river for the Golden Meadow Mill, visible from the path as you pass Poulsom Park. The railway station is across the park and you can return to Douglas from here or continue into Castletown and finish your walk at the castle.

SHORT WALKS

THE FOXDALE LINE (2.5 MILES, 1 HOUR)

This short walk follows the disused railway line which connected the Foxdale lead mines to the rest of the island's railway network at St John's. The best option is to take a bus to Foxdale and start from the old station, which is adjacent to the primary school.

The Foxdale Line was built in 1886 by the Foxdale Railway Company, an offshoot of the Manx Northern Railway, as an opportunist venture to win lucrative mineral traffic from the Isle of Man Railway.

Prior to the building of the line to Foxdale, all the ore was taken by horse and cart to St John's for onward transmission by the Isle of Man Railway to Douglas station. It then had to be loaded again into horsedrawn carts and hauled to the harbour at Douglas. The contract for the carriage of the ore came up for renewal and the Manx Northern bid was successful. A subsidiary company was formed to build the Foxdale Railway and create a direct rail link between the mines and Ramsey harbour. But it was to prove a financial disaster and resulted in the eventual downfall of the Manx Northern, everything coming into the ownership of the Isle of Man Railway.

When mining came to Foxdale it brought with it a tremendous increase in population. Public houses sprang up in its wake and it soon supported a constable and a jail. Methodism found a strong footing in the area as in Laxey. The established church appointed a chaplain to Foxdale in 1850 but it was to be

1881 before Foxdale had its own church. Public subscription and a handsome donation from the mining company resulted in the foundation stone being laid in 1874 by Mrs Cecil Hall. The church, designed by James Cowle, was consecrated by Bishop Rowley Hill on Whitsun Tuesday, 7th June 1881 as a chapel of ease to Kirk Patrick Parish Church. The village became a parish district in its own right some years later. The church can be seen on the opposite side of the valley beyond the old school.

It is hard to imagine now what this area was like at the height of the mining boom, lead and silver produced to an annual value of £50,000 at the time the railway was built. There were 350 people employed in the mines. The three main shafts were Potts, Beckwiths and Bawdens. The deepest, Beckwiths, reached a depth of 320 fathoms (1,920 feet) by 1902, yet by 1911 the industry had declined and the Isle of Man Mining Company had ceased working.

The walk starts by the old station building which is opposite the new school in Mines Road, and is all downhill at a steady gradient of 1 in 49. There is quite a wide defined track which runs from the road beside the school. This is the start of the track bed, and the building on the left is the station building. There was a shallow platform with brick edging served by a single line with a runround loop. The area presently occupied by the school was the site of the principal spoil heap from the Beckwiths mine.

A temporary siding was built into this area in the 1930s to assist with the removal of the spoil, which was mostly used in the construction of the playing fields at what is now the National Sports Centre in Douglas. The spoil from the Bawdens shaft formed a massive heap and the station was hemmed in between these two mountains of waste - a scene extremely difficult to imagine today. Beyond the station building was a small brick structure supporting a water tank for the locomotives. A single line climbed behind the

back of the station at a gradient of 1 in 12 to cross the road and enter the mines yard. Here the ore was loaded into wagons for Ramsey via St John's. This line was always referred to as 'the back of the moon' – which was exactly how the area looked after the mines had ceased working.

Before starting the walk, go up Mines Road a short distance and you might just be able to see the remnants of the crossing, with the running rails and check rails in the road surface – the only visible remains of the Foxdale Railway.

Return to the station and start to walk down the line. While the first part near the school is somewhat changed, you soon come on to the old track bed, which is quite unmistakably railway as it skirts behind the miners' cottages in Higher Foxdale. On the hillside to the right there is still visible evidence of the oldest mine in the area, particularly near the river.

Now you are very close to the road. The line ran on a high stone-built embankment before swinging left to cross the road on a steel girder skew bridge (Luke's Bridge), the road prescribing a double corner as it dropped under the bridge to continue to Lower Foxdale (the name Foxdale is an anglicised corruption of Forsdalr, a Scandinavian word meaning waterfall dale). The bridge was removed when the track was lifted in the early 1970s. You must climb through the stile in the boundary wall and cross the road to the opposite side where there are steps leading up the old bridge abutment and back to the track bed.

Now the formation can be really appreciated and you continue on an embankment towards Lower Foxdale with a view of Slieau Whallian ahead. Cross over the accommodation road to Ballamore farm (from an Irish family name – More's farm) on a small bridge. The line entered a cutting through rock as it curved left and approached Waterfall Halt, which was the only intermediate stop. Little remains of the halt.

Originally planned to have a passing loop, it was completed with only the single line and a small wooden building on the flat area to the right.

Walk straight on across the timber footbridge spanning the Gleneedle stream, a tributary of the Foxdale River. The halt served the community of Lower Foxdale and also attracted visitors to the Hamilton Falls, where the stream cascades down a rock face before joining the main river. Walk under the bridge which carries the Ballanass road over the railway (Balla n eas is Manx Gaelic meaning farm of the waterfall). You are in a short cutting under trees and can probably hear the sound of the waterfall below you on the right. You emerge to curve around the hillside with lovely views towards the central valley dominated by Greeba Mountain. The line was built on an embankment and followed the natural lie of the land. There was an old mine on the left, but nothing remains except a very overgrown spoil heap. The occasional telegraph pole is a reminder of the railway's existence.

You are now approaching Slieauwhallian farm (an obscure word which could refer to a personal name, possibly Mc Aleyn, or it could refer to hill of the whelps) and entering a wooded area. Pass under the bridge which carries an accommodation road associated with the farm and you will see that the construction was of a very simple nature and used concrete for the abutments. After the bridge the line passes through a very attractive section before curving left alongside the plantation – part of the larger Slieauwhallian plantation, neither of which existed in the days of the railway.

Unfortunately, you have to leave the line at the end of the plantation and veer off to the left to join the Slieauwhallian back road.

Follow it to the right, downhill to the Patrick Road and right again to the next junction. Before leaving the track bed, look to the right through the trees and note where the track continued on an embankment

almost forty feet high. Although now much overgrown, it still gives an indication of the amount of material needed for its construction. The line curved to the right to cross the Foxdale River on two steel spans carried on a central stone pier between two abutments.

If you like you can turn right at the junction. Walking a short distance towards the Hope will show you where the line crossed the river, after which it curved in a left-handed sweep to cross over the Peel Line and into St John's. If you return to the Patrick Road junction, you can carry on towards the village, passing what is now a car park but was once the site of the St John's station originally built by the Isle of Man Railway.

Walk further up Station Road and cross over the Foxdale Line just before the Post Office. You can look over the right-hand parapet wall and see where the line came into St John's behind Pretoria Terrace, with the embankment climbing away towards Foxdale and over the Peel line. Look over the left-hand parapet and you can clearly see the St John's terminus of the Foxdale Railway. The station was a grand building by comparison with that belonging to the Isle of Man Railway, and similar in style to the station building at Foxdale. There was a passing loop at the station, with goods sidings and the connection to the Manx Northern Railway beyond. Finish the walk here and use public transport to go on to Peel or Douglas.

DOUGLAS TOWN WALK

Starting in front of the Sea Terminal forecourt, it is worth taking time to look at this building, completed in 1962. Now offices, the circular part of the structure immediately below the spire was originally a restaurant commanding unrivalled views of the bay and harbour. The unusual roof earned it the nickname of the lemon squeezer. The building was formally opened by Princess Margaret in 1965.

The short walk around what is now the

A lasting tribute in Douglas to revered Manx poet T.E. Brown (1830-1897).

Once the home of Douglas's Royalty Cinema, now the boast and toast of AXA.

lower part of Douglas commences along Bath Place towards the bus station. Keep to the left-hand side of the road and head around the corner towards the inner harbour and the new harbour liftbridge, which replaced an earlier swingbridge. The accumulator tower and control room for the old bridge can still be seen on the other side of the harbour.

Cross the road at the bridge to the harbourside and read the inscriptions on the plaques, which have been fixed to blocks of Foxdale granite. The inner harbour was until recently a commercial harbour and was tidal. When the new bridge was installed a tidal flap was built and the enclosed basin became a yacht marina – a development which has elevated the harbour as an attractive new focal point for Douglas.

Walk along the side of the harbour behind the parked cars and cross the road opposite the Clarendon Hotel and continue along the North Quay. The old Fish Market (now the Royal British Legion Club) and the market are the next buildings you pass before reaching the British Hotel.

The harbour frontage is gradually changing but some of its past can still be traced on this part of the quay. At the junction of Ridgeway Street is St Matthew's Church, dating from 1895 and built at a time when the old heart of Douglas was being redeveloped and new streets were being driven through the town.

Continue along the quay and look for the plaque on the building on the right just before arriving at Queen Street. You will see that it was the first electricity generating station for the town. At the junction with Queen Street are the last vestiges of the old character of the area. The Liver Hotel formerly stood directly opposite and is now part of the Newson Trading block. To the right is the Saddle Hotel, and the old narrow alignment of Queen Street, winding round the rear of the quay to Quines Corner, completes the picture.

The area had many more public houses then than it has now, earning it the reputation of the 'Barberry Coast'. As you walk along the quay to the top of the harbour you will see that the old and the new have blended together to retain some of the character of the old harbour frontage. Upstream from the Douglas Bridge, a new apartment block nearing completion is further evidence of the changing face of the old riverside property – all part of the grand Development Plan for Douglas.

To continue the town trail, cross Bank Hill and walk into the railway station forecourt and across to the steps on the right leading up to the clock. At the top of the steps pause and look back at the grand building in red facing brick, built at the start of the 20th century at the time that the Isle of Man Railway Company acquired the other two railway operators.

Go through the entrance gates and cross into Athol Street and walk along the street on the right-hand side. By the start of the 19th century it represented the upper limits of Douglas, the Georgian-styled houses being the residences of merchants and the wealthy. As the town expanded this area quickly became its business centre, and still is. Much of the street has been redeveloped but here and there you can still see some of the original buildings.

Walk as far as Lower Church Street and turn right past what was once the old Court House but has now been tastefully converted into offices and a restaurant. Note on your right the new multi-storey car park. At the bottom of the hill turn left by the Isola Restaurant. It is probably the oldest surviving building of old Douglas. Opposite is the John Street elevation of the Town Hall and the site of the original fire station for the town.

Turn left and head up Prospect Hill, passing several of the national banks before reaching Athol Street again opposite the Italianate-style Isle of Man Bank headquarters. The opposite side of Prospect Hill has been redeveloped, new office buildings presenting a stark contrast in styles.

A view across Castletown Bay to the former ancient capital.

Continue as far as Hill Street and pause before turning left to look at the 'wedding cake corner' buildings – part of the administrative and parliament buildings of the Isle of Man Government. On the opposite side of the road is St Mary's Roman Catholic Church, designed by Henry Clutton and opened in 1859.

Walking along Hill Street you will note more new office development reflecting the new-found wealth of the town. At the end of Hill Street turn right into Upper Church Street and opposite is St George's Church, from which the street gets its name. Walk up as far as Circular Road and turn right, crossing over to walk on the left-hand side of the road to its junction with Prospect Hill again. Opposite, at the other end of Government Buildings, are the Rolls Office and the new Court House. Now turn left and

continue up Bucks Road, once the main route out of Douglas to the north.

Carry on as far as Rosemount, pausing to admire the fine spire of Trinity Methodist Church. Continue straight on past Prospect Terrace and the shops which were originally built as private houses, the extent of the original terrace framed by the pediments at each end. At the junction with Hawarden Avenue is Woodbourne Square, laid out in the late 19th century and one of several which retain the Victorian character of the town. Walk through the square and emerge opposite the Masonic Lodge. Cross the road and walk towards the next town square which you will see behind the Lodge. Hillary Park is totally different from the square you have just seen. Walk through it and emerge opposite the terrace of yellow brick houses and turn right, walking as far as Derby Road, where you turn left.

After a short distance look for the right turn to Derby Square opposite the Bowling Green Hotel and walk to Crellins Hill, at the top of which is the Manx Museum. Walk down the steep hill to St Thomas Church, completed in 1849. Keep to the left-hand pavement, cross the road and walk down Church Road to the promenade. Turn left, and go past the Sefton Hotel to the Gaiety.

If the Gaiety Theatre is open for conducted tours you shouldn't miss the opportunity to see it. The Gaiety is described in more detail elsewhere in this guide, so suffice to say it will be time well rewarded. Next to the theatre is the refurbished arcade which is now home to a Wurlitzer theatre organ. The arcade is also an interesting point on the town walk, giving you access to an elevated walkway above the colonnade, with commanding views over the promenade and the Villa Marina gardens. Leave the walkway by the steps at the fountain, opposite the war memorial, or complete the walk by returning to the Sea Terminal

CASTLETOWN WALK

The walk around the former capital of the island starts at the railway station. This will give you the ideal opportunity to arrive at Castletown by train and sample the delights of Victorian travel. From the station, go over the railway lines into Poulsom Park and cross the park adjacent to the children's play area, through a gate directly opposite on the bank of the Silverburn River. Turn left and walk beside the river.

Pass under the railway bridge, where you will almost certainly be accosted by the resident population of geese and ducks. Walk up to Alexander Road and cross it to join Victoria Road, continuing beside the river. Straight ahead is the imposing grey bulk of Castle Rushen, around which the town grew to become the ancient capital of the island.

The castle beckons – but first, a detour. Cross the road at School Lane and walk past Victoria Road Primary School and the unusually named Smetana Close, so called because of the town's close association with many continental musicians and through an annual music festival held in the town. Emerge past the gates of Lorne House, a former residence of the Governors of the island, on to Douglas Street and turn right.

Look out across Castletown Bay at the long peninsula of Langness, its prominent lighthouse at the southernmost tip. Walk along the pavement to the corner with Bridge Street and past the Nautical Museum – another chapter in the *Story of Mann*, telling of the island's fishing industry and the amazing *Peggy*, the oldest surviving Manx-built ship. Continue as far as Bridge House.

As you join the harbour turn left, cross the swingbridge and there's the castle in all its glory. Straight ahead on the corner is the local police station, designed in keeping with the castle by Baillie Scott. Across the road is the castle barbican and entrance. The castle is a must on your list of places to visit. It is one of the best-preserved medieval castles in the British Isles, largely because of its limestone construction, and it has remained in use throughout most of its life.

For now though, leave the castle behind by turning left and walking along the quay. Then turn right up narrow Quay Lane, leading into what is now a public car park. Ahead is the old Grammar School, one of the island's oldest buildings, incorporating part of the medieval chapel of St Mary and its structure pre-dating most of the castle.

Turn immediately right and walk into Parliament Square, which forms the forecourt to the old House of Keys building. This is where the island's Paliament met until

Douglas became the capital in 1865. It too is part of the *Story of Mann* and merits a visit. Turn left into Castle Street and into the Parade. Cross the road and catch the best view of the castle. Note also the unique one-fingered clock presented to the island by Queen Elizabeth I in 1597. The castle as it stands now dates from the latter part of the 16th century but parts of it were built as early as 1250. The dominant features are the massive keep and four flanking towers.

If you look to the right, the other end of the Parade is Market Square, which has as its backdrop the former garrison church of St Mary's, dating from 1826 but now deconsecrated and converted into offices. In the centre of the square you will also see a fine Doric column built to commemorate Cornelius Smelt, the first Governor of the island. Unfortunately the column never received a statue of the Governor.

Continue along Arbory Street – the road to the left off the Parade. On one side of the street stands the new development known as Callow's Yard, comprising shops, a restaurant, coffee shop and a pleasant open seating area within.

At the end of Arbory Street, turn right into the Crofts and admire the part of the old capital where the wealthy of the day lived. Half way along the Crofts go in through the gate on the right to the municipal bowling green and walk past the cafe and green to emerge in Malew Street. Turn left and then right to walk down Mill Street.

This area has been redeveloped under the guidance of the local Commissioners to bring people back into the centre of the town. At the end of Mill Street turn right into Hope Street and walk back towards the town centre. At the end of the street is a limestone building, formerly the National School and now converted for use as a replacement for St Mary's Church. Turn left and cross the bridge over the harbour to retrace your steps to the starting place at the railway station.

PEEL TOWN WALK

The walk around Peel starts outside the Creek Inn in Station Place – formerly the Railway Hotel and part of the town's railway heritage, though trains no longer run here. Directly opposite is the House of Manannan (a Manx National Heritage *Story of Mann* attraction), which incorporates part of the old railway station.

To start the walk head away from the harbour and turn right into Mill Road. Passing the back of the House of Manannan, you will see that the goods shed of the railway has also been incorporated into the museum.

To some extent this is still the 'industrial heart' of Peel, with the gas works on the left together with the kipper yards, the site of the old brickworks and the new electricity generating station. The chimney of the latter lacks much of the elegance of the old brickworks chimney. Peel Heritage Trust has in fact established a small museum in the brickworks weighbridge office, and the former railway station yard opposite is now a boat park, though the railway's water tower has been preserved.

Where Mill Road joins the harbour, Moore's kipper yard is on the left. This is one of very few surviving kipperies which still preserve herring using the traditional oak-smoked method – a process which summer visitors can see for themselves courtesy of a conducted tour of the smokehouse and museum. Turn right here and walk alongside the harbour (back towards the Creek Inn) and over the bridge in the direction of Peel Castle. The hill which dominates Peel (comprising Peel Hill and Corrin's Hill, the latter part distinctive for its tower) is well worth a walk to the top, as described under Coast Path Section 1: Peel to Port Erin on page 165.

As you'd expect, the imposing ruins of Peel Castle on St Patrick's Isle are an important landmark along the town walk, accessible over the causeway. Once across, look for the steps leading up to the path around the castle and follow the path to enjoy the views south over the back of the hill and Fenella beach below. The castle is also an unmissable chapter in the *Story of Mann* and well merits half a day's exploration of its ruins and history to reveal such fascinating facts as why Peel can lay claim to city status.

Return from the breakwater to the bridge at the seaward end of the harbour. The inner harbour is now enclosed by means of a flap gate, a development which has created Peel's new yacht marina. Cross the bridge and turn right on to East Quay. Walk back towards the Creek Inn but look for St Peter's Lane.

You join East Quay after passing the impressive entrance to the House of Manannan. And continue along the quayside for a short distance, passing the remnants of the old warehousing which serviced the fishing industry (for so long the mainstay of Peel's economy) but which are now taking on new life as modern waterside apartments.

At St Peter's Lane turn right and walk up the narrow street past grand stone-built houses, originally the homes of fishermen. At the top of the hill turn left, skirting the whitewashed wall which enclosed the churchyard of St Peter's Church, built as a chapel of ease to the original St German's Cathedral on St Patrick's Isle. It was demolished in 1958 but the clock tower remains and the grounds are retained as a place of quiet reflection.

As you walk along the lane, the architecture of the tower gives an indication of the style of the former church. Turn left into Castle Street and then right into Love Lane and left into Market Street. Continue down the hill to the double corner. On the second corner, continue to the bottom where it joins Crown Street. The Leece Museum, which you pass on your right, is well worth a visit to learn a little more about the town.

Turn right into Crown Street and follow it to the promenade. Turn right, and right again,

Completed in 1884, St German's was not consecrated
as Peel's 'new' cathedral until 1980.

into Market Street and walk through the opening on the left into Charles Street – a charming part of old Peel. Many of the buildings in Peel are built of sandstone and here the beauty of the stone can be seen to advantage.

Continue through Charles Street and Strand Street into Beach Street and turn left back on to the promenade. Here you will pass some of the oldest fishermen's cottages still remaining in the town. Turn right on the promenade and enjoy the fine view of the castle (which has its origins in a Norse settlement), and continue along the promenade as far as Stanley Road. Turn right and half way up the hill turn right again into Circular Road. Walk up the hill to the corner at the top and cut through the alleyway into Christian Street, turning left and then right into Mona Street. Peel had many Methodist churches, nearly all of which are no longer places of worship, but their spirit remains in their architecture.

Walk up Church Street to emerge opposite the courthouse and police station. Cross the road and enter the grounds of the 'new' St German's Cathedral. Although dating from 1884 and built as the parish church, it was not consecrated as the new cathedral until 1980.

Continue through the grounds and walk down to emerge through the grand entrance gates into Atholl Street, opposite the Methodist church. Turn right to Atholl Place and left down Michael Street, which is the town's main shopping thoroughfare. At the end of the street turn right into Douglas Street and then left at Market Place. Now you can imagine the commanding position which St Peter's Church held overlooking the old part of the town.

Cross the square and follow the church wall to Lake Lane and walk down to Station Place and the completion of the walk.

RAMSEY TOWN WALK

Your tour of the town of Ramsey starts in Market Place, opposite St Paul's Church. This dates from 1822, when it was spawned from the parish of Maughold as the town grew and the population centre gradually shifted. In earlier times Market Place was the focal point of the town and the location of an open-air market selling predominantly fish. Some stalls still open here on certain days.

Leave Market Place by way of Dale Street, passing what was the former municipal swimming pool (now destined to begin a new life as a bowling alley) and the Roman Catholic Church of Our Lady of the Sea, designed by Giles Gilbert Scott and built in 1900.

Arriving at the promenade, walk in the direction of the Queen's Pier. Dating from 1886, it is one of the surviving classic Victorian piers, constructed to allow vessels of the Isle of Man Steam Packet Company to call at all states of the tide. It is now the subject of a preservation campaign.

Opposite the pier, turn right up Queen's Pier Road and then right again into Waterloo Road to return towards the centre of the town. You will pass the old Cross on your right – the site of the Old Town Hall and the point at which one arm of the Sulby River originally discharged into the sea. Just after the Old Cross note the distinctive Mysore Cottages built in memory of Sir Mark Cubbon, Commissioner General and Administrator of Mysore in India. Adjoining is the old Grammar School dating from 1864 and replaced by the present school in 1922.

At the end of Waterloo Road turn right into Bourne Place and Parliament Street, opposite the terminus of the Manx Electric Railway. The courthouse and police station are on the left as Parliament Street curves around in that direction.

As you continue along Parliament Street, note the facades of the buildings and the dates when they were built. The town still displays a good variety of shops in its main street despite the pressures of supermarkets. Walk along as far as Christian Street before

Ramsey's tall waterfront warehouses are an umistakeable landmark.

turning left, but pause at the junction and look ahead at the classic buildings of Auckland Terrace – now more than ever the business centre of the town. To the right the old warehouses, still in use, are a reminder of the wealth and importance that this northern town once possessed.

Turn left and on the skyline ahead of you is the Albert Tower, built to commemorate a surprise visit by Queen Victoria's consort when their ship was unable to land at Douglas. Walk as far as the junction with Albert Road and turn left again. Here, on the right, is another reminder of the royal visit, in the shape of Albert Road School. It was built at the turn of the 20th century at the instigation of the then newly-formed School Board.

At the junction with Tower Road, turn right and at the end of the terrace turn left down the narrow lane, emerging in the station of the Manx Electric Railway. After protracted negotiation this was the rather ignominious end of the line when it reached Ramsey, rather than the grand entrance the

MER envisaged along the sea front to connect with the Queen's Pier. In the event the railway seems to have faired better than the pier as a visitor attraction and still provides a unique travel experience.

Walk through the station – but be mindful of tramcars moving through the area – and turn right into Parsonage Road, continuing as far as its junction with Queen's Pier Road. Turn right again and proceed past the bus station into Parliament Square. The newly-built Town Hall replaced two earlier buildings on the site and was completed in 2003.

Continue along the road, which now becomes Bowring Road, and at the first roundabout pause to look across to the left at the area occupied by Ramsey Bakery. This was the site of the station for the steam railway which once connected Ramsey and St John's, but the line has long since closed and no trace remains of the station. Carry on past the second roundabout and you cross the Bowring Road Bridge, going straight on as far as Windsor Road.

Turn right and walk along Windsor Road.

The style of the properties belies the opulence that the merchants and entrepreneurs who originally developed the town enjoyed when Ramsey was in its infancy. At the end of the road turn right into Windsor Mount. Stop at the house on the corner and read the plaque on the wall proclaiming that this was once the residence of celebrated Manx poet T.E. Brown. Walk down Windsor Mount and Ballacloan Road to North Shore Road. To the left is Mooragh Park, created on land where the second arm of the Sulby River discharged to the sea. On the right you pass the ground of Ayre United Football Club – not be confused with the Scottish club of the same name (but without the 'e'!).

Turn left on North Shore Road to Mooragh Promenade. Turn right along the promenade, which was a late development in the Victorian guesthouse boom and never really realised its potential in the way that Douglas promenade did. All of the houses were built to a very similar design and have come to represent the symbol of the Victorian era on the island.

Continue back towards the centre of the town, passing the new swimming baths at the end of the promenade before crossing the swingbridge – a major feature of the harbour. The harbour frontage ahead gives further clues to Ramsey's past wealth. Many of the old warehouse gables remain but only a few retain their original use.

On reaching the other side of the bridge turn left on West Quay to return to Market Place – your starting point.

Ramsey's very popular Mooragh Park boasts a 40-acre boating lake.

Peel harbour.

DAY
DRIVES
6 LEISURELY TOURS

As Toad would have it, you can't beat the freedom and pleasure of the open road – or touring the Isle of Man by car or motorcycle!

The six circular routes chosen here cover all regions and can be enjoyed at a leisurely pace, giving ample opportunity to visit points of interest along the way.

The accompanying maps should be sufficient for the purpose, but more detailed information can of course be found in the Ordnance Survey Landranger Map 95.

TOUR 1: 35 MILES

DOUGLAS – SIGNPOST CORNER – THE BUNGALOW – RAMSEY – MAUGHOLD – PORT MOOAR – PORT CORNAA – DHOON – LAXEY

This tour starts in Douglas at the foot of Broadway, which is adjacent to the new Villa Marina and where the Harris Promenade merges with Central Promenade.

Climbing up Broadway you leave the tourist part of town behind and as Broadway

day **drives:** six leisurely **TOURS**

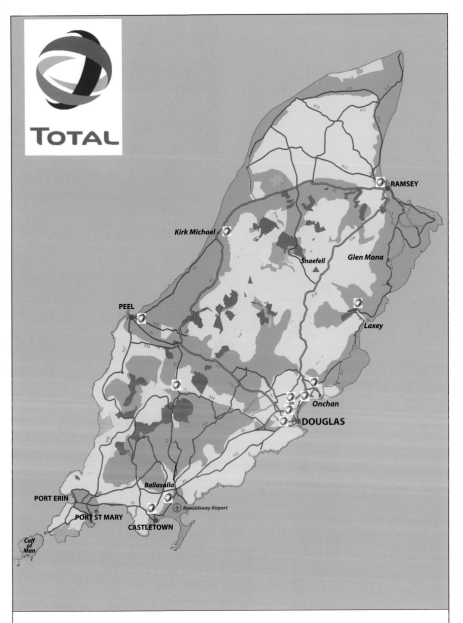

For all your TOTAL *needs -
a garage is always close at hand*

becomes Ballaquayle Road you come to the Bray Hill traffic lights. Turn right and head past the TT Grandstand (on your right).

Some three quarters of a mile along Glencrutchery Road you arrive at Governor's Bridge. Be careful here that you don't turn too quickly, and take care at the double roundabout before following the road marked Ramsey, turning up – left – by the white-painted stone wall.

For the next few hundred yards on the right you are passing the home of the island's Governor. Head on up the A18 to Signpost Corner. Leaving Cronk-ny-Mona behind, there is a distinct change of scenery as the road winds upwards to the famous TT viewing spot of Creg-ny-Baa.

Over to your left, as Kate's Cottage comes into sight, are some very good views of Douglas, and the panorama of the southern half of the Isle of Man lies before you. Take great care in choosing where to stop to take in the views, especially on the TT course as it

TOUR 1

is a very fast road.

Passing through Keppel Gate you are now in the mountains and some of the finest scenery on the island. Still on the A18 descend to Ramsey at Brandywell, just past the junction with the B10.

Directly in front of you stands Snaefell and if time permits it is well worth stopping here and catching the electric railway to the summit, from where on a clear day you can see England, Wales, Scotland and Ireland – not to mention the Isle of Man itself, of course! In 1995 the Snaefell Mountain Railway celebrated its centenary and the original rolling stock is still in use.

Past Snaefell the magnificent mountain scenery continues with the views on your right of Laxey and its valley, and the impressive sight of Ramsey and the northern plain spreading out before you. Ramsey is well worth exploring – and if you have still not picked up your free parking disc, call in at

The cross house in Maughold churchyard preserves a large collection of Celtic and Norse crosses.

Cornaa, a small hamlet near Ballaglass Glen.

Ramsey Town Hall, they will fix you up.

Maughold is the next stop. Drive along Ramsey promenade and past the Queen's Pier, watching for the signs directing traffic to Laxey (A2).

Shortly after, bear left on to the A15. A good tip on these roads is to watch out for the unmanned railway crossings as you will be criss-crossing them for the next few miles.

About half a mile past Maughold there is a small road which takes you down to the peaceful beach at Port Mooar. It's an ideal place to stretch your legs and have a picnic. Back up from the beach turn left on to the A15 and travel to Cornaa.

There is a well-preserved burial ground just past the Ballajora crossroads. Look for an old chapel on the corner, keeping it to the left, and travel uphill on the minor road (which in more recent times became the last resting place for those Quakers who remained on the island, the majority of their fellow believers escaping persecution by seeking a new life in America).

Take care approaching Cornaa as the roads are very narrow. Turn off the A15 at Cornaa

railway halt and turn down the minor road to the left.

Pass the Ballaglass Glen car park on your right and drive on until you reach a small ford where you turn sharp right for Port Cornaa. The drive down to the beach is well worth the effort, but be careful where you park, it is a popular spot with locals and sometimes the stony upper beach can cause problems if you pick the wrong place.

When coming back up this lovely wooded valley continue past the ford – on your right – and climb back up to the A2, watching out for the signs to the Dhoon and Laxey. If you are feeling energetic park opposite Dhoon station and enjoy a walk down to the shore, but remember to leave extra time for the return journey ... it can fool you! The A2 soon takes you to Laxey and there are great views all along the coast.

There is a choice of how you leave Laxey. If you are in Old Laxey then the steep road up from the harbour soon comes out on the A2 at Fairy Cottage. Or if you have been exploring around the mines then rejoin by the Electric Railway station.

Stunning Sulby – the island's most extensive glen.

On through the picturesque villages of Lonan, Garwick and Baldrine and over the railway crossing just out of Baldrine, take a left turn and over a second crossing in the vicinity of the Halfway House to Laxey (Liverpool Arms) – the road A11 is signposted to Groudle and Douglas. Groudle has a beautiful natural glen and the revitalised miniature Groudle Glen Railway.

TOUR 2: 38 MILES

DOUGLAS – EAST BALDWIN – INJEBRECK – DRUIDALE – BALLAUGH – KIRK MICHAEL – PEEL – ST JOHN'S

This journey takes its starting point at the bottom of Broadway and proceeds in just the same manner as that described in Tour 1 until the traffic lights at Parkfield Corner (St

Ninian's Church) are reached. Get into the left filter lane and enjoy the run down Bray Hill to the bottom of the dip where you take a right turn. (TT racers speed down this hill at over 150 mph – but only on race days!)

The road now winds along through an area known as Port-e-Chee, which translated from the Gaelic means Haven of Peace. Cronkbourne Village is the next destination and this is soon reached. Turn right and go up the steep Johnny Watterson's Lane (A21), turning left at the halt sign, then drive along Ballanard Road

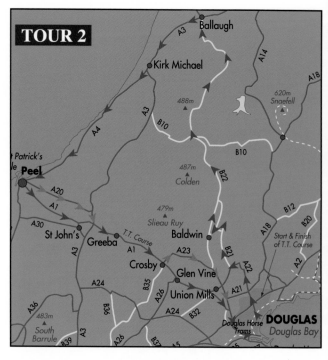

(A22) towards Abbeylands for just over a mile. At the crossroads turn left and, heading over Sir George's Bridge, make a right turn on to the B21 – the East Baldwin Road.

Between 1900-05 a three-foot narrow-gauge railway wound its way around these small valleys, carrying workers and building materials for the Injebreck Reservoir.

Keep on the B21 and move in a northerly direction until you reach the old and disused East Baldwin Chapel. Park here awhile and see if you can spot 'The White Man of East Baldwin' – a figure built into a mountain wall on the hillside as a memorial to a deemster, who perished with his horse in a snowstorm whilst on an errand of mercy. The walk up to the cairn from the bottom of the valley is strenuous, and mind you don't get your feet wet when crossing the Baldwin River, but the views are worth the effort.

Retrace your track back to Algare Hill – the small connecting road between the two valleys – and a right turn at the top brings

you along to St Luke's Church, on the site of an ancient Tynwald. Drop down to the valley floor and join the B22 by heading once more in a northerly direction. There are lots of good picnic spots around here but be careful where you park as the roads are narrow. If you like fishing, Injebreck is a good spot. From the reservoir the road climbs up between the peaks of Colden and Carraghan, eventually bringing you out on to the Brandywell Road (B10).

Just before the junction there is a small slip road which you should turn into and, by turning right and then almost immediately left, you are now on the Druidale Road. This is a single-track road for its entire length. A short drive down Ballaugh Glen brings you to the village.

Turning left at the famous Ballaugh Bridge – where TT racers become airborne for some distance! – you head south-west towards Kirk Michael, home of runic crosses and the last resting place of five bishops. Take the right fork here as the A3 becomes the A4 and head down towards Peel. This is a good road, but if you are not in a hurry stop off at Glen Wyllin, Glen Mooar or the Devil's Elbow.

It's worth spending some time in Peel. This is the only 'city' on the island, with two cathedrals, and there are some interesting shops, narrow streets, a harbour and a very fine castle. If you are out on an evening run, stay for the sunset, you won't be disappointed!

Leaving Peel behind, take the A1 to St John's, a village of great political importance to the island. An alternative route to the village is via the A20 and the connecting road through Tynwald Mills, which is well signposted from Peel. Alongside Tynwald Hill lies the Royal Chapel of St John. The village is little changed in the best part of a century.

The last part of the drive takes you along the central valley. Ten thousand years ago this was the sea bed, dividing the Isle of Man into two main parts. Moving along the A1 towards Ballacraine you come up against an island rarity – a set of traffic lights. Carry straight on towards Douglas, but just after Greeba Castle look to your left and there is the ancient roofless church of St Trinian standing in splendid isolation in its own meadow.

From here there is a choice of routes back to the capital. The main road follows the A1 to the Sea Terminal via Glen Vine, Union Mills, Braddan Bridge and the Quarterbridge. Alternatively, if time permits, why not take the A23 (the Nab Road) by turning left at Crosby and heading towards Douglas via Eyreton, the Nab, the Strang and Braddan. The A23 rejoins the A1 at the Jubilee Oak Braddan Bridge.

TOUR 3: 38 MILES

RAMSEY – POINT OF AYRE – JURBY – THE CRONK – THE CURRAGHS – SULBY – THOLT-E-WILL – THE BUNGALOW

As you wander around the northern plain the scenery changes frequently, from the fine sands of the Lhen, gravel beaches of the Point of Ayre and up to the wooded slopes of Sky Hill, Glen Auldyn, Carrick, Rock and Mount Karrin, and St Ciaran's Mount. Coupled with the winding lanes of the Curraghs it is one of the best places to tour.

The drive starts on Ramsey promenade, but before setting off be sure to take in the lovely sight of the bay and the slopes of Lhergy Frissel (Frissel's slope) – the hill with the tower set on the summit.

Driving along Mooragh Promenade you may get a glimpse of St Bees Head in Cumbria, the nearest mainland point to the Isle of Man. At the end of the promenade bear left up the hill and join the A10 by turning right. Follow this road to the lovely village of Bride. The church acts as a good landmark for miles around.

At Bride take the A16 marked for the Point of Ayre. Again it is an easy place to find because the lighthouse stands as a sentinel. This landmark was built in the early years of the 19th century by the great-grandfather of Robert Louis Stevenson. Definitely not the place to go swimming: the waters surrounding the Point are extremely treacherous.

On now to the Lhen, so reverse the route back as far as Bride and turn right and west at the church. Lovely country here with good farming land rolling down to the coast. Watch out for the sign to the Ayres Visitor Centre, well worth a visit but only open mid-May to mid-September, 2pm-5pm., Wednesdays to Sundays. Stay on the A10 and the Lhen is reached after a pleasant drive of a few miles. Watch out for the sharp turn at the Lhen Bridge. The little park close to the shore is ideal for a picnic.

Just a couple of miles further on is Jurby. Long ago this village was important to the Vikings and although it has lost something of its old eminence it is nonetheless a pleasant part of the island, and well worth exploring for its beaches, church and crosses.

Carrying on still further on the A10, look

out for The Cronk (The Hill), such as it is.
Go straight on here at the crossroads,
following the B9, and turn left at the second
road down from The Cronk crossroads – but
not counting any farm tracks or lanes. If you
have it right, it's the road coloured yellow on
the map taking you towards Dollagh Mooar,
Black Lake and the Curraghs (mire or
marsh).

Caution here because the roads are
extremely narrow and there are lots of ditches
awaiting careless drivers. Cross the A14,
approximately half way between Sandygate to
the north and Sulby to the south – and you
are still following the yellow road to Kella
and West Sulby.

Turn left at the junction and for a brief
distance you are on the TT course, on the
famous Sulby Straight (A3). Just past Sulby
Bridge is the Ginger Hall public house and
you should turn right here on to the B8,
which will bring you on to the Sulby
Claddaghs, the river meadowland.

Drive through the Claddaghs to the A14 or
the Sulby Glen Road and begin the ascent of
the glen towards Tholt-e-Will. This extremely
scenic route brings you up past the Sulby
Reservoir, built in the early 1980s to secure
water supplies well into the 21st century. The
upper reaches of the road roll across the
shoulder of Snaefell and the scenery is typical
of high moorland interspersed with
plantation.

The end of the A14 joins the A18 TT
course at the Bungalow. There is a Manx
Electric Railway station here and during
summer the Snaefell Mountain Railway
operates regular services between Snaefell
summit and Laxey, far below at the bottom of
the valley.

Turn left and travel the 'wrong way' around
the TT course – it is still a fast stretch of
road. In clear weather, summer or winter,
there are fine views of the Ayres, Scotland,
England and Ireland. Take care on the final
descent into Ramsey – there are some sharp
corners. Once into Royal Ramsey it is easy

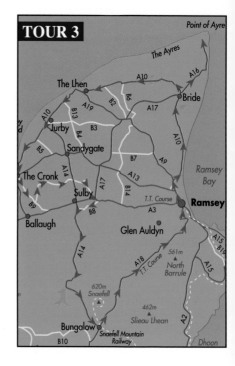

TOUR 3

to find your way around and the A18 takes
you right into Parliament Square. Turn right
just through the Square and you are into
Derby Road and West Quay. Cross the
swingbridge and on to Mooragh Promenade.

TOUR 4: 40 MILES

PEEL – ST JOHN'S – CRONK-Y-VODDY – WEST BALDWIN – BALLASALLA – CASTLETOWN – FOXDALE

Peel is a must and if you are not actually
staying in the town a visit should be a
priority. This tour takes you from Peel
through the island's lovely hinterland and
moorland, valleys and glens.

The starting point is the north end of Peel
promenade in the vicinity of the Empire
Garage. From here proceed up Stanley Road,
turning right then almost immediately left
into Church Street.

At the halt sign (the police station is across
the road) take a left and head into Derby

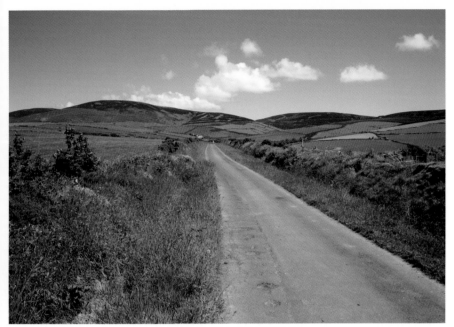

The road to Little London, a small community close to Cronk-y-Voddy.

Road and the A20, signposted for St John's.

You'll know you're on the right road when you pass the Poortown quarry, and after about a mile and a half turn right down the small road marked Tynwald Mills Centre, which is well worth a visit.

Leave the Tynwald Mills Centre complex by the opposite end and bear left on to the TT course (A3). The exit on to the main road is narrow, and sometimes approaching cars from your right-hand side may be travelling at speed, so take care.

Now you are heading up the beautiful wooded Glen Helen road and if you feel like stretching your legs, stop and stroll up the glen. From opposite the glen car park the road climbs steeply for a short distance, passing the famous TT landmark Sarah's Cottage and on up Creg Willeys Hill, Willy Syl's (or Sylvester's Crag) and on to Cronk-y-Voddy, which translated from the Manx means the Hill of the Dog. Here at the crossroads turn right for the undulating drive

to Little London.

Long ago Little London was famous for fishing but nowadays its peace and tranquillity are disturbed only by the occasional passing car or walker. Before the Second World War the Old Smithy was the home of the renowned flyer Captain Pixton, who was the first British winner of the prestigious Schneider Trophy and the holder of many flying records. The road out of Little London skirts the south-west slopes of Sartfell, which is old Norse for Black Mountain or Dark Slope. In Manx it is known as Slieau Dhoo and joins the B10 about half a mile above Bayr Garrow (Rough Road).

Just before the minor road joins the main road is Sartfield Farmhouse Restaurant. The views from here are superb and at night you can see various Irish and Scottish lighthouses.

Turn up the hill and on the way look back at the view; on clear days there are fine panoramas of the Mountains of Mourne and the Mull of Galloway. You are now heading

St Patrick's Isle
Peel
Cronk-y-Voddy
487m ▲ Colden
B10
479m ▲ Slieau Ruy
St John's
T.T. Course
A1 A23
Baldwin
Crosby
Foxdale A24
483m ▲ South Barrule
B30
St Mark's
A5
A6
Ballasalla
Santon Head
Castletown
Ronaldsway Airport
Scarlett Point
Castletown Bay
Langness Peninsula
Dreswick Point

TOUR 4

along the Brandywell Road with Colden Mountain ahead and to the right. There are a lot of cattle grids in the mountains, so be sure to take care crossing them and if you have to use the gates, please don't forget to close them after use.

Keep a lookout for the B22 turning; it should be easy to spot because it is just before Brandywell Cottage – the only building on your left since you started on the B10. Turn off to the right and head along the Injebreck Road, and if you want a good idea of what the centre of the island looks like, pull in just before the crest of the hill and you will see a countryside little changed in thousands of years.

Head down into the West Baldwin valley – an area not unlike the Scottish Highlands. At the upper end of this green and tree-lined cleft is Carraghan, which translates in English to rough, craggy or rocky place. It was chosen as an ideal spot for the Injebreck Reservoir, which has served Douglas and much of the

island for many decades.

On down the valley, keep to the B22 all the way until the Mount Rule halt sign, where a right turn puts you on to the A23 bound for the central village of Crosby. The road follows what was the edge of the south coast of the larger of the two northern islands that made up the Isle of Man at the time of the last ice age.

Go straight across the Crosby crossroads and up the B35 towards St Mark's. It is likely that at one time a cross stood somewhere near the site of the present-day village, because its name is derived from the Scandinavian word for Cross Village or Farm. The tour now follows one of the driveable parts of the Millennium Way.

St Mark's is a quiet little backwater and lies peacefully on a rise and is visible for a good distance around the parish of Malew. Once a year it comes to life with the holding of the ancient St Mark's Fair.

A couple of miles or so further on you come to the busy village of Ballasalla. In more recent times there has been an upsurge in commercial activities here. There is plenty to do in Ballasalla, including a visit to Silverdale Glen, which is well signposted.

Go straight on at each roundabout, looking for the airport and Castletown signs (A5). Pass the airport on your left and drive into Castletown. The old capital is described in detail elsewhere in this guide, and when visiting remember that the town is a disc parking area.

The journey back to Peel is fairly straightforward. Retrace the route back along the harbour in Castletown to Victoria Road and the first roundabout, where you should turn left into Alexander Road and cross over the Alexander Bridge. Carry on for a quarter of a mile and turn right into Malew Road and the A3.

Stay on the A3, climbing up the Ballamodha Straight before dropping down through the old mining villages of Upper and Lower Foxdale. Approaching St John's, the road

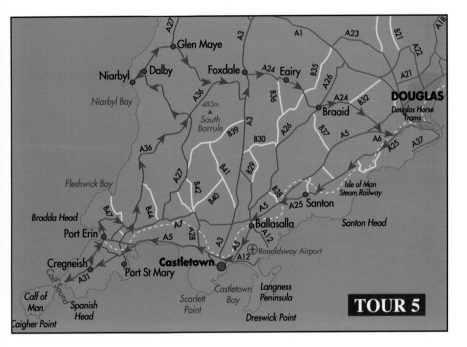

divides at a small hamlet called The Hope (not shown on many maps). Take the left branch and follow the A30 past the Forestry Department's nurseries, bearing right until you reach the halt sign in the middle of the village. A good guide as to whether you are on the correct route is that Tynwald Hill is across the road. Turn left at St John's for Peel and follow the A1 and the signs all the way to Peel promenade and the end of Tour 4.

TOUR 5: 42 MILES

PORT ERIN – THE SLOC – NIARBYL – GLEN MAYE – FOXDALE – BRAAID – UNION MILLS – DOUGLAS – BALLASALLA – PORT ST MARY – CREGNEASH

Pretty Port Erin is a good place to base yourself for a motoring holiday. Parking is easy and although parts of the village are disc zones, they present no real problems.

This drive starts on the Upper Promenade and covers the southern part of the island. It takes you from the steep cliffs and hills of the south-west, through the gentle rolling hills of Glenfaba, Rushen and Middle Sheadings to the capital, and on to the old Manx hill village of Cregneash.

Drive up the hill away from the hotels and look for the signposts to Bradda. The village nestles on the slopes of Bradda Head and is divided into west and east, although the exact boundary between them is now somewhat blurred. This is the A32 and it brings you along a gradually widening road to Ballafesson, which appears on the ancient manorial roll as MacPherson's Farm.

At the junction you pick up the A7 for a short while and at the next crossroads – marked as a roundabout – turn left on the A36, up through Ballakillowey (McGillowey's Farm). It should be noted that the Manx usually exchanged the prefix Mac for the prefix Balla as far as place names were concerned.

Just before the junction with the B44 there is a nice open picnic area, with fine views over Castletown Bay and the sweep of the

Port Erin – an ideal base for a motoring holiday.

coast right round to the villages of the Howe and Cregneash high up on the Mull Peninsula.

Driving on upwards on the Sloc Road, there are continually changing views of the landscape around almost every corner. There are many fine walks and picnic sites.

The Sloc Road takes you to the Round Table crossroads. Turn sharp left here on to the A27 and down to Niarbyl. Descending the hill into Dalby village, it is easy to see where the name Niarbyl is derived. Jutting out into the clear waters of the Irish Sea is a tail of rocks, which is how Niarbyl translates into English. Take the minor road down to the shore and spend some time on the rocky beach at the foot of the cliffs.

From Dalby the A27 continues on to Glen Maye, loosely translated meaning Yellow Glen on account of the muddy, almost clay-coloured waters of the streams running down the glen. There are a number of easy walks here.

From here carry on to the village post

office. To the side of the building there is a narrow country lane which takes you up towards Garey, translated as rough or rugged river-shrubbery. If there ever was a river up here on the high ground it has long since disappeared; perhaps the road was the river, because in wet winter weather the road does seem to double as a stream. The road is also known as the Back of the Moon Road.

Rushen Mines soon loom up and even the isolation of the mines has a particular beauty of its own. Back on to the A36 and a left turn down the mountain to South Barrule Plantation and the junction with the A3.

Head left towards Foxdale, where you take the first right and join the A24. Skirt the edge of the Eairy Dam – watch out for the ducks crossing the road – and on to the Braaid, which literally translated means throat or windpipe, as applied in the sense of a glen or sheltered vale. Carry straight on at the roundabout, head up the hill for about half a mile, and look down and across into the central valley to the view known as the Plains of Heaven.

Carry on along this road until you arrive at a major road junction where the A24 bisects the A5. Cross over and drive to Kewaigue, which translates into Little Hollow. If you would like to revisit Douglas, continue on into town; if not then just past the headquarters of Isle of Man Breweries turn through an acute right-hander and head for Santon on the A25.

Santon – in older times it was spelt Santan – derives its name from Saint Sanctan. This road is known as the Old Castletown Road and there are a number of roads leading off it down to rocky bays and isolated coves. Try them when you have time, most are off the beaten track and are not accessible by public transport.

The road takes you in the direction of Ballasalla and rejoins the A5 at a spot where the railway line passes under the main road. Stay on the A5 by turning left at the Ballasalla roundabout – the Whitestone Inn faces you directly ahead as you approach it.

Drive past the airport and skirt the edge of Castletown. Leave the town behind by using the bypass (still the A5) and drive all the way along the edge of Bay ny Carrickey (The Bay of the Rock). Turn right up past the tall stone building along Beach Road, heading for the crossroads, where you go straight on using the A31. Ignore any other roads and make for Cregneash. From here carry on down to the Sound to enjoy the totally unspoilt scenery of the Isle of Man's equivalent of Land's End.

For the final stages of the drive you return back up the hill from the Sound towards Cregneash again. Just before entering the village from the south, turn sharp left on to the minor road leading past Mull Hill and its stone circles. Dating from Neolithic times, this unspoilt area remains much as the earliest inhabitants would have known it. This is a single-track road with passing places. Port Erin nestles quietly below as you drive down Dandy Hill and back on to the Lower Promenade.

TOUR 6: 49 MILES

ONCHAN – BALDRINE – LAXEY – GLEN ROY – THE BUNGALOW – SULBY – ST JUDE'S – ANDREAS – BRIDE – RAMSEY – THE GOOSENECK – THE HIBERNIAN – DHOON – LAXEY

Onchan started life as a small village to the north of Douglas and in recent times its growth has outstripped that of the capital. You could be forgiven for thinking that it is a suburb of Douglas, but the village has its own local government and is very much a separate community.

The drive starts at Onchan Head, just above Port Jack. Follow the A11 as it runs parallel to the track of the Manx Electric Railway and passes Groudle Glen. There is a minor road off to the right, approximately half a mile past Groudle station, and a detour up this road will bring you to Old Kirk Lonan Church, well worth seeing. Completing the detour brings you out on to the A2 just to the south of Baldrine village. Carry on towards Laxey via Fairy Cottage and Old Laxey Hill – bear to the right at the filling station – to the attractive harbour.

Laxey owes its origins to the Norsemen, who named it Salmon River. Give yourself time here as there's plenty to see. From the harbour travel up the glen beside the river and when you reach the woollen mills go up the hill, under the railway bridge and straight on at the stop sign looking for the Creg-ny-Baa signpost.

You are now on the Glen Roy Road (coloured yellow on the OS map) and about to experience one of the best glen drives on the island. The glen was formed by the waters cascading down from Mullagh Ouyr, Slieau Meayll, Dun Summit, Bare or Bald Mountain and Windy Corner respectively. Care on this road is required as there are a number of blind corners, and the road is extremely narrow in places.

Eventually you rejoin a wider road, the

glen and pick them up just outside the inn at the bottom of the hill. Alternatively, Sulby Reservoir car park makes a good location for a picnic. The name of the glen translated from the Manx means Hill of the Cattlefold, and the inhabitants of the lower end of the bigger glen have traditionally been known as the Sulby Cossacks. At any time of year Sulby Glen has a beauty all of its own. In spring the east side of the glen is coloured with a haze of bluebells. At other times the heather and gorse lend their own particular splash of colour and the light always creates a special atmosphere.

A quarter of the way down the glen from the inn lies Irishman's Cottage and, high above the nearby waterworks, is the small feeder reservoir of Block Eary. The reservoir was built by German POWs and although it is a strenuous walk to reach it, it's well worthwhile. The name has changed somewhat from the original Scandinavian spelling Blakkarg but the meaning is still the same, Black Sheiling, from the peaty colour of the stream.

Carry on down the valley towards the Sulby Straight. Passing Sulby Mill go straight on to the main road and turn right on to the TT course at Sulby Methodist church. At the end of the straight, turn off the A3 on to the St Jude's Road (A17). From the West Craig crossroads stay on the A17 to Andreas. There is a subtle change in the scenery here as the landscape changes from moor and glen to low-lying well-drained marshland.

Andreas has a fine church dedicated to St Andrew, from whom the parish takes its name. The village is very much the centre of local agricultural activities. Leave Andreas by continuing on the same road, which takes you to the island's northernmost centre of population, Bride. The village lies in a little hollow of the Bride Hills and is one of the sunniest places on the Isle of Man.

Leaving Bride, travel along the A10 in the direction of Ramsey. The Bride road takes you right into Parliament Square and if you

B12, just above Social Cottage, and by turning in a south-west (right) direction, the road brings you to the well-known Keppel Hotel at Creg-ny-Baa. Turn right and head the 'wrong way' round the TT course (the A18), aiming for the Bungalow. Just past Brandywell is the highest point on the course at almost 1,400 feet.

The Bungalow actually bears no resemblance to a modern building of that name and the current site was home, until fairly recently, to a magnificent hotel made of wood and galvanised sheeting – very popular with TT fans. Watch out for the directions to Sulby and turn left on the A14.

If your passengers fancy a walk, pull up at the top entrance to Tholt-e-Will Glen. Allow them half an hour or so to walk down the

day **drives:** six leisurely **TOURS**

The top of the lighthouse tower is just visible in this view of Maughold Head.

are not breaking your journey in Ramsey then carry on following the route marked for the TT course and Douglas. High above the town at the Gooseneck there is a minor road leading off behind the TT marshals' shelter. Careful negotiation of the turn is required to get on to what is known as the Hibernian Road. This is a delightful run across the lower slopes of North Barrule and whilst there seems to be no trace of the name's origination, it is most likely that it takes its form from the same meaning as South Barrule – Ward Mountain.

As you come off this road at the Hibernian, turn right on to the A2 – the coast road – and head for the Corrany. This name is a variation of Cornaa, which means Treen, the modern version of homestead. At the Dhoon is the glen, running down to the shoreline of Dhoon Bay, and the nearby earthworks of Kionehenin. It's an ideal place to stop – and if your passengers happen to be annoying you, send them back to Onchan on the Manx Electric Railway!

Leave the Dhoon car park area by the B11, the Ballaragh Road. This is an interesting

name and although its derivation is doubtful, there is reason to believe that perhaps its original meaning was Farm of the Spectre or Apparition. Just before the end of this road, King Orry's Grave is reached.

Turn right here and you are once again back on the A2. At Laxey, turn right and cross over the railway lines into Dumbell's Terrace, known to the locals as Ham and Egg Terrace, and park the car. Looking up the valley you will see the largest working waterwheel in the world – *Lady Isabella*, the Great Laxey Wheel (which incidentally has its own adjacent car park).

The final leg of your journey takes you from Laxey along the A2 to just south of Baldrine village, where you veer left after the railway level crossing lights and on to the A11 Groudle Road (watch out for trains!).

Passing through Groudle you may catch sight of the popular Groudle Glen narrow-gauge railway as it chugs around the headland. Soon the road grants you a fine view of Douglas Bay and then Port Jack is in sight – and so is your journey's end.

ALL
ABOARD THE MANX
ELECTRIC RAILWAY

D oes the prospect of travelling at 18 miles an hour fill you with raw excitement and anticipation? Probably not. But then, the journey you are about to undertake has nothing to do with speed. It has everything to do with...well, step aboard and find out. The Manx Electric Railway awaits your pleasure.

In case you're wondering, you're at Derby Castle, at the northern end of Douglas promenade. This is the railway's southern terminus. The rustic booking office has been here since 1897. Some of the rolling stock is even older, built in 1893 but still in perfect

working order. They don't make 'em like this any more. In fact, the most recent rolling stock on this extraordinary and unique line was made in 1906 – positively brand spanking new compared with the originals.

You'll be pleased to know that the guard and driver are of much younger stock. And before the driver draws current to get the show on the road, and the guard checks your ticket, a brief word about terminology – often a point of contention on the quirky but definitely addictive Isle of Man.

The fact is, although this is called the Manx Electric Railway, there are those who would have you believe that it's actually a tramway. True enough, it is a tramcar – or trailer – you're sitting in. And, in the tradition of trams from the Victorian and Edwardian era, it is driven by electricity from an overhead power line. On the other hand, nobody can dispute that it runs on rails. Or that the words 'Manx Electric Railway' are emblazoned over the sides of the err... tramcars. So, in these pages at least, a railway it is, and no argument.

Now, are you sitting comfortably? Good. With a ting-tinging of the bell, one of Britain's great railway journeys – all 17.5 miles and 75 minutes of it – is about to begin. It's a gentle and graceful departure from the station, passing over the pointwork at the entrance to the car sheds. In busy holiday periods a good selection of the vintage rolling stock is here. Trainspotters note: there are 17 power cars and 19 trailers still in regular use.

A gradient of 1 in 24 takes you and the train up towards Port Jack – the first of 63 possible stopping places between here and the railway's northern terminus at Ramsey, your destination.

You can't fail to be struck by the novelty of road and railway running beside each other like this, in parallel, on the same level and so close together. This will change. Before long, the track will cut its own and more spectacular route that car travellers can only dream about.

So far, so good – and already, a clue as to the coming excitement. A right turn reveals impressive views over Douglas Bay; alas, all too quickly interrupted by a turn the other way to level off past Onchan Head station, and then lost completely with a sharp left past Howstrake station.

Not to worry: the descent towards Groudle brings more superb coastline into view, including Clay Head (300 feet above sea level). On the other side of the glen from Port Groudle is the Groudle Glen Railway, which runs on track only two feet wide. This

little line opened in 1896 to transport visitors to a small zoo at the seaward end, just past the reinstated and clearly visible station building at Sea Lion Rocks.

Now, already 12 minutes into the journey, it's inland to Groudle station, the original terminus of the line in 1893. A Railway Centenary plaque is mounted on a stone monument just past the station on the left. And to prove that those 1890s were a busy old time on the Isle of Man, you'll soon be passing the Groudle Hotel (1893), designed by Mackay Hugh Baillie-Scott, and the three-span Groudle Viaduct (1894), built by Mark Carine.

The Groudle coast road's still there beside you as the landscape on the left levels off and presents you with lovely views of the central mountains and up to Snaefell summit (that's it, with the pylons on top).

It soon becomes pretty obvious that you're half way to Laxey, courtesy of the Liverpool Arms (Halfway House), a pub dating from the 1860s. As the train crosses over the Groudle road and then the main Douglas-Laxey road, a single white light between the tracks tells the driver that the road traffic signals are operating.

It's not long before the village of Baldrine sneaks up besides you. On the other side are more views up to the mysterious and enticing Snaefell. Baldrine is derived from the Celtic Balla-Drine meaning place of the blackthorns. The village has a new millennium clock which is illuminated at night.

Bye bye, Baldrine and hello, Garwick. It's about 18 minutes into your journey when trees on either side of the track form a virtual tunnel and you emerge at this once-busy station. The remains of a gatepost mark the old exit from the station to the glen. Garwick comes from the Norse, Gjar-vik meaning cave or creek.

More stunning views open up before you – this time of Laxey Bay and the cliffs beyond Laxey to Maughold Head and lighthouse. The civilised 21st-century rail travel? You bet!

bay stays in sight as you pass a station with a very Manx-sounding name – Ballabeg.

Is this a rollercoaster you're riding, or a railway? You could be forgiven for wondering; not because of any stomach-wrenching ups and downs or breathtaking sharp turns, but because you're definitely riding (albeit sedately) along a rolling coastline, and a pretty spectacular one at that.

Soon you can see Laxey beach, with Laxey Head on the opposite side of the valley. Poles carrying the railway's overhead wires are also visible to the point where the line disappears over the headland on its way to Ramsey.

The intriguingly-named Fairy Cottage station is next, on the approach into Lower (or Old) Laxey. Fairy folklore is a serious matter on the Isle of Man – scoff at it at your peril. On the other hand, you can certainly take the next station with a pinch of salt; at least, the optimistic claim that South Cape is the station for Laxey beach. In reality it's an energetic walk down, let alone back up!

You are now 25 minutes into your unforgettable journey. Spanning both sides of the valley below you is Laxey village. The line ahead is relatively straight, soon passing Laxey car shed and electrical sub-station. Just before you cross the impressive Glen Roy viaduct into the station, you pass the point which was the terminus of the line when it first reached Laxey in 1894. Crossing the viaduct presents super views – down through the village and glen on one side, and the road bridge and Laxey Flour Mills on the other. Opened in 1860, the mill supplies all the flour for Ramsey Bakery as well as to local supermarkets.

Just when you thought your great railway adventure couldn't get any better, it does. At least, it could. Your arrival at Laxey station gives you the perfect opportunity to switch trains – and to experience the delights of the very uplifting Snaefell Mountain Railway, of which Laxey is the lower terminus. If you decide to go for it you can easily resume your journey to Ramsey on a later train; this is summer and they run every hour (every half-hour between Douglas and Laxey). But no, in the event you decide to give the summit of Snaefell a whirl on some other day – tomorrow maybe. Today's journey is far too enjoyable to interrupt.

However, your appetite is whetted and your curiosity demands to know more about the Snaefell Mountain Railway. Well, to begin with the train buff stuff, the 5-mile line opened in 1895 after just seven months of construction. All six of the original 1895 tramcars still operate the summer-only service. At a gauge of 3 feet 6 inches, the track is 6 inches wider than the one you're travelling on. The overall gradient is 1 in 12, the tramcars using normal wheel-on-rail adhesion and the centre rail providing an emergency braking system.

It's a tiny exaggeration to say that the railway will take you to the very summit of the highest mountain on the island (at 2,036 feet), but it'll certainly deliver you to within 46 feet of it – a short walk – and what's that between friends?

Besides the mountain railway there are other sights and points of interest for you to absorb here in Laxey. Take the parish church for example. It was completed in 1856 and built on land that was formerly part of the garden of the Mine Captain's house – now the Mines Tavern. Then there are attractions such as the woollen mill, the Great Laxey Wheel, Laxey Glen and gardens – and not forgetting the cafe in the station building. Laxey, by the way, comes from the Scandinavian word Laxa, meaning Salmon River.

With all aboard who are coming aboard now seated, it's time to leave Laxey, passing the tavern and the former goods shed and crossing the main road. Visible on the right of the valley is the famous giant waterwheel with its 168 buckets, and also on the right are the Valley Gardens – the old washing floors of

Snap! Electric versus steam at the restored Mines Railway, Laxey.

the mines.

The climb to Laxey Head is rewarded with another good view of Laxey beach and Old Laxey, and you can see how tastefully many of the older buildings have been restored. More superb views come your way, this time of the coastline ahead, as far as Maughold lighthouse. Clear days bring the Lake District into view – even Sellafield can be visible on the shoreline.

Still climbing, and beyond the main road – now on the left – you can see the village of Ballaragh. It's known for a Bronze Age stone about five feet high and decorated with spiral patterns. Looking forward you have a view towards the north of the island, along some of the most magnificent coastline in the British Isles.

Another intake of breath comes as the train reaches Bulgham and runs along a relatively narrow ledge 658 feet above that big, wide blue-green sea. This is the highest point on the line – and most definitely one of the highlights. In early 1967 an earthslip here blocked the line for several months while repairs were carried out.

The dramatic scenery continues as the train rattles on through a short cutting to run alongside Dhoon Glen and present you with a view of North Barrule (1,854 feet in height). Barony Hill, crowned by a stone circle and tumulus known as Carnane Breck, is on the opposite side of the glen.

You've now been travelling for 45 minutes and Dhoon Glen is the next station (almost 600 feet above sea level), complete with tearoom and the entrance to the glen. The walk down through the glen to the sea is effort well rewarded but deceptive – it takes longer than you'd expect.

It's onward ever onward, through farmland to Dhoon Quarry station. This is now a track storage facility for the railway but in quarrying days the siding layout was considerably more extensive, with various narrow-gauge lines and ropeways serving the two separate quarries, one each side of the MER line.

The climb out of Dhoon Quarry is steep and you can see North Barrule again. Looking forward and right you also get your first glimpses of Lewaigue and Port e Vullen (Port of the Mill), villages lying on the north coast of Maughold Head.

A long straight run takes you now to Glen Mona. The station building is on the right and the village is up on the left. Then it's into a cutting to pass under Ballagorry Bridge – the only overbridge on the whole line.

Now North Barrule is on your left and there are views up the valley towards Snaefell. The ridge has three other summits. Two are unnamed (at 1,749 feet and 1,804 feet) and at the far end is Clagh Ouyr (1,808 feet).

If you enjoy hill walking, you'll really want to take steps to explore this ridge at some point. The place to begin your ascent would be The Hibernian (easily found on OS Landranger map 95), which would mean leaving the line at Cornaa station and walking along the A15. And the exciting bonus is that whether you finished the walk on the A18 mountain road at Bungalow or on the summit of Snaefell, you could then experience the joy of descending to Laxey by the mountain railway.

Note that this enticing scenario is described as a possible future event, because today you've already decided to complete the journey to the end of the line without interruption. So, about 55 minutes after leaving Douglas, it's on past the former Ballaglass Power Station – now a private residence – to Ballaglass station and the entrance to the glen of the same name. This too is an area awaiting your discovery. Look out for the small single-arched bridge that carries the railway over the river shortly after the station.

The line heads back towards the coast, leaving the main road to its own devices for awhile. Only now do you pass the aforementioned Cornaa station and climb quite steeply to enjoy views down the glen to Port Cornaa and the sea beyond. Looking back from the right you can also catch a fine view of another ridge – not so high this time – behind Glen Mona. Again there are three peaks for the taking: Slieau Ruy (1,299 feet), Slieau Ouyr (1,483 feet) and Slieau Lhean (1,539 feet).

As for sea views, if it's clear enough you could give a little wave to the Lake District (ignore the strange looks from other passengers) and forward and right of you on the headland is the distinctive white lighthouse at Maughold. Built in 1914, the actual light is 212 feet above sea level and now fully automated.

There isn't a station called Maughold; the one serving the village is Ballajora and when you reach it you'll have been travelling for just over an hour. The station building is on the right opposite a cluster of houses. Maughold churchyard is much visited for its fine collection of carved stone crosses.

Dreemskerry is the next station – like Dhoon, once the site of extensive quarry workings, with ropeways and all the associated paraphernalia.

The progress north extends your views up beyond Ramsey Bay to Shellag Point and the lighthouse at Point of Ayre. And beyond that, visibility permitting, you should be able to see the hills of southern Scotland.

It's a good few minutes since you first caught distant coastal views of Lewaigue and Port e Vullen, but now you're practically there. Another straight stretch, mainly downhill, brings the village of Lewaigue and its same-name station to your right, and at the end of a short wooded section you arrive at Bellevue station for Port e Vullen (station building on the left, name board on the right).

There's another temptation here – to disembark and indulge in a leisurely walk along the coast to Maughold Head. There's an Iron Age fort at its summit, and colonies of seabirds inhabit the cliffs. How many little

Ballajora.

excursions is this that you've made a note of for return trips?

Not long now and you'll get your first look at Ramsey – a town with a lot of history and thwarted ambitions. The Queen's Pier, built in 1886, reaches out into the Irish Sea from the shore for 2,300 feet and is an unmistakable feature of the bay even when viewed from distance.

Ramsey (from the Norse for Wild Garlic River) comes into full view on the approach to the Ballure Viaduct (160 feet long), constructed in 1899 by Francis Morton & Company of Garston, Liverpool. The railway had reached Ramsey the year before, stopping short at the gap which the viaduct then so conveniently filled and enabled the line to reach its present terminus in the centre of town.

Weaving through the outskirts of Ramsey, the line brings you into Walpole Road. It's noticeable here that the overhead wire poles are to the left-hand side of the double track

rather than between the tracks. They were salvaged from the Douglas Southern Electric Tramway that operated along Marine Drive between the capital and Port Soderick.

The final approach to the terminus takes you behind the houses of Waterloo Road and past the tramcar sheds before crossing a road and entering the station. The former goods shed is on the left, the station building (built 1964) on the right.

A look at your watch confirms that it's taken 75 spellbinding minutes to complete this incredible journey. There's plenty to see and do in Ramsey before you decide it's time to take your seat for the return trip to Douglas.

Then again, maybe you just can't wait.

The Manx Electric Railway operates all year round and in the evening during July and August.

CYCLING
6 ONE-DAY
TRAILS

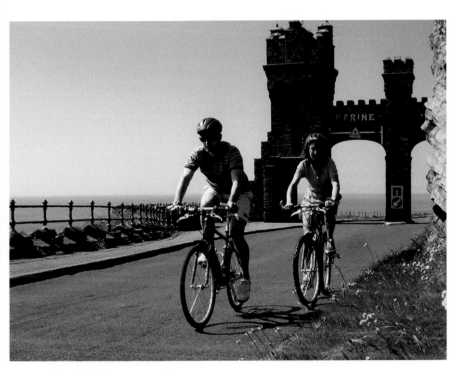

These designated circular routes vary in terms of length and the type of terrain you will encounter, and each is rated accordingly as easy, moderate or challenging, with two trails in each category – so there's something here for everyone.

The easy trails, on mainly flatter roads and lanes, are suitable for all, while the challenging rides tackle steep climbs and descents and require a much greater degree of physical fitness and cycling experience.

You should take as much care when cycling on the Isle of Man as you would anywhere else. Although many of the island's country lanes are often quiet and traffic is light, other roads and lanes can be deceptively busy.

The nature of the landscape also means that roads tend to be winding and narrow, with high hedges limiting visibility, so approaching traffic can sometimes appear unexpectedly.

You're welcome of course to bring your own bike, and cycle hire is available on the island. Details are available from the Welcome Centre in Douglas.

Happy cycling!

TRAIL 1: DOUGLAS (27 MILES)

Rating: challenging.

Major climbs/descents: Eskdale Road or Bibaloe Beg, River Glass valley at Sir George's Bridge, Ellerslie Hill at Crosby, Braaid, Crogga.

Attractions en route: Manx Museum, Douglas horse trams, Manx Electric Railway, Groudle Glen and railway, Molly Quirk's Glen, St Patrick's Chair, Port Soderick, Marine Drive.

This demanding but rewarding tour takes you out of the island's busy capital and into the tranquil countryside which surrounds it. Cycling is an ideal way to explore the small glens such as Groudle and Molly Quirk's, and the coastal road of Marine Drive provides a stunning end to the day.

The majority of the route is on quiet lanes, but you will also encounter busy main roads in and around Douglas and need to take care, particularly during morning and evening peaks. You should exercise the same caution along the promenade, which has tram lines running its entire length, and on roads around the Sea Terminal.

Start the tour at Derby Castle, at the northern end of the promenade, passing the terminus of the Manx Electric Railway and climbing towards Onchan.

After King Edward Bay Golf Club at Howstrake you come to the lovely Groudle Glen, with its miniature steam railway (seasonal). Continue alongside the MER track in the direction of Laxey, and take the first available road on your left (Bibaloe Beg Road – a short but very steep climb).

On reaching the main A2, turn left towards Onchan, but beware: the A2 is a fast, busy road, and your visibility of approaching traffic will be poor.

Cross the Whitebridge into Onchan and take the third right turn (School Road) –

cycling **6** one-day **TRAILS**

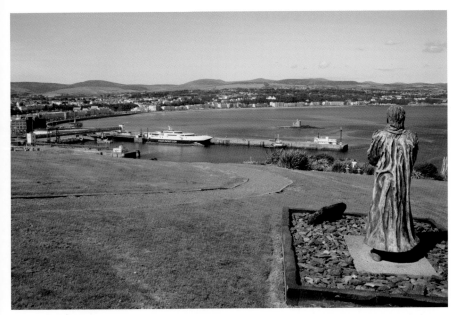

The statue of Sir William Hillary, founder of what later became the RNLI, keeps an ever-watchful eye over the bay from Douglas Head.

Onchan village, shops and pubs are 300 yards ahead.

Pass the Dowty factory, and a hairpin turn takes you down into the glen past Little Mill and steeply up the other side. Continue to Hillberry and the intersection with the TT course. Caution: traffic here is very fast.

Go left on to the TT course, right after approximately 300 yards, and immediate right again into Scollag Road. This takes you to Abbeylands Crossroads and down the steep slope into the River Glass valley at Sir George's Bridge. Follow the A22 into Strang, passing Strang Stores. At the mini roundabout turn right and follow the A23 to Crosby and the crossroads, where you cross the main A1 Douglas to Peel road. Continue up the steep hill, passing St Runius Chapel and, a quarter of a mile further on, a footpath sign to St Patrick's Chair (an ancient monument about 400 yards off the road).

The long climb brings you to Garth Crossroads, where you turn left towards Douglas. A mile further on, cross the mini roundabout at the Braaid. There is another long climb, passing Chibbanagh Plantation, and go next right towards Mount Murray Hotel, which is about a mile and a half further on. Another half a mile beyond the hotel, turn right at the T-junction on to the A5 – a busy main road linking Douglas and the airport. After a mile turn left into Oatlands Road, and go another mile and left on to Castletown Old Road towards Douglas, descending into Crogga dip and climbing out on the other side.

Take the next right turn to Port Soderick, soon passing under the steam railway at the station. Turn left shortly afterwards. Half a mile further on, go next right on to Marine Drive and proceed along its dramatic length to Douglas Head and down the hill towards South Quay – the end of the route. To return to the Sea Terminal you can either go left around the landward end of the harbour, or use the new harbour bridge.

TRAIL 2: CASTLETOWN (13 MILES)

Rating: easy.

Major climbs/descents: none.

Attractions en route: Castle Rushen, Nautical Museum and Old Grammar School (all Castletown); Hango Hill, Derbyhaven, St Michael's Fort, St Michael's Chapel, steam railway, St Mark's Church; Rushen Abbey and 14th-century Monks Bridge (both Ballasalla); Shebeg Pottery, Silverdale Glen.

Optional: rides to St Michael's Isle and Langness, both of which run close to the shore and give panoramic sea views, and to Silverdale Glen.

Far less demanding than Trail 1, this relaxing ride shows you the gentler slopes of the island's south and is suitable for all age groups and levels of fitness. The total distance of 13 miles does not include the optional routes, for which you should allow a further 7.5 miles.

Start at Castletown station (Isle of Man Steam Railway), turning right where the station approach reaches the A5. Go left at the mini roundabout and alongside the harbour, passing the Nautical Museum, and along Douglas Street.

Where College Green forks off to the right, you have the opportunity to take the optional route (as marked on the map) to the lovely Langness peninsula – a spectacular, level expanse of coastline in the island's south-east corner. This will also enable you to cross the causeway to St Michael's Isle (another optional route) and see St Michael's Chapel and the fort overlooking the bay at Derbyhaven. However, be aware that for part of the way you'll be riding alongside the Castletown links course, so look out for flying golf balls!

If you decide not to take these options, ignore the right fork to College Green and continue straight on to join the main A5 Douglas Road (which you can join from the

Langness detour by retracing your steps towards Castletown, turning right into Shore Road and right on to the A5).

Go past the airport and over the level crossing to the mini roundabout at Ballasalla, leaving the A5 by going straight on along the A26 through the village centre. At the second mini roundabout you must bear right to remain on the A26 towards St Mark's.

On reaching St Mark's, take the left-hand fork at the church to join the B30 and then left again almost immediately. In about a mile you will pass the pet cemetery.

Turn left down the B29 and continue, joining the A34 back towards Ballasalla. Both of these roads are quiet country lanes running between high Manx sod hedges, so take extra care as limited forward visibility means that traffic from either direction can be really close before you're aware of it. The terrain is almost entirely downhill.

Once back on the outskirts of Ballasalla, you have a third option (see map): turn right along a leafy lane for just under a mile and you'll reach Silverdale Glen and its variety of family attractions. Return on the same narrow lane and at the junction where you detoured off the A34, turn right and right again shortly afterwards.

You are now back on the outward route, but just before the mini roundabout turn right, approaching the ford, and cross the Silverburn River over the bridge. Rushen Abbey is on your right and the road follows the abbey wall.

After a quarter of a mile turn right at the T-junction (a busy road, so take care.) Turn left at Cross Four Roads on to Malew Road. Pass Malew Church on the Z-bend, where Manx martyr Illiam Dhone is buried.

Continue back into Castletown. Cross over the main road into the old town and, dismounting, walk along Malew Street into Market Square, where Castle Rushen stands with its one-handed clock.

To get back to the station, leave by Castle Street and The Quay, cross over the bridge at the harbour, and along the opposite bank of the inner harbour. At the mini roundabout turn right for Douglas and, a quarter of a mile further on, go left and into the station.

TRAIL 3: PORT ERIN (14 MILES)

Rating: moderate.

Major climbs/descents: Port Erin to Cregneash, Bradda East, the Sound to Cregneash.

Attractions en route: Port Erin Railway Museum, Mull Circle, Cregneash Folk Museum, Viking ship burial ground at Balladoole, Milner's Tower (Bradda Head).

Optional: rides to Fleshwick Bay, Port St Mary and the Sound.

You can really go wild on this eye-opening

The sandy beach of Gansey Bay, Port St Mary.

ride! The magnificent coastal scenery of the south-western corner of the Isle of Man rises dramatically at Bradda Head, and you have the opportunity to see the seals and seabirds which inhabit the Sound (the island's equivalent of Land's End) and to enjoy a cuppa at the visitor centre and cafe.

Start at Port Erin station (the steam railway's southern terminus), turning left along Station Road (one-way street) towards the bay. Stay on this road (which turns right to become the promenade), passing the turn to Bradda Glen Cafe. The road climbs round to the right, becoming Bradda Road, and 2 miles further on is Ballafesson.

Here you can exercise your first option: turn left for a 1.5-mile (each way) detour to Fleshwick, a rugged cove hemmed in by towering cliffs.

A quarter of a mile after Ballafesson, turn left on to the A7 Port Erin to Douglas Road. Go straight on at the mini roundabout at Ballakillowey and on through the pleasant villages of Colby and Ballabeg.

Remain on the A7 until A7 Douglas is shown as a left turn. Go straight on, which is the A28 to Castletown, passing close by Ballabeg railway station (a modest structure) and on to the junction with the main A5 (a fast road, so take care), where you turn right.

After a quarter of a mile, turn left through stone gate pillars signposted Poyll Vaaish, and you will pass the gate leading to Balladoole Burial Site – a Viking ship burial ground dating from prehistoric to Norse times.

The road continues to the coast, where you turn right at a T-junction to follow the rocky shoreline until rejoining the fast and busy main A5 at the bottom of Fisher's Hill, where you go left. The A5 runs alongside the coast of Bay ny Carrickey, before swinging right and inland, at which point you leave the A5 by forking left. Half a mile further on you come to a crossroads. You can either go straight on, or take your second option by turning left to visit the popular seaside village and harbour of Port St Mary.

This option runs along Bay View Road to

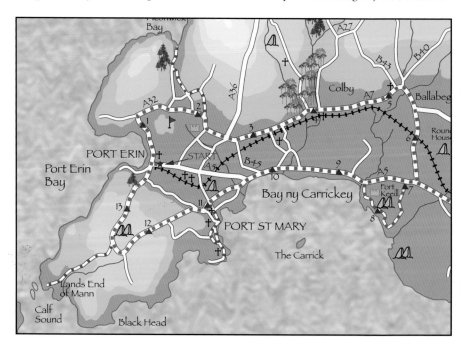

a right turn. After a quarter of a mile, turn left and left again shortly to the harbour.

To return, go along Athol Street (one-way street) and before long you will rejoin the crossroads, where you turn left into Plantation Road to continue on tour 3.

The road climbs steeply for a mile and a half, eventually reaching the interesting thatched-cottage village of Cregneash – a living museum with a farm which still uses traditional Manx farming methods. Here you can take a third option – route 3C down to the wild attractions of the Sound, with views across to the Calf of Man islet. It's a detour well worth making (there's a visitor centre and cafe) but the climb back up to Cregneash is quite severe.

After Cregneash, go on past the hilltop Meayll Circle (a unique megalithic ritual and burial site) to return to Port Erin. When you reach the promenade (called Shore Road at this point), turn right, which is blind so take care. Go uphill to one-way Station Road, opposite the Isle of Man Bank, where you'll have to dismount for the short walk back to the railway station.

TRAIL 4: PEEL (10 MILES)

Rating: moderate to easy.
Major climbs/descents: St John's to Snuff the Wind lead mine, and Garey to Glen Maye.

Attractions en route: Peel Castle, St German's Cathedral, Leece Museum, House of Manannan (all in Peel); Tynwald National Park & Arboretum, Manx Wild Flower Garden, Tynwald Hill, Royal Chapel, Tynwald Mills Centre (all in St John's); Snuff the Wind leadmine, Glen Maye waterfall and beach.

Optional: an alternative easier route (4A on the map) between St John's and (Kirk) Patrick.

Peel and its surrounding area have to be high on the list of everyone's Isle of Man cycling plans. As well as showing you the port and its impressive castle ruins, this trail takes

you through the picturesque villages of St John's and Glen Maye, with spectacular views on the climb up to Snuff the Wind leadmine.

Start at the House of Manannan and go along the quay and the promenade to the Creg Malin Hotel, turning right up Walpole Road. Go right at the T-junction at the top of the hill, shortly turning left into Church Street, signposted Douglas and South. At the far end of Church Street turn left into Derby Road and follow it out of Peel.

Passing Poortown Quarry on your left, and round the double bend, turn right into a narrow lane going steeply downhill to a stone bridge over the River Neb.

A short deviation to the right immediately after the bridge takes you to the Tynwald Mills Centre (shops and two cafes in the old mills).

Returning to the trail, continue on the narrow road through the trees and after half a mile you'll see Tynwald Hill close by on your left.

At the crossroads go straight on, across the

The Peel trail begins and ends along the impressive new-look waterfront.

Peel to Douglas road and through the village of St John's. After the Central Hotel take the sharp right turn into Patrick Road and cross the stone bridge, where the route turns left up the hill. If you wish to take the alternative easier route (4A on the map), go straight on at this point, rejoining the trail further on at Patrick.

The main suggested trail continues up the hill – very steep in some sections – for 2 miles. At the junction on the brow of the hill, near the old leadmine known as Snuff the Wind, turn right. A mile and a half later you begin the 2-mile descent into Glen Maye, emerging by the Post Office, but take care – the road is narrow and winding.

The trail turns right here on to the A27 road to Peel. However, a short detour to your left takes you to Glen Maye and its waterfall and beach.

Return to the trail at the Post Office and take the A27 to Kirk Patrick (2 miles), where the easier route 4B rejoins from the right.

Stay on the A27, over the River Neb, and climb to the Peel boundary. Half a mile further on brings you to the top of Station Hill. Turn left and shortly right and you are back at the House of Manannan – your starting point.

TRAIL 5: RAMSEY (16 MILES)

Rating: easy.

Major climbs/descents: none.

Attractions en route: Ramsey Pier (closed), Grove Rural Life Museum, Point of Ayre, Ayres Visitor Centre, Knock y Doonee (Viking ship burial site), Andreas crosses, Kerroogarroo Fort (Civil War – formerly known as Ballachurry Fort).

Optional: Bride to the Point of Ayre.

This relaxing ride can be enjoyed by all – particularly if the idea of rural tranquillity and flat, quiet, unhurried roads appeals to you. Set against the backdrop of the Manx hills, the gentle landscape of the northern plain is in stark contrast to the rest of the island. In other words, it's perfect holiday cycling country!

The gateway to it all – and your starting point – is Ramsey, a pleasant town with a busy shopping centre and harbour. So take care in the traffic.

Start at the Manx Electric Railway station and cross over Albert Street. Turn into Peel Street and take the first right opposite the police station into Market Hill – a short road leading directly into Market Place.

Turn left, then left again, on to West Quay. Follow the quayside and go right over the swingbridge, bearing right and then left along Mooragh promenade. After a mile the road swings inland and gradually climbs the cliff.

Go right at the T-junction beside the old Grand Island Hotel and follow the A10 through the small village of Bride – a

distance of about 4 miles.

At the mini roundabout you have the option to take a detour to the island's most northerly place – the Point of Ayre, marked by its distinctive red and white lighthouse. But beware of big lorries which use this road for access to the tip site and gravel pits.

Returning to the mini-roundabout, the trail continues on the A10 (to The Lhen), heading west. Follow it for 4 miles and turn left into the Leodest road (which will take you past Leodest Farm) to Andreas, a further 2 miles.

In the centre of the village, turn left at the T-junction and right at the Y-junction. Then turn right at the T-junction past the church. A quarter of a mile further on, again turn right, into Bayr ny Harrey (Manx for Road to the Ayres) and follow this quiet country lane for 2 miles.

Go left at the crossroads for half a mile and then left at the T-junction. After a mile this brings you into the village of St Judes, where you turn left at the crossroads and pass St Judes Church. Proceed along this pleasant road for 5 miles back into Ramsey.

Turn right at the T-junction into Bowring Road and cross the bridge into the centre of Ramsey. Go straight on at the two mini-roundabouts and then left (signposted A2 Laxey and Douglas) back to your starting point – Ramsey station.

TRAIL 6: LAXEY (6 MILES)

Rating: challenging.

Major climbs/descents: Laxey to Ballaquine.

Attractions en route: King Orry's Grave, Laxey Wheel & Mines Trail, Laxey Glen gardens, Fairy Cottage, Laxey Woollen Mills (all in Laxey) and Ballalheannagh Gardens.

This is by far the shortest of the 6

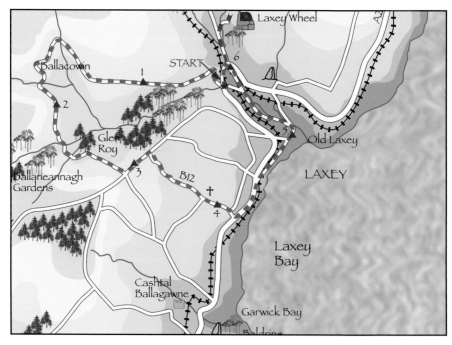

designated cycle trails, and one of great scenic beauty, but the initial climb is definitely not for the faint-hearted! And following this are several steep ascents and descents into pretty river valleys, where the road is very narrow and demanding.

You will also encounter some traffic over the first mile or so after leaving Laxey.

Start at Laxey station and New Road (A2), taking the steep hill next to the filling station in the direction of Baldhoon. This is

extremely steep to begin with before climbing more steadily.

The road is narrow and cuts a tortuous path through numerous tributary valleys until it reaches the B12, where you turn left.

Follow the road round to the right (signed Laxey) and down the hill towards the coast.

Half a mile after passing the church on your left, turn right at the T-junction and almost immediately go sharp left on to the main coast road.

Pass Fairy Cottage and South Cape and fork right down Old Laxey Hill. Within half a mile you will reach Old Laxey at the Shore Hotel, where turning left into Tent Road will show you the old harbour and Laxey promenade.

You can return to the Shore Hotel along Shore Road. Cross the old bridge over Laxey River and go left up Glen Road, at first following the river.

Cross the river and proceed up Church Hill and under the railway bridge, turning sharp right to return to Laxey station.

Lovely Laxey Bay.

CLASSIFIED ADVERTS

DOUGLAS & THE EAST

ALL SEASONS, 11 CLIFTON TERRACE, DOUGLAS, ISLE OF MAN. Tel: 0871 855 0603. Web: www.hotels-iom.com Well appointed B&B holding 3 star status close to all amenities. All rooms non smoking, free broadband and much more. From £34.00. Book online or call us.

★★★   TSL 12

ASHVILLE HOLIDAY FLATS, 24 Derby Road, Douglas, Isle of Man, IM2 3ET. Tel: 07624 315654 or 07702 859459. Web: www.ashvilleapartments.co.uk. Central location close to Villa Marina, bowling green, beach, shops. Accommodation from 2 person apartment to 2 bedroom apartments for up to 6 people. Full equipped. Pets welcome.

★★   MW TSL 12

ATHOL HOUSE, Broadway, Douglas, Isle of Man. Telephone: (01624) 629356. Web: www.atholhouse.net Family run Guest House in the centre of Douglas overlooking the Villa Marina. Approx 50yds from beach. All rooms en-suite, free Wi-Fi access. From £20.00 p.p.p.n B&B.

★★★   TSL 12

THE BEECHWOOD, 20 CASTLEMONA AVENUE, DOUGLAS, ISLE OF MAN, IM2 4EH. Tel: 07624 409482. Email: delia@beechwoodiom.com Web: www.beechwoodiom.com Centrally located, close to all amenities. The Beechwood is a comfortable B&B set just off main promenade in quiet dwellings. The Beechwood offers both en-suite and standard rooms from £20.00 p.p.p.n.

★★   12

BROOKVALE COTTAGE, MAIN ROAD, UNION MILLS, ISLE OF MAN, IM4 4AJ. Tel: (07624) 464525. Beautiful self contained cottage situated in grounds of Brookvale House. Close to shops and public transport. An ideal romantic getaway from the stresses of modern life.

★★★   1-11

CALEDONIA, 17 PALACE TERRACE, QUEENS PROMENADE, DOUGLAS, ISLE OF MAN. Tel: (01624) 624569. Email: CaledoniaHotel@hotmail.com Web: www.isle-of-man-hotel.com Charming accommodation set in elegant Victorian building. Refurbished. All rooms en-suite. Sea views from rooms looking over Douglas Bay available. Restaurant offers authentic Chinese cuisine and English breakfast. Winter rates available.

★★★   TSL P 12

DREEM ARD, BALLANARD ROAD, DOUGLAS, ISLE OF MAN, IM2 5PR. Tel/Fax: (01624) 621491. Web: www.visitisleofman.com Dreem Ard is a quiet elegant home offering beautiful en-suite accommodation with secure off-road parking. Only minutes from Douglas, yet enjoying rural tranquility. 4 Star AA Best Bed & Breakfast rating. Awarded best B&B 2007 IOM Tourist Board.

★★★★   TSL 12

EDELWEISS, QUEENS PROMENADE, DOUGLAS, ISLE OF MAN. Tel: (01624) 675115. Email: edelweiss@manx.net Web: www.isleofmantravel.com/edelweiss No steps into the Edelweiss, lift to all floors. Friendly atmosphere, we specialise in a friendly service with a friendly price. Located in the fashionable Queens Promenade, all rooms en-suite. A stay not to be missed.

★★★   TSL MEH 12

THE GREAVES, SUNNYCROFT, RAMSEY ROAD, LAXEY, ISLE OF MAN, IM4 7PD. Tel: (01624) 861500. Peace, tranquillity, magnificent panoramic views, yet situated in Laxey village near electric tram station/bus stop and shops. Homely Guest House. Good home cooking. Ideal base for walkers. Evening Meal optional. Contact Mrs Patsy Quirk.

★★★   12

GROUDLE GLEN COTTAGES, ONCHAN, ISLE OF MAN IM3 2JP Email:info@groudlecottages.com Tel: (01624) 623075. Web: www.groudlecottages.com. Only minutes from Douglas/Onchan. Self-catering cottages with panoramic views overlooking wooded glen and/or sea. Each cottage can accommodate up to six people. On site Bike hire. Catering services available.

★★★   MW 12

251

HILTON HOTEL, Central Promenade, Douglas, Isle of Man, IM2 4NA. Tel: (01624) 662662. Email: reservations.isleofman@hilton.com Web: www.hilton.co.uk/isleofman. Get lucky in the casino or bingo hall at our seafront hotel. Stunning views over Douglas Bay, just 12 miles from Ronaldsway Airport. Call to make a reservation.

★★★★ 　　　　🍴 🅿 📶 ⏚ 🔲 ♨ 🔲 ➘ ⪼ 👤 12

LAXEY CAMPSITE, QUARRY ROAD, LAXEY, ISLE OF MAN. Tel: (01624) 862623. Email: laxeycommissioners@manx.net Web: www.laxey.org Pleasant child friendly site located half a mile from the beach. Facilities on site are provided free of charge and include toilets, wash-basins, hot showers and a well equipped kitchen.

Listed 　　　　➘ 🍴 🅿 🚪 Ⓜ 🐾 MW 4-9

REAYRT NY MARREY COTTAGE, Ballakinnag Road, Isle of Man, IM7 3ED. Tel: (01624) 882025 or 07624 401428. Email: beehive@mcb.net. Set in beautiful Manx countryside with fantastic views. Short walk to beach, close to amenities. Furnished to a very high standard. Two double en-suite bedrooms. Contact: Alice.

★★★★ 　　　　🚪 ➘ 🌡 ⚒ 🅿 ❁ 🔲 📷 12

THE SEFTON HOTEL, HARRIS PROMENADE, DOUGLAS, ISLE OF MAN, IM1 2RW. Tel: (01624) 645500. Email: info@seftonhotel.co.im Web: www.seftonhotel.co.im The Sefton Hotel is a perfectly situated, relaxing, calm and beautiful four star hotel. Call us to make a booking and this year make it special; make it Sefton.

★★★★ 　　🍴 Ⓧ 🅿 ♨ ⊞ ❁ 📶 ♨ 🔲 🕯 📟 TSL 🔥 12

ST HELIERS GUEST HOUSE, CENTRAL PROMENADE, DOUGLAS, ISLE OF MAN, IM2 4LU. Tel: (01624) 624355. Email: stheliers@manx.net Family run seafront accommodation. Licenced. Lift. Standard and en-suite rooms available. Evening meals on request. Central for all amenities.

★★★ 　　　　➘ 🍴 🔲 📞 👤 ♨ 🔲 ⪼ 12

TREVELYAN, QUEENS PROMENADE, DOUGLAS, ISLE OF MAN, IM2 4NE. Tel: (01624) 616631. Email: trevelyan@manx.net A seafront catchment area. 74 appointed bedrooms, mostly overlooking Douglas Bay. Comfortable B&B accommodation run by friendly family. Close to all amenities. Licensed Bar. Lift to all floors on premises. £18.00 p.p.p.n.

★★ 　　　　➘ 🍴 🔲 📞 👤 ⪼ Ⓢ 4-10

WELBECK HOTEL, MONA DRIVE, DOUGLAS, ISLE OF MAN, IM2 4LF. Tel: (01624) 675663. Email: mail@welbeckhotel.com Web: www.welbeckhotel.com Blending the style and elegance of a Victorian building with the modern luxuries required by the traveller of today. The Welbeck Hotel is ideal for business and pleasure stays. The Welbeck is a no smoking hotel.

★★★ 　　🔲 ➘ 🍴 🔺 ⊗ 🔲 👤 🐾 🔲 Ⓢ 🕯 12

PORT ERIN & THE SOUTH

BALLAVAYRE COTTAGES, Ballakilpheric, Colby, Isle of Man, IM9 4BU. Tel: (01624) 832949. Email: peterquine41@hotmail.com. Web: www.ballavayrecottages.com. Self Catering cottage situated in heart of Manx countryside. Ideal for coastal/hill walking. Elevated position affords panoramic views of southern coastline. Award-winning warm Manx welcome assured.

★★★★★ 　　🔲 🍴 ⚒ 🅿 ♨ 🔲 ❁ 🔲 📷 12

BALMORAL, Promenade, Port Erin, Isle of Man, IM9 6AG. Tel: (01624) 833126. Email: balmoralpe@advsys.co.uk. Unique promenade position with stunning views of Port Erin Bay and Bradda Head. Relax on our balcony and enjoy the wonderful sunsets. All bedrooms en-suite.

★★★ 　　　　🔲 ➘ 🍴 📞 👤 ♨ ⪼ TSL 4-9

CNOC TAIGH, ST MARYS ROAD, PORT ERIN, ISLE OF MAN. Tel: (07624) 493824. Email: mkeggen@manx.net Website: www.harbourviewapartment.com Recently renovated house. 5 bedrooms, 3 en-suite, 1 bathroom. Sleeps 10 persons. Beautiful views of South of the Island. Private parking.

★★★★ 　　🔲 ➘ 🍴 🌡 ⚒ 🅿 🔲 ❁ 🔲 📷 MW 12

CRONK-E-DHOONEY COTTAGE B&B, Ballakilpheric, Colby, Isle of Man, IM9 4BS. Web: www.cronk-e-dhooney.com. Telephone: (01624) 834052. 4 Star clean, comfortable accommodation. Warm friendly welcome. Two rooms to let. Peaceful location. Panoramic coastal/countryside views. See website for more details/guest comments.

★★★★   ▥ ⚹⚻ P ♨⬚❄ UL S 3-10

HARBOUR VIEW, CORRIS LANE, PORT ST MARY, ISLE OF MAN. Telephone: (07624) 493824. Email: mkeggen@manx.net Website: www.harbourviewapartment.com Purpose built apartment, 3 Bedrooms (all en-suite). Spectacular views overlooking Port St Mary harbour and bay. Off-road parking.

★★★★   ▥ ⛵⚹⌂⚻ P ⬚❄ ▤ 12

KERROOBEG COTTAGE, KERROWKEIL, BALLASALLA, MALEW, ISLE OF MAN, IM9 3BB. Tel: (01624) 824410. Restored original Manx cottage. Beautifully situated in remote countryside with magnificent hill and sea views. Ideal for walkers. Large bed-sitting room, all on one floor. Sleeps four, suitable for family. Contact: Mrs Valerie Garrett.

★   ⛵⚹⌂⚻ P ▤ 4-10

MAYCROFT, 31 Droghadfayle Road, Port Erin, Isle of Man, IM9 6EL. Tel: (01624) 835080. Email: maycroftbandb@manx.net Clive & Mavis welcome you to their Edwardian home, near Restaurants, cliff walks, beach, boat to bird sanctuary, golf courses, Victorian Railway, central Port Erin. Guest lounge, DVDs, WiFi.

★★★★ **B&B**   ▥ ⌖⚻ P ♨⬚❄ ⚶ 12

ROWANY COTTIER GUEST HOUSE, Rowany Cottier, Spaldrick, Port Erin, Isle of Man, IM9 6PE. Tel: (01624) 832287. Web: www.rowanycottier.com. 5 Star Silver Award Guest House. Spectacular coastal views over Port Erin Bay and Calf of Man. Excellent walking, Victorian Steam Railway, golf & restaurants nearby. Private Parking.

★★★★★ Silver   ▥ ⚹⌂⚻ P ⚿♨⬚❄ TSL 12

SPALDRICK VIEW COTTAGE, 2 SPALDRICK VIEW, PORT ERIN, ISLE OF MAN, IM9 6PB. Tel: (01624) 814778. Email: fdaveg@manx.net Web: www.2spaldrickview.com Former fisherman's cottage with spectacular sea views across Port Erin bay. Ideal location for walking, bird-watching, boat trips, golf. 5 minute walk to village. Sleeps 6 (2 double, 2 single rooms).

★★★★   ▥ ⛵⚹⚻ ❄ SB ▤ ▥ MW 12

WESTWOOD, BALLAGALE AVENUE, SURBY, PORT ERIN, ISLE OF MAN. Tel: (01624) 836228. Email: westwoodiom@manx.net Comfortable home from home, well equipped chalet bungalow with large enclosed garden. Quiet rural location, close to amenities, steam railway, beach, golf, scenic walks. Enquiries contact Vicky.

★★★   ▥ ⛵⚹⌂ P ⚿❄ ▥ ▤ 1-12

PEEL & THE WEST

ALBANY HOUSE, B&B - PEEL
9 ALBANY ROAD, PEEL, ISLE OF MAN, IM5 1JS. Tel: (07624) 483866. Email: albanyhouseiom@msn.com Web: www.manxbedandbreakfast.com A warm Manx welcome and hearty breakfast awaits you at cosy Albany House. Pamper yourself in the luxurious, spotless en-suite rooms. Comfortably enjoy beautiful Peel's attractions plus the added convenience of close public transport.

★★★★ SILVER AWARD   ▥ ⛵⚹⌂⚻ ⚿♨⬚£ ⚶ 12

COSY COTTAGE, West View. Mrs N. Bridson, Dalby, Peel, Isle of Man IM5 3BR. Tel: (01624) 842716. Email: cosycottage@manx.net Cosy country cottage with garden in safe, peaceful village. Niarbyl cafe 10 minutes walk. Peel, post office, beach 10 minutes by car. Surrounded by beautiful glens. Walking, bird watching, sea and country views.

★★★   ▥ P ⚿⌂❄ SB MW ▥ ▤ 12

CRONK-DHOO CAMPSITE & BUNK HOUSES, Cronk-Dhoo Farm, Greeba, Isle of Man, IM4 2DX. Tel: (01624) 851327 or 07624 454416. Web: www.cronkdhoo.com. Set in meadowland overlooking central valley. Good facilities. Flat terraces, grass, hard standing for motor homes/caravans. High Standard. Pub 5 mins walk. Bunk houses TT and M.G.P.

⛺⛺⛺ Approved   ▥ ⛵⚹ ⚏⚻⚞ ⛟▥ MW 12

GORDON HOUSE HOLIDAY COTTAGE,
Patrick, Nr Peel, Isle of Man, IM5 3AR.
Web: www.gordonholidaycottage.co.uk Tel:
(01624) 843756. Comfortable, well equipped
studio apartment for two. Own private garden
area and parking. Set in peaceful countryside
between Peel and Glen Maye. Heavenly
walking country. .

★★★ 🏠🐾✂🅿🔌❑❄🛍🅾MW TSL 12

KIONE TURRYS, Douglas Street, Peel.
Tel: (01624) 842772 or 07624 433617. Email:
kt23@manx.net Web: www.peelcottages.com
The perfect, fully equipped holiday cottage,
beautifully refurbished and updated. Situated
in the heart of picturesque Peel. Many extras.
Early booking recommended. Parking.

★★★★ 🏠🐕🐾✂🅿❑SB🛍MW🅾12

THE OLD STABLE, BERK, PEEL ROAD,
KIRK MICHAEL, ISLE OF MAN, IM6 1AP.
Tel: (01624) 878039. Email: info@theoldstable.net
Web: www.theoldstable.net Quiet rural location, sea
views, near beaches, about half a mile from Kirk
Michael village and TT course. Cottage presented to
high standard, 2 bedrooms (double, twin **both en-
suite**). Ample parking, garden. Broadband & Satellite.

★★★★★ 🏠🐕🐾✂🅿🚗❑❄🛍🅾12

PEEL CAMPSITE & LEECE MUSEUM,
Peel Town Commissioners, Town Hall, Derby
Road, Peel, Isle of Man, Tel: (01624) 842341.
Web: www.peelonline.net. The best in the
west. Modern facilities, showers, washing
machines, hook-up points. Visit Leece
Museum displaying the history of Peel. Visit
the Ward Library.

♟♟ Commended 🐕🐾🅿🔌£🔍🚐M📷🅾TSL 4-9

THIE OLLEE, LABURNUM LODGE, GLEN
MAYE, ISLE OF MAN, IM5 3BJ. Tel: (01624)
842121. Email: info@thieollee.com Web:
www.thieollee.com Cottage for two adjacent to
main house in tranquil setting. Quality
accommodation, own garden, private parking,
mid week and short break bookings. Just perfect
for that relaxing break.

★★★ 🏠🐾🖐✂🅿❑❄SB🛍 MW 12

WHITEHOUSE COTTAGES, MAIN ROAD, KIRK
MICHAEL, ISLE OF MAN, IM6 2HE. Tel: (01624)
621705. Email: mandcnivison@manx.net Web:
www.whitehousecottages-iom.com Two bedroomed
cottages next to farmland and two minutes by car to
beach. Log stoves, beams. Dogs welcome. Hills and
glens nearby. Contact: Marilyn Nivison, 32 Snaefell
Crescent, Onchan, Isle of Man, IM3 4NH.

★★★ 🏠🐕🐾✂❄🛍🅾12

WILLOW NOOK COTTAGES, COOIL
SHELLAGH FARM, KIRK MICHAEL, ISLE OF
MAN, IM6 1AU. Tel: (01624) 877745. Email:
info@willownook.com Web: www.willownook.com
Three beautiful five star cottages sleeping four, four
and two people. Sea views, sunny patios, gardens.
Situated amongst farmland half mile from village.

★★★★★ 🏠🐾🐕✂🅿❑❄🛍🅾3-10

RAMSEY & THE NORTH

BALLACHRINK FARM HOUSE, BALLACHRINK
FARM, BRIDE, ISLE OF MAN, IM7 4AP. Tel: (01624)
880364. Email: ballachrinkfarm@manx.net Web:
www.ballachrink.co.uk Bed and Breakfast. Come and
enjoy a break in our spacious farmhouse. Airy,
comfortable rooms and quiet surroundings make an
ideal base from which to discover the magic of the
Isle of Man.

★★★★ 🏠🐕⛺✂🅿♿❄SB MEH 12

BALLACRYE BEG (SELF CATERING),
Ballacrye Farm, Sandygate, Isle of Man, IM7 3BS.
Tel: (01624) 898003. Email: kerrison@iom.com
Beautiful cottage adjoining Manx Farmhouse.
Lovely country setting. Wildflower meadow,
large garden, mountain view. High quality spacious
interior, Manx stone fireplace, woodburning
stove. Sky Freesat. Private entrance. Parking.

★★★★ 🏠🐕🐾✂🅿❑❄🛍🅾12

BALLAVARTEEN HOLIDAY COTTAGE,
BALLAVARTEEN FARM, NASSAU ROAD, RAMSEY,
ISLE OF MAN. Tel: (01624) 880801.
ballavarteen@manx.net Web: www.ballavarteen.com.
Tastefully converted single storey 2 bedroomed detached
cottage. Idyllic location on small working farm, offering
high quality accommodation. Enjoy countryside on the
private south facing patio.

★★★★ 🏠🐕🐾🖐✂🅿❄🖐🛍🅾MW 12

BALLURE HOLIDAY HOMES,
BALLURE, MAUGHOLD, ISLE OF MAN, IM7 1AG.
Tel: (01624) 813104. Email: carrick@mcb.net
Web: www.ballureholidayhomes.com Six detached
fully furnished three bedroomed bungalows, each
sleeping up to six adults with spectacular views
over Ramsey and the North. Contact Anne and
David Craine.
★★★　　　🏠👣🐕🍴🅿️Ⓜ️🔌🔲♨12

KILLEABRAEGGA HOLIDAY COTTAGE,
Sulby Glen, Isle of Man. Tel: (01624) 816445.
Traditional Manx Cottage. Lovely glen setting.
Sleeps four adults.　Children and pets
welcome. Oil AGA. Sky Television. Coal fire.
Central location, near to many hill walks.
Fishing on reservoir.
★★　　　👣🅿️🕭🔲❄[SB]🔲🔲12

OROTAVA, 14 WESTLANDS CLOSE, RAMSEY,
ISLE OF MAN, IM8 3PU. Tel: (01624) 814233.
Email: orotava@manx.net　www.orotavabnb.com
Friendly, comfortable accommodation. Twin with PB,
double en-suite.　Excellent breakfasts.　In quiet
cul-de-sac 10 minutes Ramsey town centre. Ideal for
golf, walking, fishing holidays.　TV and Broadband
router which signals into all rooms.
★★★　　　🏠👣🅿️🍴🔲🅿️👣❄12

PRIMROSE LODGE, SLIEU LEWAIGUE, MAUGHOLD,
ISLE OF MAN, IM7 1BH. Tel: (01624) 816105 Mobile:
07624　450305　Web: www.primrose-lodge.com
Converted barn finished to very high standard. Open plan
upstairs, fully fitted kitchen, washing machine, dishwasher,
microwave, TV, 2 en-suite Bedrms downstairs. Beautiful
country views. Ramsey/Douglas bus stops outside.
Ramsey town/beach 2 miles.
★★★★　　　🏠👣👣🅿️🅿️❄🔲3-11

KEY TO SYMBOLS

TOUR OPERATORS
Ɛ	Everymann Holidays
ᶆ	Magic Holidays
P	Premier Holidays

DISABLED SYMBOLS
♿	Accessible One
🦼	Accessible Two
🧍	Accessible Three
👁	Partially sighted

SELF-CATERING
🚐	Electric hook-ups
M	Gas/Electricity charged extra
🔌	Linen provided
🚿	Showers on campsite
⎔	Washing machine/drying

SERVICED & SELF-CATERING
▥	Central heating
🐎	Children welcome
🐕	Dogs welcome
🐕	No dogs
👔	Guest laundry/laundry service
🏋	Gym/Leisure facilities
⬍	Lift
🛏	Ground floor bedrooms
🚭	Non-smoking
P	Private parking
☎	Public telephone available
Ⴑ	Residential liquor licence
☕	Tea/coffee making facilities in all bedrooms
☎	Telephone in all bedrooms or sc units
🖵	Television in all bedrooms or sc units
£	Accepts major credit cards
❄	Garden
⁙	Group rates on application
⛾	Public Liquor Licence
🏊	Swimming pool (indoor)
📞	Modem point in bedroom
UL	Unlicensed (alcoholic drinks not served)
S	Special diets provided
🏛	Conference Room
SB	Short breaks offered
12	Open all year
⌨	On Line Booking
MW	Mid week bookings

Monks Bridge

USEFUL
INFORMATION

BUS & TRAIN SERVICES

For up-to-date timetable and fare information, call Isle of Man Transport on 01624 662525 or the Welcome Centre on 01624 686766.

CIRCA

For information about disabled facilities, contact 01624 679153.

ENTERTAINMENT

Villa Marina & Gaiety Theatre Complex. Tickets 01624 600555. For information and what's on: www.villagaiety.com

FERRY SERVICES

For details of routes, services, fares and special offers contact the Steam Packet on 01624 661661 or visit www.steam-packet.com

FLYING TO THE ISLE OF MAN

For details of airports and airlines see page 10.

FURTHER READING

Other Isle of Man books published by Ramsey-based Lily Publications, the island's leading publishing house, include:

Air of Mann (aerial views)
Churches of Mann
Lorne House
Lucky Little Devil! (Norman Wisdom's own story)
Mann Ablaze
Profile of the Isle of Man
Profile of the Isle of ManProfile of Castletown
Saving the Gaiety
Story of Mann
This Island Now
Three Legs in the Irish Sea
Trains & Trams of the Isle of Man
Tram, Train & Foot
Visions of Mann
Wild Flowers of Mann

THE ISLE OF MAN TRANSPORT SERIES

Ailsa Years
Aircraft
Buses
Coastal Shipping
Post-Nationalisation
Trams
Twilight Years

■ Other Isle of Man books, published by Ferry Publications (sister company of Lily Publications) include:

Ferries of the Isle of Man
King Orry
Life & Times of the Steam Packet
Steam Packet 175

All titles listed are available direct from Lily Publications, PO Box 33, Ramsey, Isle of Man IM99 4LP. Tel: 01624 898446. Fax: 01624 898449. Email: lilypubs@manx.net
Website: www.lilypublications.co.uk

■ Many other books about the Isle of Man, and a comprehensive list of Manx titles, are available from Lexicon Bookshop in Strand Street, Douglas. Tel: 01624 673004. Fax: 01624 661959. Email: sales@lexiconbookshop.co.im
Website: www.lexiconbookshop.co.im

HARBOURS

■ Douglas. Good shelter except in NE winds, very heavy seas in NE gales. Harbour

Fairy Bridge.

The steep western hills roll down to the sea.

Master 01624 686627.
- Laxey. Sheltered except in strong NE/SE winds. Harbour dries out. Port Manager 01624 861663.
- Peel. Good shelter except in strong NW to NE winds, when entry should not be attempted. Harbour Office 01624 842338.
- Port St Mary. Very good shelter except in E or SE winds. Inner harbour dries out. Port Manager (also for Port Erin and Castletown) 01624 833206.
- Ramsey. Very good shelter except in strong NE/SE winds. Harbour dries out. Port Manager 01624 812245.

ISLE OF MAN LAW

The Isle of Man has a strong anti-drugs policy and illegal possession of banned substances can lead to imprisonment.

ISLE OF MAN STAMPS

You can buy Manx stamps online at www.gov.im/stamps

ISLE OF MAN VISITOR WEBSITES

The main website for visitor information – including details of accommodation, events, attractions, activities, TT and motorsport, travel information, special offers and much more – is www.visitisleofman.com

The Isle of Man Government website is also a mine of information and has a comprehensive index: www.gov.im

LICENSING LAWS

The Isle of Man permits 24-hour opening for pubs, bars and off-licences. This means that all licensed premises, including nightclubs, restaurants and the Douglas casino, now have the option to serve alcohol 24 hours a day but only within their stated pre-arranged opening times.

MANX NATIONAL HERITAGE & THE STORY OF MANN

For opening times, admission prices (where applicable) and other information about Manx National Heritage sites and Story of Mann attractions, call 01624 648000 or visit www.gov.im/mnh or www.storyofmann.com

MANX WILDLIFE TRUST

The Trust's shop, at the Tynwald Mills Centre in St John's, has a great variety of leaflets, books, maps and other information about Isle of Man wildlife and habitats. Call 01624 801985 or visit

Corrins Hill, Nr Peel.

www.wildlifetrust.org.uk/manxwt

MOTORING LAWS AND INFORMATION

■ Drive with care. Isle of Man roads and lanes are narrow and should be negotiated with care and consideration.

■ Mobile phones. It is an offence to use a hand-held mobile phone while driving. • Parking discs. These are required in some of the larger towns and villages and are available free from Isle of Man Steam Packet vessels, the Sea Terminal, airport, car hire companies and local Commissioners Offices.

■ Seatbelts. Similar seatbelt laws to those in the UK and elsewhere apply.

■ Touring caravans are not permitted on the Isle of Man without a permit, but tenting campers and motorhomes are welcome.

TOURIST INFORMATION: THE WELCOME CENTRE

Located at the Sea Terminal, Douglas, and formerly known as the Tourist Information Centre, this open 7 days a week: Monday to

Saturday 8am–6pm and Sunday (May to September) 10am–3pm.

For information call 01624 686766, fax 01624 627443, or email tourism@gov.im

From the Republic of Ireland call +44 (1) 8744455.

TOURIST INFORMATION POINTS

Open all year:

■ Airport 01624 821600

■ Ballasalla 01624 829526• Onchan 01624 621228

■ Peel 01624 842341 or 845366

■ Port Erin 01624 832298 & 835858

■ Port St Mary 01624 832101

■ Ramsey 01624 810146

Seasonal only:

■ Castletown (by visit only)

■ Laxey Heritage Trust 01624 862007

TYNWALD PARLIAMENTARY WEBSITE

■ www.tynwald.org.im

Derbyhaven sits on the shoulders of Langness.

Everything you have ever wanted to know about the beautiful unspoilt Isle of Man

Churches of Mann

Isle of Man churches, chapels and keeills in words, pictures and music. Accompanied by a wealth of large format photographs by Miles Cowsill and Vicky Harrop. Author Jonathan Kewley. The book also includes CD of organ music by Gareth Moore.
192 pages 280 x 225mm
£28.50 (inc p&p)

Realising the Dream at the TT

Commissioned by Honda, this book covers the history, events and excitement of Honda's involvement with the Tourist Trophy Races on the Isle of Man. With text by expert Mick Duckworth, it includes a wealth of historical photographs (many previously unpublished in Europe), Honda results, facts and rider profiles.
192 pages A4 style
£24.50 (inc p&p)

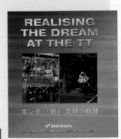

Isle of Man by Tram, Train and Foot

This book traces the history of the Manx railway system and also includes the fascinating history of mining and other interesting industries on the Island. The book also contains a series of walks which allows the reader to follow the history of the Isle of Man transport system and its heritage.
A5. Colour and black & white. Price £7.40.

Visions of Mann

Replaces our successful Spirit of Mann which is now out of print. Featuring a wealth of colour photographs by Miles Cowsill and Vicky Harrop it covers all seasons on the Island. Accompanying text by Manx writer Stan Basnett.
168 pages A4+
£25.50 (inc p&p)

Three Legs in the Irish Sea
Tree Cassyn ayns Mooir Vannin

The Isle of Man is not part of the UK or the EU. Head of State is the Duke of Normandy – who is female. Use of a simple three-letter word in public is almost tantamount to treason. This book portrays the quirks of the Isle of Man in a delightfully lighthearted way packed full of stunning photography.
168 pages 250 x 225mm
£24.00 (inc p&p)

COMING SOON

The All Round Guide to Wildlife on the Isle of Man

This new book will be published in early 2011 and will contain a wide variety of information and details on how to enjoy the many aspects of wildlife on the Isle of Man. Produced to A5 style in full colour. The publication will contain articles by leading experts on wildlife. Maps and sites to visit also included. Price £7.40.

ALL-ROUND GUIDE

Isle of MAN

BY FAR
THE MOST
COMPREHENSIVE
GUIDE

Beautiful, unspoilt, deeply relaxing, self governing – and in many ways different from anywhere else in the British Isles. Here in this expanded and completely revised edition of Lily Publications' bestselling guide is the full story of what makes the Isle of Man such an interesting and memorable place to visit.

CONTENTS INCLUDE

attractions & activities

beaches & resorts

churches

day drives

events

fishing & golf

glens & gardens

history & heritage

lighthouses

myths & legends

queenies & kippers

railways & trams

street plans & maps

TT & motorsport

visitor centres

walks & cycle trails

xtraordinary facts

yachting & sailing

£5.95

Published on the Isle of Man
by Lily Publications Ltd

ISBN 978–1–899602–49–0

9 781899 602490 >

East & West Runton

TWO VILLAGES, ONE PARISH

G.F. LEAKE

Poppyland
Publishing
w.poppyland.co.uk

Other in-print titles in this series
An Acle Chronicle / Brian Grint
Blakeney: Have you Heard about Blakeney? / Peter Brooks
Cley: Living with Memories of Greatness / Peter Brooks
Cromer: the Chronicle of a Watering Place / Martin Warren
Great Yarmouth: History, Herrings, Holidays / Charles Lewis
Holt: Georgian Market Town / Peter Brooks
Poppyland: Strands of Norfolk History / Peter Stibbons & David Cleveland
Potter Heigham: Heart of Broadland / Olga Sinclair
Sheringham: the Story of a Town / Peter Brooks
Southtown and Gorleston: The Mouth of the Yare / Colin Tooke
Swaffham: in the Pedlar's Footsteps / David Butters
Weybourne: Peaceful Mirror of a Turbulent Past / Peter Brooks

First published in 1988.
Second edition published in 2006 by Poppyland Publishing, Cromer NR27 9AN

ISBN 0 946148 75 9
   978 0 946148 75 2

Picture credits
Cromer Museum: page 17
G. F. Leake: pages 1, 9, 21, 25, 28, 29, 30, 31, 33, 37, 39
Poppyland collection: pages 5, 19, 29
Poppyland Photos: pages 2, 6, 7, 15, 40
Randall/Salter Magic Lantern Collection: page 13
H. H. Tansley: page 8

Designed & typeset Garamond by Watermark, Cromer NR27 9HL
Printed by Printing Services (Norwich) Ltd

Front cover: Runton from the air, October 2005, East Runton village sign, West Runton common, early 20th century.
Back cover: Spring tides attack the cliffs and defences, West Runton 2006